"Through a great combination of data, practical advice, and new thinking, the authors show how to individualize the way organizations treat their employees—and make it pay off! I really enjoyed it."

—Edward E. Lawler III, Distinguished Professor of Business, Marshall School of Business, University of Southern California and author, *Talent: Making People Your Competitive Advantage*

"The mass customization techniques that have proliferated as a customer service tool are finally being applied to the workforce. *Workforce of One* is the first comprehensive look at why 'now' is the time and how to make it work. Rich in strategic and practical examples, this book represents a major advance in human capital management applicable to any business looking to chart a course for the future."

—Harold Scott, former VP of HR, Harley-Davidson

WORKFORCE of one

SUSAN M.
CANTRELL

DAVID
SMITH

Workforce of one

Revolutionizing
Talent
Management
Through
Customization

Harvard Business Press
Boston, Massachusetts

Library of Congress Cataloging-in-Publication Data
Cantrell, Susan M.
    Workforce of one : revolutionizing talent management through customization / Susan M. Cantrell, David Smith.
        p. cm.
    Includes bibliographical references and index.
    ISBN 978-1-4221-4758-0 (hardcover : alk. paper)   1. Personnel management.
2. Organizational effectiveness.   3. Employees—Coaching of.   I. Smith, David.   II. Title.
    HF5549.C285 2009
    658.3'01—dc22

                                                                    2008056019

To Zbysek, Sally, Bob, and Edward, with thanks for
their love and encouragement, without which I would never have
had the courage or confidence to take on this long
and often seemingly endless project!

—*Sue*

To Claire, Christian, and Natalie, your spirit and support
take me to new places every day!

—*David*

Contents

Acknowledgments   *ix*

Introduction   1

PART ONE

Toward a Workforce of One

1. The New Management Imperative   11

PART TWO

Four Paths to a Workforce of One

2. Segment Your Workforce   61
3. Offer Modular Choices   87
4. Define Broad and Simple Rules   109
5. Foster Employee-Defined Personalization   129

PART THREE

Cultivating a Workforce of One Organization

6. Designing Your Own Workforce of One   157
7. Workforce of One Challenges and Solutions   189

Contents

8. A Call to Action for HR   211
    Building Your Workforce of One Capability

    Conclusion   235
    The Future of Workforce of One

    Appendix   239
    How Many Employees Have Customized Work Experiences?

    Notes   *241*
    Index   *261*
    About the Authors   *269*

Acknowledgments

This book has benefited by the significant contributions made by other people, whom we would like to thank for their generous support and insights throughout the process of developing and refining our ideas and finally putting them down in book form.

Our deepest gratitude goes to Peter Cheese, the former managing director responsible for Accenture's Talent and Organization Performance service line globally, and Robert J. Thomas, director of Accenture's Institute for High Performance. Peter and Bob have not only been generous sponsors and enthusiastic supporters of this project, but they have been critical in sharing their insights and experiences to help us shape our thinking and significantly improve the ideas we present in this book.

Our deepest gratitude also goes to Karen Wolf of Accenture and Darcy Lake Kerr, Vice President for Accident Insurance Fund of America, formerly with Accenture of Accenture. They have been with us every step of the way since we started writing this book, both contributing significantly to the broader thinking on the issues we've tackled and helping us with the details of producing a book in final form. They have been nothing less than outstanding and deserve significant credit for their hard work and unending enthusiasm.

Our thanks also go to Tom Davenport, who believed in this project from the very beginning, and who was always there to discuss insights and his experiences and to lend his sharp mind when we needed it most. Tom has been an invaluable mentor and colleague, and one whom we treasure and respect deeply. We also thank Tom for introducing us to our wonderful and gifted Harvard Business Press editor, Melinda Merino. Without Melinda's insights and suggestions, this book would not be what it is today. She played a crucial role in shaping the book, and we thank her for always stimulating our thinking and pushing us to new heights. Lucy McCauley also provided extremely valuable editorial suggestions and comments.

Many people reviewed this manuscript in its various forms. We would like to thank David Gartside, Cathy Farley, Peter Cheese, and Bob Thomas in particular for providing an extensive review of the manuscript and helpful comments to improve it.

Before we even started writing this book, the book was several years in the making. Early on as far back as 2004, Jeanne Harris, Jane Linder, Paul Nunes, Robert J. Thomas, Jim Benton, and David Light all contributed their thinking as we worked through the initial ideas of workforce of one. Jeanne, David, Bob, and Paul also later helped us learn the ropes of book publishing and provided their insights into the book proposal and book writing process. We also thank Nicole Di Paolo Foster and Susan Miele, who worked hard in 2005 and early 2006 to help us flush out some of the initial ideas, conduct an extensive secondary literature review, and write initial Accenture research notes to get our preliminary thoughts on paper and in published form.

Later on in the process in 2007, we conducted a whole new round of secondary research. Many research assistants helped us with this. They include Kristi Fasteson, Lucy Walline, Anne Lin, Whitney Walker, Liz Kim, and Lara Cohen. Our thanks also go to Rachel Barere, who helped provide some insights into the workforce of one survey design, and to Janice Beebe, who helped us with the many logistical details of producing this book.

Throughout the process of developing the concepts in this book, we benefited from many discussions: with dozens of employees who told us about their work experiences and talent management practices that did or did not work for them; with HR and senior business leaders who told us about what they were doing in their own organizations; and with colleagues who were either subject matter experts or consultants who could share their experiences working with numerous companies. The latter included Maureen Brosnan, Claude Ferguson, Markus Lamers, Rich Westphal, Elizabeth Hopkins, Sharon Klun, Michael L. Nicholus, Elizabeth Craig, Keri Halperin, Ian Page, David Gartside, Prithvi Shergill, Andrew James, Anthony Abbatiello, Paul O'Keeffe, Warren Dodge, Cathy Farley, Jill Smart, Elizabeth Wood, Kim Sillence, William Hildreth, Geoffrey M. Halaburt, David Metnick, Donald Mccurdy, Ellen McCarthy, Daniel Harley, Jennifer Jaramillo, Leo Aguerrevere, and Nat Robinson.

Finally, and most importantly, we thank our families for their constant support, encouragement, and emotional nourishment: the Cantrells and Brezinas—Zbysek, Edward, Sally, and Bob; and the Smiths—Claire, Christian, and Natalie.

Introduction

IMAGINE FOR A MOMENT that the organization you work for today is designed to fit you, rather than demanding that you fit it. This organization would help people learn in exactly the way they learn best, and it would reward and motivate them in precisely the way they are motivated best. It would enable people to design a career customized to their innate strengths and interests. And it would allow people to fluidly change their work experience as their personal and professional needs cycle and change. In essence, this organization would no longer treat its workforce as a single homogeneous entity, but rather each and every employee as a *workforce of one* with unique needs, aspirations, and preferences that vary over time.

As a human resources professional, you know how deeply fulfilling such a workplace could be for employees and what a positive effect such individually relevant and personalized systems would have throughout the organization. But we know what you're thinking: isn't this just a pipe dream? We're here to tell you that it isn't. This book is about how more than a dozen companies are leading the way in creating a customized experience for their people—not only to engage, attract, and retain them, but also to unleash their people's full potential as human beings to better contribute to their organizations' performance and profits. Through customization, these cutting-edge companies have done the remarkable: they have altogether transformed HR so that it is no longer just a value saver, but rather a true value *creator*. We've spent the last several years helping organizations navigate the practical ramifications of creating a customized experience for their people without sacrificing important organizational needs like control, scalability, and manageability. This book distills the insights we gained from that work to launch you on your own journey to managing each employee as a workforce of one—and help enable your organization to outperform the competition and gain real, sustainable advantage in the marketplace.

> *What is a workforce of one?* It is an approach to talent management that tailors people practices and policies to individuals and groups of employees throughout the organization, with the goal of improving individual and organizational effectiveness.

We all know, of course, how customization already has revolutionized the way companies treat their customers. Amazon.com and Netflix were built on the notion of providing personalized home pages and product recommendations tailored to individual preferences, and Dell famously revolutionized the PC business by enabling customers to custom configure their own computers. In an era such as ours, when you can customize everything from your own postage stamp to medicines to your iTunes playlist, it makes sense that organizations would figure out how to customize offerings for their most important resource—their people. And it seems imperative to do so: talent and knowledge have been cited as one of the few competitive advantages we have left.[1] Just as customization fundamentally transformed the way companies relate to customers and the kind of value those companies receive in return, so can it fundamentally transform the way companies relate to their people—while *multiplying* the value of employees and their ability to help their organizations compete.

Think about it: because everyone has different abilities, work styles and preferences, and motivations to work, no single way of treating an individual is ever likely to be the *best* way. Yet as HR people know perhaps better than anyone, the way companies manage their people to date has been largely a one-size-fits-all affair. To ensure efficiency, equality, and fairness, they train everyone on the same knowledge and in the same way, they rank people on the same performance criteria, and they provide the same set of rewards, assuming everyone is motivated by the same thing. Most organizations—with their formalized processes and lists of standard competencies, training, and linear lockstep career paths—operate under the assumption that most employees are the same, or that they should be reshaped until they are.

To be sure, this approach has generally served organizations quite well in the past, especially when it came to achieving control and scalability as companies went global, and in the interest of equity. But that approach no longer applies to the realities of today's business environment: a "perfect storm" of events and trends is pushing organizations to break through the old standard employment deal. In fact, at no time in history has customization for employees been more sorely needed than the present. Organizations are now facing their most diverse workforce yet—not only in terms of age, gender, and ethnicity, but in terms of life pursuits, cultural norms, and key values as well. In an era of substantial foreign competition, mobile employees with rising expectations, more complex knowledge work, and a shortage of qualified workers, today's generic people practices will be quickly rendered obsolete—and increasingly detrimental to the bottom line.

But make no mistake: customization isn't simply "the killer app that can 'win the war for talent' " (as one HR executive put it) when times are good and talent battles are hard fought. It is a business imperative when times are troubled and companies contract, as they are at the time of this writing. To resiliently bounce back in the face of crisis, organizations will need their employees' help more than ever. They will need to do more with less and will be forced to find new ways to multiply the value of their existing talent and harness their employees' full productivity potential. Without employees' discretionary energy and unflagging commitment, companies will be hard pressed to successfully navigate their way through turmoil and position themselves for success when market conditions rebound. Many of the customization practices profiled in this book can help organizations and their employees nimbly adjust to rapidly changing business conditions during an economic downturn. And as we'll show in this book, customization is not about throwing more money at HR (a poor business practice no matter what the economic climate). It's about using HR budgets in a more targeted manner to maximize the value of every dollar spent.

The good news is that technology advances in the past few years are finally allowing organizations to offer customization in a truly cost-effective, scalable, and manageable manner. In fact, technology has enabled organizations to achieve what they have not even been able to consider before: no less than radically transform the very practice of talent management, from managing a single monolithic workforce to managing a workforce of one.

Some employers are already introducing choice and variation in such areas as employee benefits and job assignments in an effort to recognize the differing needs of individuals. And many organizations have begun to introduce customized practices for their high-performing or most valued employees. But most companies have not yet begun to tap into the depth of this opportunity through applying customization in creative new ways across a vast array of people practices to their entire workforce—let alone approach customization in a strategic, thoughtful, proactive way. To be competitive in the marketplace, companies will need to understand and address the diverse needs of the individuals they hope to attract and keep—and in a way that works best for the organization's unique strategy, culture, and types of employees. Our hope is that this book will spur you, the HR manager, to action, and provide a useful, practical guide to managing talent in a way that enables both the individual and his or her organization to become the best they can be.

Why We Wrote This Book

Our journey to writing this book began with a puzzle and a question. A few years ago, we had developed a measurement tool to assess and benchmark the effectiveness of an organization's people practices.[2] After conducting thirty-five hundred surveys in more than sixty organizations, we found that the extensive implementation of what are widely regarded to be "best practice" processes, although important and statistically linked to business results, was not what mattered most to business performance. Rather, the single most important factor contributing to superior business results was *how supported* employees felt by their organization's people practices.

Yet our data revealed that in most organizations, even in ones that had extensively adopted standard "best practices" like across-the-board 360-degree performance feedback or extensive use of e-learning, employees still do not often feel supported. In fact, rather than associating people practices with performance improvement, most employees associated them more with needless bureaucracy, wasted resources, and discouraged individuals. This was the puzzle.

Our guiding question then became, What *would* help employees feel more supported by their organization's people practices and enable a consequent improvement in business results? Our statistical data didn't tell us, so we conducted dozens of exploratory interviews with line managers and employees. Our goal in this phase of the research was to look at people practices from the point of view of the *employee*—the ultimate customer of HR offerings. For the most part, we heard stories about how people practices, even ones widely considered best practice, had inhibited rather than helped employee performance because of their rigid, cookie-cutter approach that rendered them irrelevant. We heard how managers had lost key employees because of HR-imposed salary and reward restrictions; how employees had learned little from training that was chronically misaligned with individual learning styles; how high-performing people had opted out of their organizations when they bumped up against limiting, linear career paths; how employees were not motivated by the standard (usually financial) rewards and incentives; and how standardized performance appraisals and competency frameworks no longer reflected the individualized nature of work in today's knowledge-oriented economy.

As a result of these stories, we surmised that the single biggest improvement organizations could make would be to become directly relevant to individual employees' unique needs and circumstances. To really make a difference in their performance and productivity, employees told us they wanted to be treated as individuals with unique and differentiated needs. Hence the "workforce of one" concept was born.

Just how an organization could successfully create a customized approach to talent management didn't become clear until we studied more than one hundred companies in detail, in part by conducting interviews with more than seventy executives in forty-seven organizations. Ten of these turned into in-depth case studies where we explored every possible way an organization worked to customize its people practices, the organizational challenges faced, and why a company's particular approach worked well for that organization.

While we identified no single company that felt it had it "all figured out" and was done with its customization efforts, we did find leaders like Best Buy and Microsoft that were further along in their journey than most toward a workforce of one organization. One of these organizations happens to be the firm we work for, Accenture, the consulting, technology services, and outsourcing company. In the interest of transparency, we can tell you right up front that we have treated Accenture like any other organization in the course of our research; we report on Accenture's practices in this book only when we feel they are truly innovative or can help you understand how companies can effectively manage their workforce as a workforce of one. Throughout this book, you'll see not only how Best Buy, Microsoft, and Accenture manage their workforces as a workforce of one, but also how a whole series of leading companies (including Procter & Gamble, Deloitte, The Container Store, Royal Bank of Scotland, and Men's Wearhouse) are all deliberately applying principles of customization learned from marketing to their people practices.

At the same time, we supplemented our interviews with a major synthesis of cutting-edge scholarship and thinking on talent management, including the critical work our Accenture colleagues Peter Cheese, Robert J. Thomas, and Elizabeth Craig had done on the concept of talent-powered organizations, and validated our exploratory interviews with employees by conducting a survey of 557 U.S. employees in midsize to large organizations.[3] And as word got out about our research and thinking, several organizations asked us to help them navigate their own journeys of managing their people as a workforce of one.

The heart of our learning revolves around a framework we hope will help spur creative thinking about how to customize your own people practices, and serve as a guide for creating a customized approach to people management that suits your unique organization. The framework presents four manageable, scalable approaches an organization can take to customize its people practices while maintaining control and alignment with business strategy.

In this book you'll learn, for example, how:

- Harrah's and Sprint Nextel segment employees based on employee behaviors; and how Accenture segments based on employee networking styles and wellness profiles (strategies we call *segmentation approaches* to customization).

- Microsoft provides a wide variety of choices to enable employees to custom configure their work environment; and how Booz Allen Hamilton redesigned some jobs so that the tasks can be modularly configured by an individual based on interest and skill (strategies we call a *modular choice* approach to customization).

- Google and W. L. Gore broadly define jobs to allow for individuals to shape them to suit their strengths and preferences; and how Best Buy more broadly defines work by task and outcome, not time, and broadly defines competencies to ensure they are relevant and meaningful to an individual's work and passions (strategies we call *broad and simple rules*).

- Software company Taleo is developing software that will enable companies to analyze promotion and transfer histories to identify common customized career paths of employees (and then use social network technology to help employees identify and network with people who have taken similar paths to the ones they want to take); and how hiring managers at Forrester Research and a joint venture of DaimlerChrysler, Mitsubishi Motors, and Hyundai get to know potential employees in a more individualized way by engaging them in simulated work tasks (strategies we call an *employee-defined personalization* approach to customization).

In the process of studying these companies and others, we saw first-hand how customization fosters a workforce that is happier and more engaged, and how organizations achieve marketplace advantages through improved employee performance and productivity. Why? Because when rewards, learning, and jobs are customized to individuals, greater motivation and learning result, and people's work tasks become better aligned with their actual strengths. Customization also improves companies' ability to attract and hire top talent by customizing recruiting practices toward specific, desired individuals (and enticing them with a customized experience once they join); moreover, it increases engagement and lowers turnover costs because people who receive customized offerings feel more satisfied in their jobs.

How This Book Is Organized

We have divided this book into three parts. In part I, you'll learn more about the concept of workforce of one, why it works, and why it is so desperately needed—based on six key trends we've observed that are driving organizations toward this approach. We'll present data from our employee survey and explain how the concept is different from other contemporary management concepts like employee empowerment or individualized, one-off employee deals. We'll conclude with a diagnostic that will help you determine how (or if) your organization could benefit from a workforce of one approach, and whether your organization has specific conditions that make workforce of one particularly suitable or important.

Part II will focus on each of the four customization approaches, with one chapter devoted to each. Our goal here is to present an array of rich illustrations of the approaches in practice to help stimulate your thinking about how you might implement a particular customization approach. We'll conclude each chapter with a brief analysis of the inherent advantages and disadvantages of each approach, to help you decide whether it might be appropriate for your organization, and with a summary of our recommendations for using each approach.

Part III will offer some tools and ideas to help you build and manage your own workforce of one organization. In chapter 6, we'll provide you with a guide to help you determine how to create your own unique path toward managing your workforce as a workforce of one by choosing which customization approach or approaches to emphasize based on your specific business needs and types of employees. We'll conclude that chapter with an inside view into how leading workforce of one organizations have chosen different customization approaches best for them.

Chapter 7 addresses many of the organizational challenges inherent in a workforce of one approach. It addresses important questions like these: When everyone's employment experience now varies, how does an organization instill a sense of fairness? How does an organization maintain company unity while focusing on individuals? How can an organization practically manage a multitude of diverse talent management practices with some consistency and control, not to mention limited resources?

Chapter 8 is a call to action for HR professionals to develop their own workforce of one organizations. It provides a road map for how HR can get started to develop an altogether new mandate and sets of skills and capabilities to support a more nuanced and granular—but ultimately more effective—approach to managing talent. The chapter concludes with a brief look toward the future of customized employment experiences.

Who Should Read This Book

This is the first solution-oriented book to address how a wide range of people processes and practices can more effectively improve workforce performance by becoming more personalized, relevant, and tailored to every employee. As such, it was primarily written for those responsible for designing an organization's people practices—whether these people are HR staff, senior leaders, or even people in other functions, such as IT or real estate, whose practices also work to support people's performance at work. This book applies to any company striving to customize its people practices, from large multinationals to rapidly growing start-ups seeking ways to scale without losing a personal touch.

The great organizations of today and tomorrow capitalize on difference, and they provide supporting structures to enable individuals to bring out their best at work. This book is about how companies can take a more nuanced approach to their people, and about how they can make their talent management practices relevant to every employee. It's about creating an environment where individuals can flourish, all while still allowing organizations some measure of control and manageability. But don't get us wrong: this is not just about the individual. It is a business imperative not only when competition for top talent is tough, but when people's performance and productivity can spell the difference between business success and failure. In an age where "granularity will be king," as an article in an *Economist* publication pointed out not long ago—where quantum mechanics breaks matter parts down to the subatomic level, and where each parcel in the supply chain can be marked with a radio-frequency ID tag and tracked and managed individually—it is time for our talent management practices to catch up.[4]

So let's begin with a basic exploration of the workforce of one—what we have come to think of as the new management imperative—starting with a quick glimpse at how Best Buy has already applied these principles to great success.

Part One

Toward a Workforce of One

Our individuality is all, all, that we have. There are those who barter it for security, those who repress it for what they believe is the betterment of the whole society, but blessed in the twinkle of the morning star is the one who nurtures and rides it, in grace and love and wit, from peculiar station to peculiar station along life's bittersweet route.

—Tom Robbins, *Jitterbug Perfume*

The New Management Imperative

A transformation is underfoot. An increasingly diverse workforce, increased job complexity, businesses that depend more than ever on the performance of their people, and the growing demands from people for customized work experiences are all pushing companies away from the paradigm of standardization and uniformity.

—Cheryl Kozak, vice president of human resources, Travelers[1]

THE WORLD KNOWS Best Buy today not only as one of the most successful electronics retailers, with 2009 sales topping $45 billion, but also as one of the best places to work.[2] For Brad Anderson, CEO of Best Buy from 2002 to 2009, those two elements, people and performance, are deeply connected—for better or worse.

Back in the 1970s, when Anderson joined the company, Best Buy was a boutique-style audio electronics dealer; today, the company is the largest consumer electronics retailer in North America. Since Anderson became CEO, revenues have more than doubled, earnings per share have increased over 25 percent, and its stock price has soared, even faring much better than competitors in the 2008/2009 economic downturn.[3] Ultimately, the company's dramatic improvement in financial results meant making an intentional, holistic commitment to providing not only its customers with highly relevant, tailored products and services, but its employees with a highly tailored, *customized* work experience as well—a far cry from the one-size-fits-all people practices that Best Buy had adopted in the 1990s as a strategy to help it cope with its significant growth at the time.

Anderson's plan started with a decision to relentlessly pursue a customer-centricity strategy by learning about Best Buy's customers as individuals, inside and out, and then providing them with highly relevant, tailored shopping experiences. But that new customer focus simply wouldn't work without improved performance from Best Buy's key asset, its people. Anderson, Brian Dunn (then president and COO and now Anderson's successor as CEO), and their HR team knew that it was the company's employees who would make or break the company's ability to deliver on the new strategy. Only through the combined human effort, strengths, and skills of Best Buy's people could the company hope to understand its customers and design experiences uniquely relevant to their diverse needs, aspirations, and desires. More important, they realized that fostering a more productive, high-performing, motivated workforce would mean doing for employees *exactly* what Best Buy had just done for customers: namely, address the problem at the level of the individual to meet people's needs in highly relevant and tailored ways.

Engaging the full power of its diverse set of employees—and winning in the marketplace—meant nothing less than deliberately creating work experiences that leverage each Best Buy employee's unique set of talents, needs, and preferences. So today at Best Buy, employees can define their own customized career paths, and they have great latitude in shaping their own jobs, allowing Best Buy to take full advantage of each employee's unique strengths. But the company also works to unleash people's passion and discretionary energy by catering to their unique interests and life goals (e.g., is she a new college grad looking to rise quickly in the company, or is he a seasoned retailer hoping to grow and learn in his current position?). Rewards, benefits, and even compensation plans like long-term incentives (for eligible managers and executives) are now customized based on what uniquely motivates an individual—fostering greater employee engagement and motivation at work. What's more, performance appraisals aren't generic checklists of standard, often ill-suited criteria as they are in most companies; rather, they are so broadly and simply defined that they can be customized locally to the work a person actually performs. And enabling customization in things like when and where people work means that many of Best Buy's employees can work in ways that are most productive for the individual.

To achieve this level of customization, Best Buy has developed some highly innovative practices—such as its much-touted Results-Only Work Environment ("ROWE") begun in 2004. By simply and broadly defining work in terms of results, Best Buy's ROWE initiative has freed many of its corporate employees to do their work wherever, however, and whenever they wish—as long as they achieve the results set out for them. The program has been so successful that Best Buy has spun off a start-up company, CultureRx, to promote it to other companies.

New technology is also helping Best Buy create other innovative new practices, many of which were unheard-of even several years ago before new technology emerged to make them possible. For example, technology easily enables the company to now administer a customizable long-term incentives program that gives eligible employees the ability to configure their own incentives from a menu of options. And technology now allows the organization to make "smart" learning choice suggestions based on various employee attributes; create highly relevant user-generated learning content that can be shared on YouTube- or Wikipedia-like internal applications (resulting in a better-skilled workforce); and create a dynamic listing of people and their skills, training, and personal aspirations and interests to foster the kind of Facebook-style internal social networking that allows for fluid job movement and highly customized career paths.

Best Buy's new approach to its people, says Tina Decker, head of HR operations, has put talent at the very heart of its strategy. "If we want our employees to provide a highly individualized experience to our customers using their own judgment in a fairly open-ended way, then our employees need to have that same experience as an employee with respect to their work experiences. This has radically redefined the way HR supports its employees in nearly every respect."[4]

The company's ongoing work to customize its people practices already has earned Best Buy today a strong reputation as an employer of choice, with customized talent offerings that have produced a highly engaged and high-performing workforce boasting a minimal attrition rate. Ultimately, the combined customer- and employee-centric approach has helped the company achieve a stunning financial performance by any measure; the company also credits this approach with helping it flexibly adapt when business conditions change, as they did during the 2008/2009 economic downturn.

Later in the book, you'll learn more about how Best Buy has successfully customized its people practices to improve results. You'll also encounter in-depth explorations of three additional companies—Procter & Gamble, Men's Wearhouse, and Royal Bank of Scotland—as well as look at how other leading organizations, in fact, are successfully customizing their people practices. But for now, our point is that Best Buy and other pioneering companies are using an approach to managing their people—what we call *workforce of one*—that many companies today have not hit upon.

Meet Your New Customers: Your Employees

If all of this talk about customization sounds familiar, that's because it is. Ever since Stan Davis introduced the "far-out" concept of mass customization in his book *Future Perfect* in 1987, nothing short of a revolution in marketing has occurred over the past twenty years.[5] And for more than a decade now, companies like Best Buy—as well as everyone from Nike to LEGO to Capital One—have been finding ways to customize experiences for consumers, achieving superior results by treating customers as a "market of one."[6] This veritable "customization revolution" in marketing has led companies to identify individual consumers based on categories such as, for example, a Texas cowboy or an urban African American teen, and to "unbundle" product features for custom configurations, such as Dell does with its build-to-order computers. But it has also led companies like Amazon and Netflix to dynamically present information based on our own previous buying behaviors—and to encourage us to write reviews, thereby allowing consumers themselves to define and create value that is uniquely relevant for them.

But as we illustrated with our opening story of Best Buy, leading companies are increasingly applying this same logic to employees, not viewing their workforces as single monolithic entities but rather viewing each person as a "workforce of one" with distinct and unique needs and preferences—all to maximize employee performance and achieve an advantage in the marketplace. Improving how people perform through customized work experiences could even be considered the "last" competitive advantage, one that's thus far untapped. Just as organizations have become expert at understanding their customers and proactively delivering them customized experiences to great success, companies that customize for employees can look forward to enjoying a sustainable market advantage (see table 1-1).

But customization isn't just good for employees and the productivity and performance of our workforces; it is good for the very function of HR itself—positioning HR to become the true strategic powerhouse it was meant to be. Customization literally *transformed* the marketing function, taking marketing in completely new directions and opening up whole new ways of relating to customers, for both their benefit and that of the organization. And the revolution isn't over yet—most recently, the notions of Web 2.0 user-defined content, smart crowds, collective intelligence, and companies "cocreating" value with customers have taken hold. As C. K. Prahalad writes in his recent book, *The New Age of Innovation*, customization for individual consumers continues to nurture a new age of innovation and entirely new ways of competing and creating value. Customization has

TABLE 1-1

Customizing for customers *and* employees: good for the organization

Potential benefits of customizing for customers	Potential benefits of customizing for employees
• Increase revenues	• Increase workforce performance and productivity
• Improve customer satisfaction	• Improve employee engagement
• Increase value of existing customer base	• Increase value of existing employee base
• Improve customer retention	• Improve employee retention (and reduce turnover costs)
• Attract and acquire the most profitable customers	• Attract and hire the most talented employees
• Reach a larger, more diverse market	• Tap a larger, more diverse employee base— which can breed innovation and help organizations more effectively serve a diverse customer base
• Use resources more effectively through more targeted investments of marketing dollars	• Use resources more effectively through more targeted investments of HR dollars
• Respond more flexibly to a dynamic business environment and changing consumer tastes	• Respond more flexibly to a dynamic business environment and changing employee tastes
• Create a unique advantage by crafting a customized customer experience difficult for competitors to duplicate	• Create a unique advantage by crafting a customized employee experience difficult for competitors to duplicate

transformed consumers from passive recipients to cocreators of compelling individual experiences, one at a time. In this new world of strategy, N=1 (there is one customer).[7] The concept of customization is now poised to revolutionize whole other fields as well; according to Harvard Business School professor Clayton Christensen, recent advances in technology promise to fundamentally transform our entire educational system, customizing learning for all.[8]

Customization can revolutionize HR too. By applying the concepts that have served us so well in our marketing function to our people function next door, this book will help HR unlock new and hidden sources of value by managing its people as a workforce of one. Just as customization elevated marketing from a side function to a truly *strategic* function engaged to help beat competitors, customization can help elevate HR to the top of the CEO's strategic agenda. HR can become an integral part of how the company competes, helping CEOs to truly create a talent-powered organization and deliver on the oft-cited idea that "people are their best asset."[9]

But how, you might well ask, is the workforce of one really new or different from what many companies are already doing? After all, lots of companies have customized learning or are offering things like choices among benefits. But companies like Best Buy and others that we will illustrate in this book are doing things that most organizations haven't even thought about yet. This isn't just flextime or flex benefits or letting people choose where they want to work. Rather, it's about implementing customization broadly and extensively in a proactive, coordinated, and thoughtful manner to achieve the best possible results for both employees and the organization. What we are talking about is a whole new ball game—real customization on a level never practiced before.

Old Model—New Needs

Unfortunately, few employees today experience the kinds of people practices that workforce of one pioneers like Best Buy foster to maximize their people's full potential. Consider this shocking statistic: only 6 percent of the 557 employees we surveyed strongly agreed that their human resource department significantly supported and improved their performance at work. We think it's no coincidence that the same small percentage strongly agreed that their human resources practices were highly relevant to them. This means that a full *94 percent* of employees do not fully believe that the practices specifically designed to support them at work are relevant or helpful in improving their performance! In general, more people disagreed with these statements than agreed with them—implying that they may view employment practices more as a barrier to performance improvement than as an enabler (see figure 1-1 and table 1-2).

This is bad news not only for individuals looking to flourish and develop to their potential, but for their organizations too. When people practices aren't relevant, organizations risk poor employee performance. But they also risk losing people altogether—and failing to attract others in markets where good talent may be difficult to find.

After all, how can companies hope to maximize the performance of a workforce of *individuals* when they treat them all according to the same set of cookie-cutter practices? How can companies get maximum performance from their employees when they fail to offer learning that's tailored to how individuals learn best, or optimize rewards, feedback, and incentives based on how individuals are motivated best? It's a bit like expecting a multitude of different plants and flowers in a garden, each a unique

FIGURE 1-1

Relevance of most people practices today

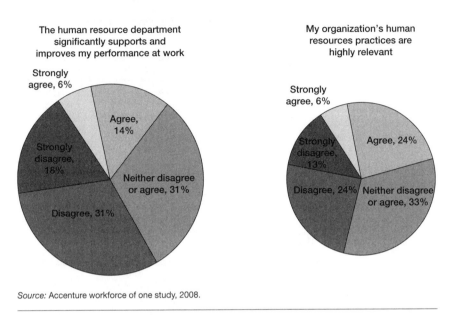

The human resource department
significantly supports and
improves my performance at work

My organization's human
resources practices are
highly relevant

Source: Accenture workforce of one study, 2008.

specimen, to flourish under exactly the same light, soil, and moisture conditions. If we want the garden to reach its full glory as a unified whole, we must carefully attend to the particular needs of different plants in different ways.

Today more than ever, such a tailored, personalized approach to managing human resources is critical. Companies have more types of "plants" to contend with in their "gardens" than ever before. The collective face of the workforce has changed significantly, but organizations have not changed with it. No longer can we count on the fact that an organization's employees will look like one another. In an age of globalization, virtual work, freelancers, an unprecedented four generations in the workforce at once, and more women in the workforce than ever before, we face an increasingly diverse workforce with diverse needs and expectations from work. And even when people don't vary on such dimensions, they are still likely to have vastly different aspirations and needs at work because they have differing personalities and interests (see "The Case of Jill and Helen"). In short, diversity can no longer be understood on just the standard diversity dimensions we have relied on in the past, such as generation, gender, or geography; to really maximize performance, organizations need to begin taking a much more sophisticated look at diversity by capitalizing on difference

TABLE 1-2

Traditional people practices: what employees say

	One-size-fits-all examples	Employee comment
When of work	Companywide work schedule	"I need a different schedule to accommodate child care; I'd be more effective at work if I weren't worried about picking up my kids late again! And besides, I'd be more productive if I could work when I feel I'm at my best."
Where of work	Generic cubicles	"My job requires concentration, but I sit in an open space where I can't get any work done!"
Rewarding and compensating my work	Pay determined by HR based on position; cash-only rewards	"I lost a top performer because of HR-imposed caps on pay."
Definition of my work	Job tasks are standardized and specifically defined, leaving no latitude for interpretation	"I could achieve better results through 'soft selling' than the prescribed way of the hard sell."
Career development at work	Standard, linear, lockstep career paths	"Our new, more 'sophisticated' system slots people into pre-determined roles based on experience and skills. But we either promote people to their level of incompetence, or mistakenly assume that the job a person is most qualified for is the most satisfying. So now many people leave the firm—and we lose that potential talent."
Learning at work	Generic training classes	"Executive education courses are a waste of time. Most people don't learn the same way, but the courses assume they do. And the information tends to be so generic that it's hard to apply to specific situations."
Appraising my work	Generic assessment criteria and method of appraisal	"Performance appraisals are merely a bureaucratic exercise to set merit increases. They don't help me improve my performance, because the criteria I'm rated on don't align with what I actually do in my job."

across a whole new host of dimensions: values, motivations, strengths, learning styles, wellness profiles, mobility, life stage, and more.

The trouble is, most organizations haven't caught up with this new reality of shifting workforce demographics and needs. Our survey revealed that few employees feel their organizations excel at meeting the needs of a diverse workforce on many dimensions. In fact, fully 25 percent of employees feel that their organizations do not excel at meeting the needs of *any* of the seventeen different types of diversity profiles we named (see figure 1-2). What's more, HR leaders themselves report that their HR departments need to do some catching-up. One Hewitt Associates study, for example, found that only one-third of HR leaders feel that their staffs have the skills to serve a diverse workforce, and only 22 percent feel they have the skills to serve a global one.[10] And a growing number of business articles highlight executives' increasing concerns that HR practices are too inflexible and rigid to provide significant organizational value.[11]

And there's more: evidence suggests that many standard HR practices no longer seem to be working as intended. Only 8 percent of respondents in a study by the Human Resource Institute believe performance appraisals contribute significantly to individual performance, and by some estimates, only 10 percent of employees feel very satisfied with their organization's training.[12] Although we could attribute these results to any number of factors, our interviews with employees point to one key reason that people practices may now be failing: because trying to satisfy a workforce's needs with one broad, standardized stroke is no longer working. A bevy of academic studies suggest the same.[13]

And yet, despite the value that customized people practices will likely provide, evidence suggests that few organizations now offer them. Our survey revealed that only about 10 percent of employees currently enjoy customized experiences, with a third to a half agreeing that they have only somewhat customized experiences. (For more survey findings, see the appendix at the end of this book, How Many Employees Have Customized Work Experiences?) Although many companies *are* increasingly using a customized approach to manage their people, the survey results reflect the fact that in most organizations, there's still much work to be done.

None of this is to place the blame on the shoulders of HR. As we illustrated with the Best Buy example and will continue to show throughout this book, standard HR practices have in fact served organizations quite well for many years. HR has pursued these standardized policies for very good reasons—the need for fairness, consistency, and efficiency not being the least of these. In the last decade especially, as large companies implemented large enterprise systems and globalized at the same time, most organizations have galvanized their efforts and technology resources

The Case of Jill and Helen

Jill and Helen are both high-performing first-level U.S. managers who head IT development projects at a *Fortune* 500 consumer products company. Yet for all the similarities in their nationality, gender, job titles, and even job descriptions, they couldn't be more different both in how they each approach their work and in what they need from the company to perform at their best.

Jill, an energetic twenty-nine-year-old who was recently married, lives to work. "I am success oriented and trying to position myself on the fast track to a leadership spot," she explains. "I like leading people and having the power to set policies and direction, and I don't mind the lifestyle and financial affluence that comes along with it!" She puts in long, hard hours and excels by fast decision making, attention to detail, networking, and playing "ambassador" by representing her team's work to others and bringing back fresh ideas. She craves rapid, constant feedback even if it's negative. Jill also admits she has trouble focusing on one thing for extended periods and prefers jumping from project to project. Her preferred learning style? Through experience or else self-directed, short segments that are visual or auditory in nature.

Helen, on the other hand, at fifty-two years old, isn't after money, power, or advancement. She cashed in on lucrative stock options a decade ago and is well on her road to a comfortable retirement. For Helen, work is about the fun of solving logical analytical puzzles and about contribution—both in creating IT products to improve others' lives and in mentoring her people. "I love my work and am very good at it," says Helen, "but I want a balanced life where I also have time to care for my aging parents and explore other interests, like photography, travel, and charity work." Highly focused, Helen learns best by blocking out periods of quiet time for reading or discussion with others. She doesn't need constant feedback—in fact, she explains that "truthfully, any negative feedback I receive makes me just want to shut down and work less."

Given two such dramatically different people as Helen and Jill are, you'd expect they would need radically different things from an organization. Yet their company treats them largely the same—and misses getting the best from either. Both work in standard cubicles, but Jill would be more effective if allowed to rotate among each of her teams in open team rooms, and Helen needs more quiet space for concentration and conversations with subordinates. And although the standard up-or-out career path toward higher levels of management works well for Jill, it doesn't for Helen. "I'm just not interested in rising to the top," Helen explains. "I would rather make lateral moves to explore other interests and keep close to the technology and analytical problem solving I love." Both work upwards of fifty hours a week in the office, but Helen concedes she could be even more effective if she put in less time, to keep her mind fresh. If allowed to temporarily downshift with a sabbatical or reduced office hours, Helen feels she could become reinvigorated at work and achieve her goal of settling her parents into a nursing home nearby.

The two also differ in how they need to be compensated and rewarded. Rather than being paid in wages and a yearly cash bonus, Helen would be more motivated by personalized rewards, like the ability to volunteer on company time or even a whimsy trophy award like a Kate Spade handbag. But Jill would prefer to take as much compensation as possible in growth-oriented stock awards or perhaps a discount on a luxury kitchen for her new condo. The standard benefits package does little for either: Helen would like more medical coverage or "green" benefits she would care about, like a discount on a hybrid car or care for the elderly; for Jill, the medical coverage is more than she needs—she'd rather receive pet insurance for her beloved golden retriever or a health club membership.

When it comes to performance management, the one-size-fits-all approach likewise fits neither of them. Jill's ability to act as an ambassador, for example, isn't listed as a competency—and she's offered no learning opportunities to help her build on this strength. The performance appraisal criteria are so irrelevant, in fact, that Jill and Helen's superior ignores the appraisal form each year and writes, "See attached," to address their abilities and "areas for improvement." Moreover, the once-a-year feedback provided is too late and infrequent to really help Jill stay on track; and for Helen, it takes her months after receiving the feedback to feel inspired to work again. Both are marched through the same classroom and online training, even though Helen already knows 60 percent of the content, and even though both would be able to absorb and apply the material much better by having the content delivered to them in a different way—podcasts or simulated games for Jill and self-study material for Helen.

Sums up Helen, "I would perform best if my company was more like a good parent. Parents don't do the same thing for every child; rather, they create an environment where each child can thrive and develop based on his or her differing needs and temperaments." Adds Jill, "I don't understand why I can customize my cell phone ringer to songs I like, my credit card terms based on my financial situation, and my clothes to fit my body type—but am unable to have customized learning, rewards, and career experiences at work! I'd like My Work, My Way."

FIGURE 1-2

Do organizations meet the needs of today's diverse workforce?

My organization's employee practices do an excellent job of meeting the needs and preferences of people with different (multiple-answer responses accepted):

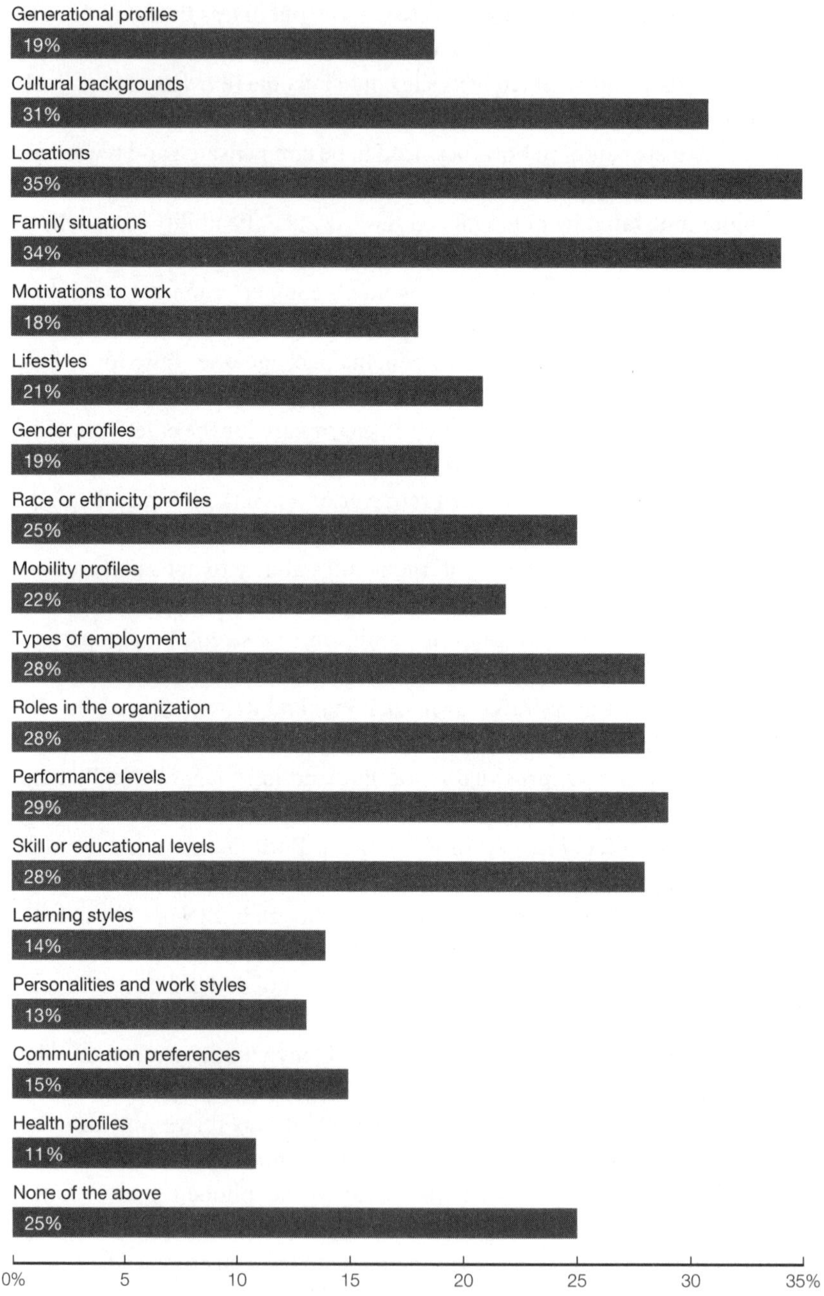

Generational profiles
19%

Cultural backgrounds
31%

Locations
35%

Family situations
34%

Motivations to work
18%

Lifestyles
21%

Gender profiles
19%

Race or ethnicity profiles
25%

Mobility profiles
22%

Types of employment
28%

Roles in the organization
28%

Performance levels
29%

Skill or educational levels
28%

Learning styles
14%

Personalities and work styles
13%

Communication preferences
15%

Health profiles
11%

None of the above
25%

| 0% | 5 | 10 | 15 | 20 | 25 | 30 | 35% |

Source: Accenture workforce of one study, 2008.

toward standardizing their people practices. The goal, of course, was to achieve a global view of their people and operate consistently as a unified organization rather than as a series of fragmented parts based on geography or business unit—where each did things differently, not from solid business reasons or to serve diverse employee needs, but more because of history, acquisitions, or the desire for autonomy. To be sure, organizations have spent years trying to gain control by applying one set of rules to everything from the benefits and rewards offered to how employees are trained and evaluated—all to provide one solution that met the needs of most of the workforce most of the time.

But today some of those very same reasons for standardization (e.g., an increasingly globalized and diverse workforce) now demand a new and very different solution. Couple this new environment with the fact that technology and HR infrastructure have advanced enough to enable new solutions in a scalable, manageable fashion (more on this point shortly)—and we are looking at a veritable sea change as HR becomes ready to adopt a new model of managing people to suit a new era. In fact, HR professionals now face a great challenge over the next decades: nothing less than to find ways to capitalize on the growing complexity of the workforce. Employees' desire for individuality, personal growth, and self-realization means crafting tailored practices to bring out their best in a systematic, manageable, and thoughtful way.

The Good News About Standardization

So why hasn't all of this been done before? With all of the benefits that customization offers, why didn't HR departments everywhere start doing this long ago? The answer is as complex as it is fundamentally simple: technologically speaking, *HR departments haven't been able to do this until now*. To be sure, new HR software has enabled more efficiency and scale, among other things. But while organizations have used new technology to customize products and services, they've yet to apply it to customizing their talent offerings—specifically, to smoothly managing multiple people practices in highly transparent, cost-efficient, and scalable ways. Nor have most companies applied the technology they have for tracking, monitoring, and managing data toward achieving superior *workforce performance*.

This brings us to an interesting paradox we've discovered—and some good news: all the hard work of standardization and control that organizations have spent so long achieving, especially through technology, doesn't need to be tossed out in order to pursue the kind of customization we're talking about. Indeed, much of that same standardization that HR has by necessity pursued for so long is actually an important foundation enabling customization. A workforce of one approach is thus not a return to the chaotic lack of people management or a hodgepodge of one-off deals of the past before HR put some controls in place. As we will show, the four approaches to customization that we propose are in fact built on standards, which is precisely what makes them controllable and manageable—but standards that allow flexibility rather than sameness. So what we call "segmentation" and "modular choice" merely expand the number of standard practices and options available; our "broad and simple rules" are standard but flexible enough to accommodate an individual's unique needs; and "employee-defined personalization" is supported by standard management and technology practices.

So now that organizations have defined a baseline platform for standard processes, they can more easily add an additional layer of complexity—by using a workforce of one approach to radically expand the number and variety of standard practices, for example, or to broaden them to be more flexible. Likewise, now that companies have integrated HR processes and data across the entire employee experience (from discovering talent to defining talent needs to developing and deploying that talent), they can look strategically at the *whole* employee (and customize accordingly), rather than viewing individuals as a series of fragmented parts.

A solid infrastructure to support HR processes helps too—this may include getting the fundamentals like payroll working to gain employee trust; establishing a shared services center for efficient and consistent processing of transactions like those involving benefits administration; and capturing standard data on employees or jobs that can be managed and tracked in a data warehouse. Without such an infrastructure, it would be hard, for example, to understand patterns in different workforce segments, track the various choices employees make, or offer all jobs for employees to view on a common platform. A traditional HR service delivery model provides a standard infrastructure to support continued flexibility and complexity inherent in a workforce of one approach.

In short, all this hard work HR organizations have done in the past decade now enables an organization to more easily administrate a greater variety of people practices. But don't confuse a workforce of one approach with the variety of people practices companies sometimes offer employees to accommodate division-level autonomy or because of the organization's history of acquisitions. In a workforce of one approach, variation exists, but only in a highly coordinated, controlled manner—and only when there are good, strategic business reasons for how variation can maximize employee performance. To achieve a coordinated and strategic approach to customization, most companies first need to go through the evolutionary

FIGURE 1-3

The evolution of talent management

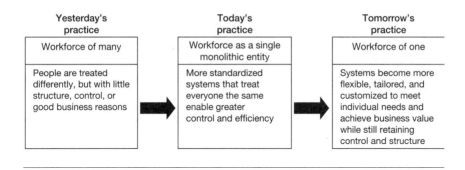

Yesterday's practice	Today's practice	Tomorrow's practice
Workforce of many	Workforce as a single monolithic entity	Workforce of one
People are treated differently, but with little structure, control, or good business reasons	More standardized systems that treat everyone the same enable greater control and efficiency	Systems become more flexible, tailored, and customized to meet individual needs and achieve business value while still retaining control and structure

stage of *reducing* uncontrolled and nonstrategic variation to build a common platform from which to support strategic, controlled customization.

All of this is to say that we believe that managing a workforce as a workforce of one will represent the next major phase of HR's journey in transformation after standardization and harmonization of people practices. Now that most organizations have already wrung all the costs they can out of the system by standardizing on a one-size-fits-all solution in their pursuit of efficiency, the next phase will be to pursue *value* by leveraging off of a common infrastructure and standardized framework to make employment practices relevant to every employee in a more granular, customized people management approach (see figure 1-3). This will enable organizations to continue to reap the benefits of standardization (efficiency and control) while also being locally relevant and customized to every employee.

Before we move on to describing each of our four workforce of one approaches, let's look first at six major trends today that we believe are converging to transform the organizational "workplace" into a "myplace" that more closely fits employees' individual needs.

Six Trends Driving the *Work*place to Become *My*Place

You are likely familiar with some of the key trends driving the workforce of one (see figure 1-4), especially the last three; but we present them here along with three newer trends we've identified, because, together, they represent important pieces in this larger picture of change emerging in today's workforce.

FIGURE 1-4

Key trends driving the workforce of one

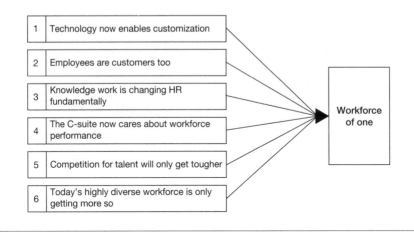

Trend 1: Technology Now Enables Customization

As we started to discuss earlier in this chapter, perhaps the most exciting new trend driving a more customized approach to talent management is the development of increasingly sophisticated technology and supportive HR infrastructure. All of this makes a workforce of one model easier and more cost-effective to implement. Business intelligence and analytics has spurred a revolution in the way companies compete; workforce of one pioneers are now developing people intelligence to likewise revolutionize the way they create highly relevant and differentiated employee offerings.[14]

Yet, to date, technology has merely accelerated the speed and ease by which traditional HR operations and transactions are handled, and allowed organizations to finally apply consistent HR practices across the workforce. Fortunately, companies can use all of that hard-won standardization as a kind of root system, enabling a workforce of one approach to blossom.

Technology in the future, however, will help enable a very different organizational goal from standardization and uniformity—it will allow companies to differentiate the workforce and manageably apply more granularity to how they treat their people. Technology has enabled ever-closer relationships with customers, so why not with employees? Just as with consumers, technology can span the bridge—organization to individual, and individual to individual. For example, technology can help an organization:

- Know employees. Employee data can now be captured and mined on everything from demographics and behaviors to communication or e-mail patterns, to determine customized offerings. Organizations can now get to know their workforce in a bottom-up way based on real data, rather than making top-down assumptions that often don't fit reality or that quickly become outdated.

- Customize for employees.

  - Selectively push out customized offerings—including targeted, personalized messages, learning and job opportunities, or personalized information such as might be found in a role-based portal—based on smart algorithms and artificial intelligence that predict what an individual needs and values.

  - Break down information on things like learning content, performance appraisal criteria, benefits, or even job activities into smaller chunks, keep track of it, and modularly configure it to create a custom offering.

  - Model and automate customization decisions to make sure they are right for individuals and stay within reasonable bounds—like determining the best benefits package based on modeling a person's risk tolerance and financial profile, or modeling trade-offs and implications of different decisions.

  - Make information necessary for customization more easily available to individuals and their managers—like what reward options they have, who in their network knows what they need to know or has followed a similar customized career path to the one they desire, or what jobs they may pursue next in a customized career path and their readiness for each opportunity.

  - Capture knowledge and information from employees themselves and enable them to easily share it when and how they desire in a customized fashion via YouTube-like videos, podcasts, and blogs—and enable others to rate, apply, and edit the information for a continually improving knowledge base.

  - Enable people to work anywhere, anytime, thereby creating customized schedules and work environments.

- Manage customization in a controlled and transparent way. With the help of technology, HR professionals can now monitor what employees choose and what customized talent management practices specific employees receive. They can now accommodate differences but still roll data up for a central view or drill down for individual visibility.

- Predict the impact of customization on performance. Through the use of analytics, organizations can now predict and drive different types of employee behavior, and model employee behavior's impact on performance.

Considering how important technology is to customization, and its recent radical advances, it's no wonder that the talent management software market is booming: such software leads the technology growth in organizations and is projected to expand over the next five years by 12 percent annually.[15] According to many analysts, talent management software—especially enterprise resource planning (ERP) systems—is growing ever more flexible and able to handle a greater variety and complexity of people practices. And service-oriented architecture (SOA), which enables different systems to more easily share information, only promises to make them even more flexible. Using SOA, for example, multiple computer systems to support different segments of the employee population could work seamlessly together. More advanced and cheaper technology will make a workforce of one approach to people management an increasingly affordable proposition. And with today's improvements in HR infrastructure, organizations can now flex to accommodate differences among individuals much more effectively than they could even just a decade ago.

Trend 2: Employees Are Customers Too

As we already began to touch on earlier in this chapter, people over the past decade have become so used to making purchases tailored to their needs and preferences that they almost take it for granted. Whether we are talking about clothes or computers, vehicles or home amenities, customization has eroded the belief that one size must fit all in most aspects of everyday life. In fact, it's hard to imagine a world without it.

The same people who've gotten used to such a variety of customization as consumers are now demanding greater customization as employees. (Only 28 percent of employees we surveyed did *not* feel a heightened expectation for customization at work today based on their experience with customization as consumers.) The demand for customization is especially strong among our next generation of workers who have never known anything different. After all, they've grown up amid a revolution in consumer technology that allows for transparent, honest, and customized information via blogs, electronic social networks, discussion boards, and the like. Says Don Tapscott, who has studied the "Net Generation" extensively, this generation demands customization in everything—from the products they buy to job descriptions, to working environments, to compensation programs. They also tend to value self-determination and autonomy, and have a consumer-focused approach to work, asking questions like "What value are you giving me for my time?"[16]

Accordingly, employees have become less comfortable with the status quo and are pressing to change policies, procedures, and programs or are negotiating exceptions to them.[17] These attitudes are consistent with employees' heightened expectation that they will have a voice in the organization—an increasingly accepted social norm.[18] And as employees become more valuable in today's knowledge economy, yet less loyal or dependent on any single organization, they have greater power to negotiate employment conditions that suit them.[19]

That's why companies need to take a deliberate approach to customization—or find themselves forced to do so in far less desirable ways, as employee pressure mounts. By proactively customizing people practices, companies have the chance to customize in a way they can live with, rather than in a way they cannot.

But there may be an even more important reason for organizations to take this expectation—demand, even—of customization seriously: applied to the workplace, customized employee experiences can unlock people's passion and commitment in their jobs. As scientists continue to explore human behavior, they find that people are very different from one another indeed—they learn differently, react to stress differently, and are motivated differently.[20] When people practices become irrelevant because they don't accommodate such differences, they fail to unlock passion and productivity and instead become exercises in needless bureaucracy.[21] When we aren't allowed to bring our whole selves to work, hiding key parts of ourselves in order to fit the corporate standard, work becomes more about compliance than commitment. Both the organization and the individual lose out when people's natural strengths and talents are made to conform to generic practices.

On the other hand, organizations that offer customized work experiences grant people tremendous benefits, including what Carl Jung calls *individuation*—the process of psychological differentiation that leads to greater self-realization and fulfillment.[22] Under these conditions, people are far more likely to perform to their potentials and to better balance work with life pursuits.

Trend 3: Knowledge Work Is Changing HR Fundamentally

Everyone knows how the growing amount of knowledge work has made jobs far more complex today than ever. In the past, not only did people have more uniform lives, but they also had far more uniform jobs. Life was more stable; jobs more predictable. The advent of the knowledge economy has changed all this. Knowledge workers (or professionals who use knowledge as the primary component of their jobs) now constitute about 34 percent of the labor force and are responsible for most of the economic growth in the past decade.[23] Meanwhile, knowledge-oriented companies have grown rapidly, as evidenced by the doubling of the ratio of market to book value over the past twenty years.

But what fewer people might understand is how all of these new knowledge workers are affecting HR. When work is more fluid and knowledge–based, it becomes harder to standardize work and related talent management practices based on job title or position alone.[24] Job titles are less relevant when work is complex and integrated or when it's performed through teams or assignments. Many organizations now find it more meaningful to tie compensation, rewards, and learning programs to employees' assignments or other criteria like preferences rather than to formal job titles because people who share job titles often do very different work. Such was the case with Jill and Helen in our sidebar earlier in this chapter. And our research reveals that they aren't unique—more than half of employees today with the same title and level do very different work from one another (see figure 1-5).

It comes as no surprise that most of the workforce of one pioneers we profile in this book, like Microsoft, Capital One, and Google, are

FIGURE 1-5

Same job title, different job

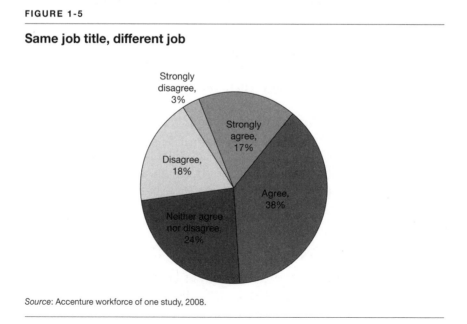

Source: Accenture workforce of one study, 2008.

knowledge-based organizations looking for a more flexible talent management model for a new era. Knowledge workers often demand more flexibility, autonomy, and fit between themselves and their work environment. And when an organization can no longer rely on static job titles or organizational charts to determine what practices are relevant to a particular employee, it is time for talent management practices and policies to change so that they fit the individual, not just the job.

Trend 4: The C-Suite Now Cares About Workforce Performance

Given the fact that economists now view people and their performance as the last competitive advantage and critical to the success of the organization, more executives are now willing to embrace a more sophisticated, nuanced, yet undoubtedly more complex talent management model.[25]

Take a few workforce of one mavericks, for example. Royal Bank of Scotland took a more customized approach to people management after an internal study revealed that its people practices and the performance of its people significantly affect business results. Even as the bank has suffered significant losses in the wake of the financial crisis at the end of this decade, the bank still knows that the performance of its people is vital to its ability to bounce back. And Procter & Gamble has developed unique human resource and organizational practices that often feature customization based in part on the realization that with a marketplace value of $200 billion, only $50 billion now resides in the form of tangible assets (plants and inventories).[26] This means that 75 percent of its value (as measured by stock price) is in the form of intangible assets—its brands and its people! It is no surprise then that effective talent management is at the top of CEO A. G. Lafley's agenda.

Research shows that like P&G and Royal Bank of Scotland, most organizations have no longer relegated HR or talent management to the shadowy recesses of the business. They are now front and center, among executives' most pressing responsibilities, taking more than 20 percent of CEOs' time.[27] And no wonder, when study after study—our own included—has found statistical proof that business performance is positively linked with people and their effective management.[28] Indeed, we found significant correlations between business results and how supported employees feel by their people practices.[29] What's more, our studies show that employees themselves feel that customized people practices would improve their performance at work (see figure 1-6).

Clearly, customization is not just an attraction and retention tool, a "nice to have" that might disappear in recessionary climates when talent markets become less heated. Rather, it is vital to improved people performance and

FIGURE 1-6

Employees say customization would improve their performance

My performance would improve at an organization where:

When I work is based on my unique needs and preferences

61%

My physical work setting is highly conducive to the work I do and suits
my unique needs and preferences

69%

My mix of benefits can be customized based on my unique needs and preferences

54%

My mix of cash, stock options, and other forms of compensation can be
customized based on my unique needs and preferences

59%

The incentives, recognition, and rewards my organization gives me are
relevant, meaningful, and tailored to what motivates me best

73%

Performance appraisals are relevant, meaningful, and tailored based on
what I do and how I receive feedback best

67%

What, when, and how I learn is based on my unique needs, preferences,
and learning style

70%

My organization supports me in a customized career path where subsequent
jobs are based on my unique interests, needs, and capabilities

72%

My list of job responsibilities can be tailored based on my unique strengths
and interests

72%

My organization customizes its recruiting approach based on a candidate's
unique characteristics

59%

Hiring decisions are based on a rich and thorough understanding of the
whole person and their unique traits, strengths, weaknesses, and capabilities

61%

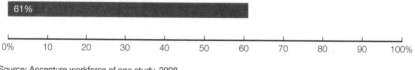

| 0% | 10 | 20 | 30 | 40 | 50 | 60 | 70 | 80 | 90 | 100% |

Source: Accenture workforce of one study, 2008.

productivity—a must-have when businesses must squeeze more work out of fewer people during economic cutbacks, and when they often must quickly reskill their people to handle a changed environment. Customization is thus a business imperative for organizations whose success depends on the performance of their people—no matter what the economic climate. As more executives realize this critical link, they will increasingly ensure that their people practices are as relevant as possible for improving every employee's performance and his ability to make an impact on the bottom line—even if it means giving up a one-size-fits-all approach in favor of a more complex one to do it.

Trend 5: Competition for Talent Will Only Get Tougher

Just when economists have determined that people are more important to a company's financial results than ever before, talented people are harder to find than ever.[30] This is true even during times of economic downturn, since companies see hard times as an opportunity to attract the best talent—and end up vying with other companies for it. It's often hard to retain top talent too, in part because people are changing jobs more than ever before.[31] With employee turnover costing as much as 10 percent of revenue, turnover can be an expensive proposition. We can see evidence of the talent shortage everywhere—from Dow Chemical expecting 30 percent of its twenty thousand workers to retire by 2012, to competitors like Yahoo!, Microsoft, and Google publicly (and legally) battling it out in the headlines to keep their talented people.[32] In such an environment, more companies will be looking to attract and retain workers with a unique employee value proposition— and to wring better performance and productivity from the employees they have. These are two key reasons Microsoft has moved to a customized workforce of one talent management model that it dubs "myMicrosoft," meant to reflect the fact that HR practices will vary based on individual needs and preferences. Two of its basic tenets? "Don't copy standard best practices" and "Think tailoring to individuals instead of one-size-fits-all."

When good talent is difficult to find and keep, recruiting practices that are customized to individuals will be more effective in targeting the people the organization hopes to hire. And potential employees will be enticed by the promise of a customized experience once they join. The evidence supports that notion: a full 80 percent of the employees we surveyed said they would be more attracted to an organization with customized people practices than one without, and 78 percent said they would more likely remain at an organization with more customized people practices. (To see how employees thought specific customized practices would affect their attraction and retention, see figure 1-7).

FIGURE 1-7

Employees say customization would attract and retain them

I would be more likely to be attracted to and remain at an organization where:

When I work is based on my unique needs and preferences
67%

My physical work setting is highly conducive to the work I do and suits my unique needs and preferences
78%

My mix of benefits can be customized based on my unique needs and preferences
84%

My mix of cash, stock options, and other forms of compensation can be customized based on my unique needs and preferences
73%

The incentives, recognition, and rewards my organization gives me are relevant, meaningful, and tailored to what motivates me best
83%

Performance appraisals are relevant, meaningful, and tailored based on what I do and how I receive feedback best
75%

What, when, and how I learn is based on my unique needs, preferences, and learning style
73%

My organization supports me in a customized career path where subsequent jobs are based on my unique interests, needs, and capabilities
78%

My list of job responsibilities can be tailored based on my unique strengths and interests
79%

My organization customizes its recruiting approach based on a candidate's unique characteristics
55%

Hiring decisions are based on a rich and thorough understanding of the whole person and their unique traits, strengths, weaknesses, and capabilities
71%

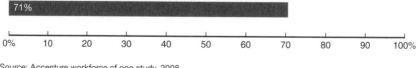

0%   10   20   30   40   50   60   70   80   90   100%

Source: Accenture workforce of one study, 2008.

Trend 6: Today's Highly Diverse Workforce Is Only Getting More So

Consider the workforce on which *The Organization Man* was based: IBM's, the epitome of homogeneity when the book was published in 1956.[33] Today, IBM has adopted many workforce of one management practices to accommodate the needs of its highly diverse employees: some 375,000 people working on six continents (90,000 of whom it recently hired from developing countries like Brazil, China, and India), 40 percent of whom don't work in the office at all, and 30 percent of whom are women.[34]

The story of IBM's growing diversity is echoed in countless organizations across the globe, driven by changing social, demographic, and economic trends. According to an International Labor Organization study, women represent 40 percent of the global workforce, with 70 percent of the developed world's women employed full-time.[35] Moreover, the number and types of family structures has so rapidly grown that the old model of a breadwinner dad and a stay-at-home mom accounts for just one-tenth of households in the United States today.[36] And there's more: an unprecedented four and sometimes even five generations are now in the workplace at once—and research suggests that each generation has different perceptions, attitudes, and behaviors vis-à-vis work ethic, skill building, rewards, and more.[37]

Likewise, fewer employees today want the standard full-time job. A survey of baby boomers looking toward retirement, for example, revealed that only 6 percent want to work full-time; most would prefer to cycle between work and leisure or to work part-time.[38] And across all age groups, fewer people than ever are seeking more responsibility and advancement in their jobs.[39]

Consider, too, that "going global" no longer means simply putting Americans or Europeans on foreign soil or relegating low-end jobs to cheaper locations; companies are now facing a "multipolar" world where there are multiple centers of economic power and activity and where superpowers like the United States, Japan, and Europe no longer call all the shots. This means that workers worldwide, in different levels and job types, are now more than ever before likely to work side by side in virtual communion. Accordingly, technologies enabling virtual work have led International Data Corporation (IDC) to predict the number of worldwide mobile workers to reach 1 billion by 2011.[40] And in another trend, the U.S. Department of Labor now estimates that over 30 percent of the country's workforce now enjoys some type of alternative contractual employment arrangement.[41]

Fortunately, companies today seem to understand that a diverse workforce can help improve decision making, avoid groupthink, and operate better in a global environment where customers are also diverse. And when talent markets are hot, companies will have to proactively seek out even more diversity, tapping unmined talent sources like women reentering the workforce after having children or older retired workers. They may also leverage a broader spectrum of work relationships, like seasonal employment, ageless internships, or on-call work. And even in recessionary climates characterized by extensive cost cutting, diversity will likely grow—as companies look to import workers or export work to places where workers are more plentiful and less costly.

As workers become more diverse and seek a wider array of career paths, their demands from employers will become increasingly unique. And that's what is driving companies like PepsiCo and other workforce of one leaders to radically transform HR toward customizing their people practices. Explains Greig Aitken, group head of employee engagement at Royal Bank of Scotland, "With a diverse workforce managing 42 brands in 53 countries, we've found it impossible to make one decision and satisfy every employee . . . this simply doesn't work anymore."[42]

Why Workforce of One Works

Given the trends just described, clearly companies need a new model if they hope to manage today's workforce and draw out the best from every employee. Workforce of one, in which employees are managed through highly tailored people practices, is this new model. But the question remains: just how can an organization achieve customization and myriad employment arrangements without devolving into chaos? Workforce of one works because it avoids such a scenario. It enables organizations to achieve customization in a highly structured, coordinated, and scalable way that retains some degree of organizational control, consistency, and manageability while meeting individuals' needs (more on exactly how this is accomplished shortly).

Equally important, a workforce of one approach avoids a key problem that today's HR departments often bump up against: in their quest to be all things to all people, they end up reducing what is offered to the lowest common denominator. For example, one manager may have problems handling conflict, while another has trouble giving productive feedback—yet they both get put together in a course on engaging employees. Neither gets what they need to be effective. And although standardization can bring efficiencies, giving people what they don't want or need is wasteful and inefficient. Workforce of one is not about spending lots more money on talent management; it is about wisely spending money in a more targeted, effective way to achieve the best results. It is about transforming HR from a value saver into a value creator.

And unlike many recent popular management ideas arguing for the end of hierarchy, workforce of one is still largely a top-down, structured, rules-based approach to customization. Workforce of one is not about granting people unlimited freedom or empowerment, or transforming employees into free agents who work for themselves, for example. Our survey suggests that a full 74 percent of employees don't want to take full responsibility for developing their own "human capital" and would rather do so with the help and support of their organizations. Left to their own devices and with little enabling structure, most people feel overwhelmed and end up doing little about it.

Moreover, workforce of one is not about transforming HR into a "strategic business partner." Although in theory a laudable goal, recently such focus has sometimes forced HR to neglect the role of employee advocate or people-performance improver. As HR departments have been increasingly aligned with finance and partnering with senior executives, they've often found it almost unavoidable to treat people like numbers. Meanwhile, employees' needs sometimes get neglected, affecting their effectiveness. So, while there has been lots of talk in the last decades about how HR must fit with the *business* goals it hopes to serve, we believe HR must now reassert its fit with the *employee* goals it hopes to serve as well.

Workforce of one is a return to focusing on employees and their needs—albeit in a much deeper way than merely the old-school attention to employee grievances or protecting employee rights. And it radically deepens traditional notions of diversity and inclusion as well. Instead of stand-alone training or hiring programs that address difference, or striving to give everyone the same employment deal to ensure no discrimination, the idea of capitalizing on difference becomes so embedded into an organization and its everyday operations that the very *structure* of its people practices and policies changes to flexibly capitalize on individual differences. Workforce of one is about bridging the needs of the collective *and* the individual; about aligning people practices with strategy *and* with individual needs; and about achieving superior business performance *through* achieving superior individual performance. It is a win-win mentality where employees and their needs are not sacrificed at the expense of the needs of the business.

Workforce of one works too because it isn't about special treatment or customization for just the leadership ranks, the elite, or the most valuable employees. Although we recognize that customizing for these types of employees can be a valid strategy as part of an overall approach to customization, focusing exclusively on such narrow segments ignores the performance improvements that can occur in the bulk of the workforce that can really drive business results.

But perhaps most important, workforce of one works because it is not about making individual one-off side deals. The trouble with these individually negotiated arrangements between boss and employee is that they are difficult to control, scale, or manage consistently or fairly. Without a common, supporting organizational structure and framework for customization, such deals can quickly turn into favoritism. With these arrangements, it is also difficult to ensure that customization is done appropriately and optimally, and achieve visibility into exactly how people are managed. Such arrangements also aren't good for employees, who find themselves reliant on the whims of their boss regarding how to shape their work to suit their unique needs.

Yet because companies increasingly rely on these one-off arrangements (Denise Rousseau estimates that between 25 percent and 40 percent of employees now have them), clearly organizations are already feeling the pressure to customize people practices.[43] But rather than do this in a reactive, scattershot way, a workforce of one approach allows companies to bring customization "out of the closet." They can deliberately and consciously establish practices, policies, and standards that make customization a commonplace, well-thought-out event for all.

One final point before we move on to describe each of our four approaches to creating a customized employment experience: workforce of one works because it has adopted tried-and-true lessons from marketing. As we pointed out earlier, customizing for employees is a lot like customizing for customers. Great customer service does not assume that one department—sales and marketing—take sole responsibility for customer interaction. Product managers, call center representatives, even support staff in most organizations today must understand and often interact with customers. Similarly, it is precisely because people practices have largely been shunted off to one department—HR—that they often fall short. Our research presents an alternative solution: share the burden. Instead of one-size-fits-all HR programs, with workforce of one talent management becomes more of an individualized, close-to-the-action responsibility of every manager and employee—supported by organizational practices and processes that are customized to the individual.

And like marketing, workforce of one does not assume there is one yellow brick road to success. Rather, it is a strategic philosophy and "meta-model" that can generate multiple ideas regarding how to create the right kind of customized people practices for the unique needs of an organization and types of workers by varying the types of customization approaches and practices used. For this reason, we believe that most organizations can find a customization approach that works for them. This is true whether they are autocratic or democratic in nature, whether they operate in regulated or nonregulated industries or countries, and whether most of their employees earn minimum wage or whether they are mostly highly paid professionals.

A few organizations, however, will have characteristics that will make a workforce of one approach not suitable: if the organization is so small (e.g., forty employees or less) that it doesn't need a structured, methodical system for managing talent; if the performance of an organization's people makes little difference to its success; if an organization does not wish to significantly improve the quality of its employees' lives in the interest of social responsibility; or if an organization is simply not yet ready to engage in a new and more complex way of managing its talent. But even if any of those things are the case, a company may eventually be forced to pursue customization anyway, just to keep up with competitors. We believe that for organizations to thrive in the next era, eventually workforce of one will become imperative for nearly all companies. (See the assessment "Is a Workforce of One for You?" at the end of the chapter for a closer look at how you can benefit from a workforce of one and if you have conditions that make workforce of one particularly suitable or important.)

The Four Workforce of One Approaches to Customization

After a comprehensive study of more than one hundred companies, we have determined four distinct ways that an organization can customize using policies and practices in a structured, rules-based manner (see figure 1-8). Each of the four approaches can enable an organization to meet *both* the collective needs of the business and its strategy *and* the needs of an individual. Each approach can also enable an organization to maintain relative degrees of control, consistency, and scalability.

As we'll show throughout this book, the four workforce of one customization approaches are not mutually exclusive and can be easily used alone or in combination with one another. An organization need not use all four approaches, nor use just one. Although all four customization approaches can move an organization toward its customization goals, each customization approach does have distinct advantages and disadvantages, challenges related to fairness, control, administration, or transparency, and different management and resource implications, as we'll show in subsequent chapters. Some customization approaches are more HR driven, for example, with HR defining the details of the people practice—thereby

FIGURE 1-8

The four workforce of one approaches to customization

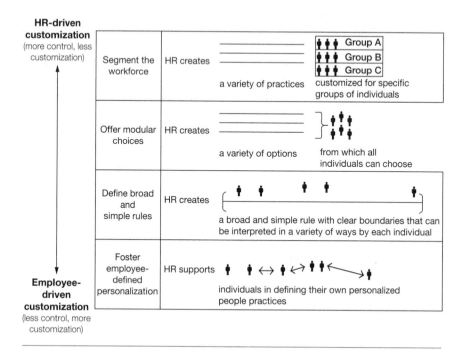

enabling the organization to maintain significant control. Other approaches are more employee driven, with employees themselves designating the details of the people practice (with organizational support)—thereby enabling the organization to attain a greater level of individual customization while allowing for somewhat less organizational control. For these reasons, we have found that different organizations tend to favor some approaches over others when designing an overall workforce of one blueprint that works best for them. Favoring all four approaches is not necessarily better than favoring just one or two approaches; the idea is that an organization should focus on the approach or approaches that work best for it.

An organization, therefore, can do one or more of the following.

Segment the Workforce

This approach borrows straight from marketing. Just as organizations group customers based on shared preferences and needs and create tailored experiences for each group, organizations can likewise group employees based on shared preferences and needs and tailor people practices for each group. Employees may be grouped by any relevant criteria, such as value to the company, role or workforce, and age or generation. Advances in business intelligence and analytics have spurred a revolution in how companies are now segmenting their workforce, allowing them to segment in increasingly meaningful and germane ways. Companies are now creatively grouping their employees on such varying dimensions as learning styles, values, personality, wellness profiles, mobility, behavioral patterns, and even networking and communication styles. Because executives spell out specific human capital practices at a detailed level for each given segment, control is maintained. Organizational choices regarding how to segment and what to provide each segment can also thus be easily aligned with the business's needs.

Offer Modular Choices

Think of this approach to customization as similar to the concept behind the McDonald's Happy Meal® product; just as you can choose from a predefined list of which types of food (an apple or yogurt? a hamburger or chicken nuggets?) and prizes (a clown or a dinosaur?) to include in your child's McDonald's Happy Meal®, this approach lets employees or their managers select from a list of predefined, limited choices based on what suits their needs and preferences best.[44] Cafeteria benefits plans or allowing employees to select their own rewards from a set established by the organization are common examples of modular choice. But companies are now offering modular choices in innovative ways across their talent management practices—thereby radically transforming everything from learning to compensation, to work space, to even jobs and careers. Like segmentation, modular choice works on the premise of creating a greater variety of specific people practices to reflect the greater variety of types of employees. But with segmentation, the organization largely dictates or suggests which practice each employee receives. With modular choice, on the other hand, the same set of options are offered to all, so employees actively participate in tailoring their own people practices. Because the set of choices is always deliberately chosen by the organization, the organization maintains control and can align choices with its needs. And as the success of McDonald's Happy Meal® has shown, this approach offers significant scalability and manageability.

Define Broad and Simple Rules

An alternative to creating a greater number and variety of specific people practices is to not define highly specific people practices at all. Rather, an organization can create an organizational rule so broad and simple that it can be flexibly interpreted in many different ways by individuals or their managers. The organization maintains control because the rules always have clear boundaries, or guardrails; as long as an employee stays within them, he can act in a way that suits him best.

Think back to fourth grade science class; the concept is similar to what we learned about taxonomy classification schemes like genus and species—where kinds of things are arranged in hierarchical chains in which the subtype must obey the constraints of the supertype above it. If we define our rules in a broad sense, then within that broad rule a whole lot more diversity can exist than if we narrowly define a rule. So to make the analogy, if we more broadly define *vehicle* rather than *car*, then a whole lot more diversity can exist, as long as the constraints of being able to transport something from one place to another are still met. *Vehicle* encompasses all types of cars, but also bikes, trucks, motorcycles, planes, trains, or intergalactic spaceships for that matter.

Applied to human resources practices, a classic example of a broad and simple rule would be a broadband compensation scheme that collapses the organization's job worth hierarchy into fewer, wider, yet more flexible salary ranges. Using a broadband compensation scheme, a line manager has the freedom to tailor a compensation package to fit the unique needs of an employee and situation—as long as she stays within the bounds of the defined salary range. Although this gives more freedom to employees to define the details of their people practices (allowing for more customization), the organization still decides just how the rules are defined and the limits to place on the rules. But this approach is no longer confined to compensation practices only; leading companies like Best Buy are now breaking new ground by creatively using the approach to completely restructure how they define jobs, careers, hiring, place and time of work, and more.

Foster Employee-Defined Personalization

The three customization approaches we've described thus far involve HR or some other central organizational group clearly defining people practices. With an employee-defined personalization approach, however, the employee or her manager largely defines the practice. Instead of performance criteria defined by HR, the manager decides what kind of informal feedback to give and when. Instead of learning content predefined from on high, an individual learns in a highly personalized coaching session, through on-the-job experience or simulations, or from peers through wikis or blogs. Instead of having career paths that are centrally defined, an individual defines his own career path and fluidly moves about the organization based on his personal networks. Technology has spurred a host of innovations in the employee-defined personalization area in the last few years, allowing organizations to more easily support employees in defining everything from their own schedules to jobs to compensation. In the consumer space, the idea of consumer-defined personalization has become quite popular. Consumer-generated content abounds: we can post and view each other's videos on YouTube, learn about what others know of a subject on Wikipedia, and create personalized networks and content representing ourselves to others on Facebook and other similar social networking sites.

Although this approach grants the organization the least amount of control, the organization still decides which employee-defined personalization practices it will support and how—enabling it to maintain some degree of control, consistency, and alignment with business needs. Employee-defined personalization is still about consciously and deliberately establishing practices to support employees. HR may not specifically define them, but it does play a very important role in fostering the practices and enabling them through incentives, technology, and cultural change. With employee-defined personalization, HR takes more of a supporting role by fostering everyday talent management practices that are woven into the very fabric of people's work lives. But these are still somewhat structured activities, consistently applied to the workforce, and centrally supported and enabled.

Throughout this book we'll show how each of our four approaches to customization differs from one another in practice. For example, take performance appraisals. With segmentation, HR makes a centralized decision about what types of appraisals will be used for different segments of employees—more rigorous performance appraisals may be provided for people performing the most critical jobs, for example. With modular choice, HR may enable managers to select from a limited set of choices of performance criteria to suit the different types of work performed by employees reporting to them. With broad and simple rules, HR may broadly define a single set of assessment criteria and give managers the freedom and responsibility to refine its details to suit a given employee in an open-ended way. With employee-defined personalization, managers may give frequent, informal, verbal feedback whenever employees need it, with HR providing little or no structure. HR may provide tools and techniques to help managers give this feedback, and it may also offer incentives to motivate managers to give the feedback, but appraisal becomes more of a general business practice rather than specifically an HR practice.

In this book, we'll see how some pioneering companies are using one or more of our customization approaches to manage their workforces as a workforce of one. "Thirteen Workforce of One Pioneers" offers a profile of companies we consider groundbreakers in this area. They are either pioneering novel and innovative ways to customize, or extensively adopting customization practices in a strategic and holistic fashion across a wide

Thirteen Workforce of One Pioneers

Segmentation and/or modular choice pioneers

Accenture

What makes it a pioneer: The consulting, outsourcing, and technology services company is a leader in segmentation (segmenting its workforce in seventeen different ways) and modular choice (across eight different dimensions). At the highest level, Accenture segments all employees into one of four workforce categories based on their primary role and skills. Innovations include segmenting people based on personal communication and networking style, health and well-being, and providing modular choices related to extended career break options and choice of job activities including volunteer assignments. Such customization has helped Accenture improve workforce engagement and retention, be recognized by publications like *Fortune* and the *Financial Times* as an employer of choice, and outperform its industry peers for five consecutive years.[45]

Capital One

What makes it a pioneer: Leader in using analytics to support segmentation and modular choice. For example, it uses data analysis to segment intended hires based on proven criteria that distinguishes high-performing employees.[46] Its employee database (including SAT scores, college grade-point averages, health benefit information, and number of children at home) is also used to identify the best staffers for assignments, to segment universities based on whether they produce top performing employees, and to tailor communications and programs such as work/life balance seminars.[47] It has created some highly innovative modular choice options related to work settings.[48] It was also one of the first companies to offer employees iPods as an alternative format option for learning.[49] Recognized by *Fortune* both as a top company for developing leaders and as a top company for which to work.[50]

Deloitte Touche Tohmatsu

What makes it a pioneer: Pioneered the groundbreaking modular choice Mass Career Customization™ concept as well as extended career break options with its "Personal Pursuits" program.[51] Extensively uses a number of other customized practices, such as modular choices regarding workplace; segmentation by generation and geography; and employee-defined personalization practices like job rotations, an organization-wide coaching initiative, employee referrals, employee-defined recruiting content, and talent-interest databases that enable more customized career paths.[52] Consistently ranked as an employer of choice and best place to work by publications like *Fortune* and *BusinessWeek*.[53]

Royal Bank of Scotland

What makes it a pioneer: Leader in using analytics to support segmentation. The bank segments its workforce in fifteen different innovative ways—such as targeting customized benefits information based on life stage. It stands out especially because of its sophisticated use of analytics to look at multiple segments at once to get highly granular in its offerings. Also offers a wide range of modular choices across many dimensions, including benefits, rewards, and time. Since it began pursuing segmentation in 2004, the bank has improved employee engagement and productivity—which in turn has been statistically linked by the bank to improvements in customer satisfaction and business results. The bank now cites customized people practices as one factor helping it navigate through challenging conditions related to the 2008–2009 economic downturn.

Tesco

What makes it a pioneer: The world's third-largest grocer pioneered a highly innovative modular choice approach to benefits, compensation, training, and development by using its database to understand individual employee values, motivations, and orientations toward work to determine the most relevant set of options.[54] Extensively offers other modular choices related to work time, for example, and gives managers a choice of diversity training courses based on the demographics of their store.[55] Also uses many employee-defined personalization practices: a shift-swapping scheme; temporary job try-outs; employee-identified job recruits; and experience-based learning through a novel apprenticeship program.[56] These initiatives, as part of a broader human resource-led business strategy, have helped Tesco take the lead in the U.K. retail sector.

(*continued*)

Broad and simple rules and/or employee-defined personalization pioneers

Best Buy

What makes it a pioneer: Extensively uses broad and simple rules and employee-defined personalization practices to help it provide a customized consumer experience. Its Results-Only Work Environment, for example, allows employees to customize their jobs, schedules, and place of work. Employees also can customize by defining their own learning experiences, career paths, and performance feedback. A customized talent management approach has helped Best Buy achieve some of its industry's lowest turnover rates, improve productivity and engagement, become an employer of choice, and ultimately has contributed to a strong bottom line.

Container Store

What makes it a pioneer: Extensively relies on broad and simple rules and employee-defined personalization practices. The company operates without an employee manual, for example, relying instead on a few simple HR guidelines, and it broadly defines compensation based on contribution to revenues.[57] It also customizes through employee-defined recruiting; fluid, cross-functional job movement to allow customized career paths; and jobs designed to fit people's skills, abilities, and talents.[58] One result: for ten years in a row, the company has placed near the top of the *Fortune*'s list of "100 Best Companies to Work for in America."[59]

Google

What makes it a pioneer: Uses broad and simple rules and employee-defined personalization in innovative ways, such as enabling some employees to spend a certain amount of time on projects they choose; using unique and highly personalized recruiting and hiring practices; and fostering extensive peer-to-peer and experience-based learning.[60] Notable for using data-based metrics to support these practices: e.g., it measures employees based on how many people they recruit or how often they host "tech talks" to help others learn from their experience.[61] Eschews many forms of segmentation, however, famously offering generous benefits to all and refusing to segment based on potential.[62] As a result, turnover is a low 5 percent, and Google has reached employee productivity rates previously unheard of; its average employee generates $1.24 million in revenue each year.[63] It has also consistently ranked at the top of the list on *Fortune*'s Best Companies to Work for list.[64]

Men's Wearhouse

What makes it a pioneer: Pioneered customization by broadly defining rules to allow customization on nearly every work dimension—e.g., jobs, careers, compensation, timing of work, place of work, performance goals, rewards, and hiring practices. Offering such a customized work experience has enabled Men's Wearhouse to attract and retain top performers who are extremely engaged with the company's brand and to improve workforce performance—ultimately helping the company achieve superior financial results compared with competitors.

PepsiCo

What makes it a pioneer: Extensively uses employee-defined personalization practices in over a dozen ways, more than any company we studied. Has recently been expanding into other customization areas as well, such as offering modular choices with respect to total rewards. PepsiCo has such a strong commitment to customization that it is one of PepsiCo's six long-term strategic imperatives for talent sustainability. Recognizing differences and providing tailored people practices has helped PepsiCo become a recognized leader in diversity and leadership development; an employer of choice; and one of the world's most successful companies—PepsiCo ranks as one of the most profitable U.S. *Fortune* 500 companies, and *BusinessWeek* named PepsiCo in its 2009 Best Performers List.[65]

W. L. Gore

What makes it a pioneer: The maker of GORE-TEX® fabric and other fluoropolymer products uses broad and simple rules extensively, and defines them more broadly than any company we've seen.[66] For example, employees have no job titles and are confined only by broad functional areas in the scope of their work, and salaries are set by very broad parameters related to strategic contribution.[67] These practices have helped the company thrive in a rapidly changing business environment, achieve a mere 5 percent voluntary turnover rate, and be ranked among *Fortune*'s Best Places to Work for twelve consecutive years, often earning the top spots.[68]

(*continued*)

Pioneers that focus on all four customization approaches

Microsoft

What makes it a pioneer: Extensively uses all four customization approaches as part of its "myMicrosoft" strategy (which provides individualized people practices) launched in 2005. Segments its workforce in eleven different ways; offers modular choices regarding work setting, time, compensation, benefits, and career paths; applies broad and simple rules across six dimensions including hiring practices, and uses ten different employee-defined personalization practices. Notable especially for using technology to support many employee-defined personalization practices—such as its expert profiling system, its system to capture and share informal feedback, and its technology-supported peer-to-peer learning and employee-defined recruiting initiatives. Customized people practices have helped the company retain its personal touch and respect for the individual, but in a scalable fashion. Customization has also helped Microsoft improve employee engagement and stem key defections to competitors—consistently making *Fortune*'s "Best Places to Work" list while remaining one of the world's most profitable companies.[69]

Procter & Gamble

What makes it a pioneer: Extensively uses all four approaches in its human resources practices. Segments its workforce in at least thirteen different ways including by demographics, geography, and performance/potential. Customization options exist for learning and development, career pathing, place of work, recognition, and more. These approaches have enabled P&G to develop a strong reputation as an employer of choice with high employee engagement and low attrition.

variety of practices. Four of these companies—Best Buy, Men's Warehouse, Procter & Gamble, and Royal Bank of Scotland—we'll profile in some detail later in this book.

Yet many other organizations also are already starting to use some of these workforce of one approaches, even if they don't identify them as such. Our evidence suggests that, in fact, the majority of organizations are now embarking on an evolutionary path toward customized people management. The six broad-sweeping trends we outlined earlier are making change inevitable, pushing most organizations toward some form of customization, even if those solutions aren't always ideal (such as making one-off deals). So whether employees are aware of it or not, they already may have experienced the nascent beginnings of a workforce of one approach in their own organizations—for example, if they participate in a flexible benefits plan, if they work from home one day a week, or if their pay is customized based on work performance.

Many of the new developments in people management, in fact, show a move toward a workforce of one approach. Recall that about a third to a half of employees are already experiencing at least moderate degrees of customization. Every one of the forty-seven organizations in which we interviewed executives uses at least one workforce of one practice, and most executives agreed that more were sorely needed. But whereas most organizations have just a few one-off customized practices, only a few real leaders have taken a holistic, deliberate, and extensive approach to customization across a wide array of practices as part of their major strategic philosophy.

Yet executives are clearly steering their organizations this way. Nearly half of all employees we surveyed told us their organizations are getting better at offering employee practices that are highly relevant and that meet individuals' unique needs; only 21 percent disagreed with this statement (see figure 1-9). And without exception, all of the HR and senior executives

FIGURE 1-9

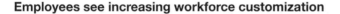

Employees see increasing workforce customization

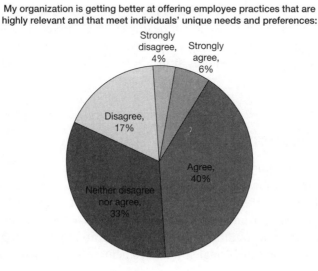

My organization is getting better at offering employee practices that are highly relevant and that meet individuals' unique needs and preferences:

- Strongly disagree, 4%
- Strongly agree, 6%
- Disagree, 17%
- Agree, 40%
- Neither disagree nor agree, 33%

Source: Accenture workforce of one study, 2008.

we asked told us that the trends described in this chapter would make it likely that they would pursue a more customized approach to talent management in the future. Likewise, in a Hewitt survey of HR executives, 35 percent said that they now tailor their HR products and services to a diverse workforce, 30 percent said they will do so in the future, 26 percent said they might do it in the future, and only 9 percent said that they were unlikely to do so.[70] Other studies echo these findings.[71]

All of this is good news for human resource departments, and for organizations as a whole. Yes, managing employees as a workforce of one sounds like a daunting task. After all, it's an entire paradigm shift—from organizations designed to battle the inherent individuality of each employee to ones designed to embrace it. And to be sure, as we'll see in this book, managing a workforce of one won't always be easy. It will present new challenges for both HR and employees alike that will need to be overcome, and new skills and capabilities that will need to be developed.

But today's workforce and economic trends are demanding a new solution, and there are very practical, manageable ways of achieving it. Companies that take a deliberate, well-thought-out approach to customization that works for their own organization will have a significant advantage over competitors. (To determine how much workforce of one could help your organization and whether your organization has unique conditions that make workforce of one particularly suitable or important, see "Is a Workforce of One for You?") Only by helping employees to become the best versions of themselves can organizations hope to become the best they can be.

In the next four chapters of this book (part II), we will describe our model by laying out in more detail the four distinct approaches an organization can take to customizing its people practices. Let's begin now by exploring in depth what, exactly, it means to segment your workforce.

Is a Workforce of One for You?

To help determine how managing your workforce as a workforce of one can help your organization, we created two diagnostic tools. Just fill out each part as instructed to determine the kind of benefit you may receive from a workforce of one approach, and whether you have specific conditions in your organization that may make a customized approach to talent management particularly suitable or important.

Part A: How Could My Company Benefit from a Workforce of One Approach?

DIAGNOSTIC 1-1A

Is a Workforce of One for You—Part A

	RATE ON A SCALE OF 1–5 (5 GREATEST, 1 LOWEST)	
	A	**B**
	Importance to the success of your business in the next five years	**Where your organization is today**
1. Having a competitive advantage when it comes to the talent at all levels of the organization		
2. Having a competitive advantage when it comes to the leadership talent of the organization		
3. Being an employer of choice with well-structured employee value propositions		
4. Having high employee engagement		
5. Attracting and hiring talented people		
6. Achieving high performance from your people through maximizing their full potential		
7. Retaining high-performing people (and reducing turnover costs)		
8. Maximizing the return of each investment dollar spent on talent		
9. Increasing the productivity of your organization		
10. Promoting innovation through a diverse employee base		
11. Growing your customer base through a diverse workforce		
12. Eliminating one-off side deals between manager and employee that can raise fairness questions, decrease organizational control, and result in less-than-optimal employment practices		
Total (add all numbers in column A and then all numbers in column B)		

Determine which quadrant you fall in on the following grid by placing the total in column A (importance to your business's success in
the next five years) along the vertical axis and the total in column B
(where your organization is today) on the horizontal axis. Then use
the following scoring guide to help you determine the benefits you
may achieve from managing your workforce as a workforce of one.

SCORING GUIDE 1-1A

Workforce of one benefit assessment

<table>
<tr><td></td><td>60</td><td></td><td></td></tr>
<tr><td rowspan="2">Importance of talent to your business success in the next five years (column A)</td><td></td><td>Category 1—
high-impact
business
transformation
opportunity</td><td>Category 2—
high-impact opportunity
to maintain leadership
position and propel
you even further ahead
of the competition</td></tr>
<tr><td>30</td><td>Category 3—
may not be a business
imperative, but could be a
high-impact social
responsibility and corporate
citizenship opportunity</td><td>Category 4—
may not be considered a
business imperative, but
could be an opportunity to
reexamine the impact of
your people on business
performance</td></tr>
<tr><td></td><td>0</td><td>30</td><td>60</td></tr>
</table>

**Today's talent performance score
(column B)**

Scoring Guide

- If you fall within Category 1: Your organizational philosophy
  and vision align with workforce of one, but your current
  people performance probably lags behind that of industry
  leaders. Managing your workforce as a workforce of one will
  give you the opportunity you've been looking for to really
  transform your business and elevate HR to a high-value,
  strategic function—enabling you to tap into the dormant
  value of your employees to help drive significant improvements in business results. You should read on; in this book
  you'll find many insights and lessons to accelerate your journey toward a workforce of one.

- If you fall within Category 2: Congratulations—you are likely
  a leader when it comes to managing talent. Your philosophy
  and approach point to a workforce of one approach, and

you're likely already looking for new and innovative ways to continue getting the best from your people for maximum business advantage. But you have a significant opportunity to use a workforce of one approach to gain even better employee performance and keep ahead of the competition—or else risk losing your leadership position as competitors adopt more compelling, customized people practices.

- If you fall within Category 3: Workforce of one may not be a business imperative. You may not need or want to use a workforce of one approach for business reasons in the next few years, but you might consider doing so to significantly improve the quality of your employees' lives and help them realize their full potential as human beings. There is much opportunity for you to achieve major advances in the area of social responsibility; we've seen some organizations start their workforce of one initiatives with solely their employees' well-being in mind, only to find that as they progressed, they received the added benefit of improved business results as well. But for companies in this category that seek neither the business benefits nor added well-being for employees, your organizational philosophy does not align with workforce of one, or else your timeline for achieving the benefits of a workforce of one may be too long. If this is the case, you'll likely do best by focusing your energy and resources in other areas.

- If you fall within Category 4: You are a true rarity—you likely have high-performing, highly engaged, and satisfied employees, yet you don't see your people as a critical driver of your business performance. You are probably therefore unlikely to be investing in people processes and practices that effectively support your workforce to maximize its contribution. There is a real opportunity here to reexamine whether or not your people truly don't contribute to your business's success. We believe that upon careful study and fact-based research, most organizations will find that their high-performing, highly engaged people are a hidden and unrecognized asset that in fact contributes greatly to the company's success. If this is the case, you will benefit from managing your workforce as a workforce of one; doing so will help you finally turn your attention to supporting your people in ways that foster ever-greater levels of workforce and business performance. If this is not the case, then continue with business as usual; workforce of one is probably not for you.

Part B: Do I Have Specific Conditions in My Organization That Make Workforce of One Particularly Suitable or Important?

All organizations can manage their workforces as a workforce of one and reap significant benefits from a more customized talent management approach. But some organizations have certain conditions that make a workforce of one approach particularly suitable or important. Take this quiz to find out whether your company falls in this category.

DIAGNOSTIC 1-1B

Is a Workforce of One for You—Part B

	RATE ON A SCALE OF **1–5** (5 GREATEST, 1 LOWEST)		
	A	**B**	**C**
	How much of this condition do you have?	**How much of this condition do you expect to have in 5 years?**	**Score Column A + B ×10**
1. **A highly diverse workforce.** Organizations with highly diverse employees may find a workforce of one approach particularly amenable as a way to effectively address everyone's needs in a controlled and scalable fashion.			
2. **Large proportion of employees who work primarily with knowledge.** Customized talent management practices are particularly important for knowledge-based organizations, since standardizing work based on job title or position alone is increasingly irrelevant for knowledge-based workers.			
3. **Large number of employees who expect customization based on their experiences as consumers or as members of the Net Generation.** Employees who are accustomed to customization in their everyday lives will expect it in the workplace, and will be more likely to effectively use customized people practices.			

DIAGNOSTIC 1-1B *(continued)*

	RATE ON A SCALE OF **1–5** (5 GREATEST, 1 LOWEST)		
	A	**B**	**C**
	How much of this condition do you have?	How much of this condition do you expect to have in 5 years?	Score Column A + B ×10
4. **Technology and infrastructure in place to help facilitate customization.** Organizations that have already laid the ground work of having a solid HR infrastructure and a mastery of fundamentals like payroll will find it easier to adopt a workforce of one approach. Likewise, organizations that have spent time harmonizing their HR practices on a standard platform, and those that have standard employee data, will find customizing people practices easier to achieve.			
5. **A strategy of customizing products or services for consumers.** We have found that those organizations who find it important to customize their products and services for consumers tend to more readily embrace customizing their people practices—in part because it sometimes helps them achieve their consumer customization strategy, and in part because they have already developed skills and knowledge about customization that they can now apply to a new area.			
6. **Senior executives who take a talent-powered approach to achieving results.** In organizations with strong executive support for talent management and who view people as a primary source of competitive advantage, executives will be much more likely to support a more complex and sophisticated talent management model to help them achieve their goal of improving workforce and business performance.			
7. **Loose (rather than tight) government, industry, or union regulations and rules.** Countries where the workforce is relatively fluid and there is flexibility in how employment can be structured (for example, the United States and New Zealand) are apt to be more open to a greater number of individualized employment practices than countries with tighter government regulations and stricter labor rules (such as Belgium and France). Even companies in countries where employment regulations are comparatively loose may			

(continued)

DIAGNOSTIC 1-1B *(continued)*

	RATE ON A SCALE OF 1–5 (5 GREATEST, 1 LOWEST)		
	A	**B**	**C**
	How much of this condition do you have?	How much of this condition do you expect to have in 5 years?	Score Column A + B ×10
still be highly regulated by unions, or need to use caution in how aggressively they pursue customized practices in particular areas.			
8. The ability to sustain multiple organizational cultures and types of people rather than just one. A few organizational cultures thrive by employing a single type of person. For example, if you aren't an outgoing female who values a pink Cadillac, you might not fit in the homogenous culture of Mary Kay Cosmetics. For these types of organizations, the customization advocated in a workforce of one approach may allow too much diversity to thrive, thereby undermining the single culture and homogeneity that such businesses have successfully relied on.			
9. An industry that favors more customized work arrangements. Some industries are more open to varied employment conditions by virtue of their competitive requirements. Advertising, consulting, financial services, and entertainment are among those that need highly independent and driven people to be successful. In return, they have been more than willing to offer flexible work arrangements to attract and retain top talent.			
10. A strong culture of fairness. An organization's values will play an important role in determining how open it is to flexibility. If employees don't feel that the company operates with a sense of fairness, they will not support the new policies and practices.			
	TOTAL: _____ *(add the numbers in column C)*		

Scoring Guide

Fill in your total number on the dashboard below to determine whether you have unique conditions that make a customized talent management approach particularly suitable or important for you.

Part B scoring guide

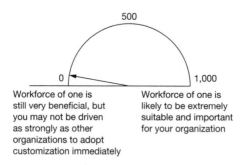

Workforce of one is still very beneficial, but you may not be driven as strongly as other organizations to adopt customization immediately

Workforce of one is likely to be extremely suitable and important for your organization

Part Two

Four Paths to a Workforce of One

What difference does it make if we follow different routes, provided we arrive at the same destination?

—Mahatma Gandhi

Segment Your Workforce

I think, as an HR community, we're starting to offer more customized employee value propositions. We've already done the work of standardization and reaping efficiencies out of the HR system; now we're tailoring our value propositions to engage and enhance the performance of very diverse workforces.

—Nancy Reardon, senior vice president and chief human resources and communications officer, Campbell Soup Company[1]

AS THE WORLD'S GREAT philosophical, spiritual, and political leaders throughout history have told us, many different paths can take us to the same destination. Likewise, when it comes to crafting people practices that are highly relevant and tailored to individuals, organizations can choose one or any combination of our four different approaches to achieve their goal—segmenting the workforce, offering modular choices, defining broad and simple rules, and fostering employee-defined personalization. It's a matter of organizational preference and choice. The end destination, however, is the same: work that is sculpted to fit lives, instead of lives that are sculpted to fit work.

We'll begin by exploring the segmentation approach to customization in this chapter. Just as marketers have been deftly dissecting consumer populations for decades—they have us pegged as suburban moms, clothes-conscious teens, techno-geeks, and the like—companies can segment a workforce into discrete groups that share similar characteristics. The segmentation approach to customizing people practices works by breaking down the monolithic concept of a workforce into more granular, meaningful parts. This allows an organization to craft distinctive practices to manage each segment.

Although many companies use *segmentation* to refer to how they group employees into meaningful segments merely to understand their workforce (an important undertaking for any of our four customization approaches), we define segmentation more narrowly: as the creation of differentiated practices for specific groups of employees. HR leaders can apply any meaningful categorization schemes, but they should be relevant and germane to the organization's specific workforce and situation at hand.

One important note before we look at some of the innovative segmentation schemes companies are using today. Segmenting any population always begs the question: is this differentiation or discrimination? Differentiation can help a company get maximum performance from its workforce and happier and more engaged employees, but discrimination is something no company wants. As we'll see toward the end of this book, when we look at the challenges that come with customization and explore solutions, segmenting by some classes that may be legally protected such as gender, ethnicity, or generation can be tricky. Companies need to approach customization carefully to ensure it complies with all applicable labor and other laws and ensure they customize in a fair, ethical, and legally defensible way. What's more, the trend toward collecting an increasing amount of personal employee data—from credit histories to personality to data about who employees e-mail—in order to segment them more meaningfully can also engender negative feelings of a "big brother" looking over employees' shoulders or raise important data privacy concerns. Later in this book we'll look at some of the practical steps organizations can consider taking when collecting data to differentiate their workforce.

Types of Segmentation Schemes

It used to be that organizations segmented primarily by rank, tenure, or function—or by administrative or legal segments (like those employees who are exempt from the United States Fair Labor Standards Act versus those employees who are nonexempt from the Act). But these forms of workforce segmentation don't take into account the real motivations or needs of employees. We're now seeing leading employers segment their workforce *strategically*—in increasingly sophisticated ways to meet differing individual needs and preferences, ultimately helping people perform at their best. These organizations are using business intelligence and analytics to create more meaningful segments based on needs, value, and expectations. Technologies that enable a data-based understanding of employees have created a new window that allows companies to see into the very hearts, minds, and behaviors of their people.

Let's look now at the ways that organizations are strategically segmenting their workforces—by life stage or generation; gender and ethnicity; geography; role or type of workforce; and value—plus some more unusual new ways to segment, such as by personality, learning style, and strengths; health and well-being; and behaviors and values. Our intent is to offer a variety of highly innovative examples of how to segment a workforce to help you determine the kinds of segmentation schemes that ultimately might work best for your organization. (See "Possible Ways to Segment Your Workforce.")

Life Stage or Generation

Take a look at your workforce, and you'll likely see a range of age groups—each with its own behavioral tendencies in the workplace. The baby boomers are likely trying to climb the career ladder and achieve visible symbols of success. Meantime, the Millennials probably view career development more in terms of a web rather than a ladder, seek meaning and service in work, prefer a lifestyle where work and life are integrated into a seamless flow, and thrive best with constant feedback. As research increasingly shows that people of the same generation tend to have common work styles and expectations of work, organizations are now applying customization based on generation to talent management practices ranging from work schedules to training to performance appraisals.[2]

Dow Chemical, for example, successfully attracted and retained employees in the tight labor market of the mid-2000s by offering flexible hours and three-day workweeks to veterans looking to phase into retirement. To its younger workers, on the other hand, Dow offers opportunities to develop green technologies and work to improve the living standards in developing nations.[3] And Deloitte Consulting offers people over fifty the opportunity to rejuvenate by redesigning their careers; if selected by a ten-member global selection committee, these employees work with the committee to customize an entire second career with Deloitte. Selected employees can restructure their jobs—choosing to work only part-time or choosing mentoring assignments rather than consulting gigs, for example. The company created the program in an effort to retain its best senior partners; because consulting is such highly demanding work, these people typically left the company at age fifty when their pensions vested.[4]

Many companies now use such special programs to retain workers close to retirement to stem the brain drain or to attract younger workers just entering the workforce. But increasingly, companies are tailoring their

Possible Ways to Segment Your Workforce

This chapter covers many segmentation schemes, but not all. Here's a checklist of possible segmentation schemes your organization may want to consider:

- By employee demographic
  - Age or generation
  - Life stage
  - Gender
  - Ethnicity
  - Education level
- By employee relationship to the company
  - Tenure in the job or organization
  - Professional stage
  - Level
- By geography
- By work roles
  - Nature of work (e.g., knowledge worker or member of the creative class, specialists versus generalists)
  - Profession or role
  - Workforce

people practices for much more intrinsic reasons—simply because workers of different generations often go about their work and learning very differently and therefore need different, tailored people practices to excel. Since younger Millennial workers typically perform better with extremely clear goals and frequent feedback, for example, PricewaterhouseCoopers now allows younger workers to determine when they get reviews, and even requires some bosses to get second opinions on evaluations to ensure that goals are ambitious enough and feedback is clear.[5]

An innovative twist on the oft-touted generational theme is to segment on the broader dimension of professional or life stage. P&G Beauty, for example, segments employees based on the points in their careers where they have a compelling need for assistance. Explains Keith Lawrence,

- By value
  - High-potential
  - High-performing
  - Most critical to the organization's success
  - Most sought-after in the open market
- By type of work relationship (e.g., business partner, contractor, general public)
- By personality
  - Learning or thinking style
  - Relationship or networking style
  - Strengths
  - Personality type
- By health
  - Mental health
  - Physical health
- By values and behavior
  - Engagement with work
  - Meaning and value of work
  - Most likely to leave
  - Mobility
- By intended hires

director, P&G Beauty human resources, "How well these needs are met contributes to employees' perception of the company as well as to their performance."[6] Efforts were initiated to map out these critical stages and develop unique products and services to better meet the unique requirements of individuals at each stage. This included efforts to improve the new employee onboarding experience and more sophisticated resources to help individuals who were moving into new jobs who are identified through a monthly-generated report of employee data.

Likewise, Royal Bank of Scotland carefully segments to whom it distributes certain HR information: if you're a twenty-year-old with no kids, it won't bombard you with information on child care vouchers. "Rather than send the same lengthy seventy-page document out to everyone," explains director of reward Trevor Blackman, "we use digital printing and communications to reorder, add, or delete text and photos to create customized communications that emphasize the benefits we think will be most relevant to the individual based on their particular stage of life. It's like what Amazon does, where we can say people like you have chosen these particular things, and you might find them valuable too."[7] The result? Big improvements in usage of relevant benefits, which in turn leads to more engaged employees: employees who take three or more items in the flexible benefits programs, Blackman says, are up to 20 percent more engaged than those who don't participate.

Gender and Ethnicity

In a workforce of one approach, the traditional notion of diversity is turned on its head; rather than HR pushing a lot of programs that attempt to equalize everyone, it is about recognizing that different diversity segments may have different needs, requiring very different support. We now know from experience that things such as health and retirement benefits, authority, and job satisfaction have different meanings, depending on one's race or gender.[8] Author Sylvia Ann Hewlett, for example, found that women (in contrast to men) tend to find connection to colleagues, time-out or flexible arrangements, recognition from bosses, and giving back to the community more important than compensation.[9]

Many organizations, therefore, are differentiating their people practices to help these groups perform at their best—while being extremely careful to ensure they do so in a fair and legal way so that one group is not marginalized at the expense of another. We aren't talking here about the typical mentoring, leadership development, and networking events for specific affinity groups based on ethnicity or gender found in most organizations. The real leaders in this space are making sure these activities and others are customized to the specific needs of those who use them.

Both Accenture and University of Pittsburgh Medical Center, for example, customize their people practices based on fact-based research revealing that different minority groups tend to have different needs. When Accenture conducted research (including focus groups and extensive data analysis) as to the major obstacles confronting different minority groups in obtaining leadership positions as part of their effort to ensure diverse representation at the highest levels of the company, for example, it discovered that different populations tend to confront different obstacles. Some groups, for example, tend to feel that lack of visibility and sponsorship are their biggest barriers; others tend to feel that they are sometimes held back by the *perception* of others that they are sometimes too deferential and not aggressive enough in their leadership style. Explains Accenture's U.S. inclusion and diversity lead Dalila Asha Stitz, "What we found isn't surprising; most companies would have probably found the same thing. What makes us unusual is that we acted on these findings by creating tailored development programs based on the specific needs of each group. We created training courses that include a specialized leadership program for one group that strongly emphasizes networking and one that emphasizes leadership styles and ways of combating people's often mistaken perceptions for another."[10]

Likewise, when research revealed that African Americans were underenrolled in the 401(k) plan at University of Pittsburgh Medical Center, the organization created targeted financial seminars aimed specifically at African Americans.[11] Research has shown that such targeted plans can make a difference, since different ethnic groups often have very different attitudes toward retirement. For example, whereas Asians tend to focus less on individual gains and more on how retirement plans benefit the entire family, Latinos tend to have shorter time horizons about the future and therefore tend to undersave for retirement. African Americans, for their part, tend to spend more for home and college than for retirement.[12]

Gender differences also come into play. PricewaterhouseCoopers, for example, discovered higher turnover among women than men, despite the fact that it hired them at the same rate. Research revealed that the company's female workers often felt disconnected at client sites and while traveling, and that the heavy workload interfered with other goals in their lives. Accordingly, women are now assigned partners to discuss their goals and work, and work has been redesigned so that instead of each partner being an individual entrepreneur, partners now share a group of clients and staff members. This has resulted in more teamwork and reduced workloads for many. As a result, the number of female partners increased by 30 percent, and turnover among females fell from 24 percent in 2001 to 16 percent in 2006. Sums up Jennifer Allyn, the director of gender retention and advancement at PricewaterhouseCoopers, "We thought to be fair, you had to treat everyone the same. But we suddenly realized to retain people, we had to treat different people differently."[13]

Increasingly, companies are also catering to diverse populations in new and innovative ways to find bright and able people off the beaten track to get a leg up in heated talent markets. JetBlue Airways, for example, staffed its entire reservations department with mostly stay-at-home moms who can take reservations while caring for their households.[14] And Eli Lilly's operations in Japan overcame the hiring difficulties it faced by targeting women, whose employment opportunities are more limited in the male-dominated culture of Japanese firms.[15]

Geography

At Google Ireland, many employees enjoy cycling, so the company offers its people in Ireland a *cycling plan*—a benefit in which the company contributes toward the cost of a bicycle.[16] Microsoft, for its part, found that the Chinese are so accustomed to fast change that they must promote its Chinese workers much more rapidly than employees in other cultures or risk losing them altogether.[17] And to attract top employees in many Indian cities, Deloitte offers free company-organized transportation that shuttles employees from pickup points to its offices.[18]

In a global economy, many organizations are finding that they need finely crafted talent strategies that can accommodate growing numbers of people from different cultures, with different customs, values, beliefs, and practices. A Towers Perrin survey confirms that potential employees value different things in different countries: in the United States, competitive base pay is the most important factor; in Brazil, career opportunities; in China, chances to learn; in Japan, challenging work; and in Spain, work-life balance.[19]

Accordingly, companies like Royal Bank of Scotland are now tailoring everything from leadership development and benefits to rewards and work-life balance programs based on the particular engagement drivers of people in different geographies. To help customize these people practices, the bank conducted its own internal study and found stark differences of engagement drivers, depending on the employees' country of origin; Americans want health care, while Brits with socialized medicine don't need this—they rank integrity and trust in the management team as more important. The Japanese care most about the organization's values, putting pay for performance (a commonplace practice in the United States) at the bottom of their list, while in the United States, personal development is considered most important. The bank even segments by geography within a country; it analyzes data like engagement rates by city, for example, to fine-tune its strategy location by location, with data-based performance dashboards for each. Explains Greig Aitken, group head of employee engagement at the bank, "We are really striving to take an evidence-based approach. Most companies have surveys, but they often don't act on them . . . We do extensive statistical analysis to pinpoint exactly how to drive engagement in customized ways by location."[20]

Growing markets like India and China often have particularly great cultural variances. In India's family-based culture, for example, some companies have been known to foster loyalty by encouraging parents of employees to visit the workplace and by sending them letters of thanks and recognition regarding their children; this would be considered highly unusual in America or Great Britain. In China, where personal relationships are likewise paramount, hiring individuals recommended by employees works particularly well, but practices like 360-degree performance reviews, popular in the United States, are rarely effective in China.

Role or Type of Workforce

Imagine your employees being able to log in to their work computers and click on information that is precisely tailored to their job needs—including real-time access to relevant knowledge, training, simulations, networks of experts and collaborators, progress on critical performance metrics, process methodologies, relevant applications, and productivity tools. As with the way Netflix offers customized movie suggestions based on your prior movie selections, the more that people use the site, the more relevant the content becomes. Call center employees at British Telecommunications (BT) now enjoy such a customized environment—and agents report that the confidence they have when performing their jobs has improved by 23 percent. What's more, the resulting efficiencies in handling calls have led to a savings of US$6 million.[21] BT employees are not alone; 36 percent of 251 companies surveyed now report that they tailor HR and training support to each workforce's distinct needs (see figure 2-1).[22]

FIGURE 2-1

Percentage of companies that segment by workforce type

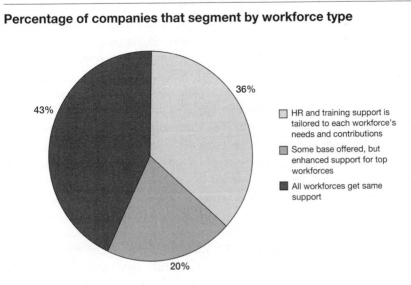

HR and training support is tailored to each workforce's needs and contributions

Some base offered, but enhanced support for top workforces

All workforces get same support

Source: Accenture high-performance workforce study, 2006.

Workers in different roles, for example, may be motivated by different things—a scientist by being given the chance to deliver a paper; a customer service rep by a ticket to the movies. A study by the Center for Effective Organizations found, for example, that the factors that motivate and retain managers are often quite distinct from those for technical professionals.[23] When Best Buy segmented employees by role, for example, it found that store associates weren't motivated by the standard stock option reward, compared with operational staff, because store associates often have more immediate bill-paying needs. For this segment, Best Buy now offers a profit-sharing program called Blue Crew Bucks, where employees earn a percentage from every dollar made above the company's profit plan. Explains John Waiden, executive vice president of the customer business group, "How do we do this [employee centricity] in a cost-effective manner? The same as with customers. We look for groupings of employees that have shared needs and we ask them what they want."[24]

Other companies are finding that as they change their business models, the one-size-fits-all approach no longer works. When Accenture expanded from consulting into the outsourcing and IT services businesses, it briefly tried to manage the new employees under the same set of talent practices such as expected career progression in a pre-defined period it had long used for consultants. But the outsourcing business required a different model. The company therefore created new career models for nonconsulting employees that focus on developing deep skills, independent of time served in a position, to motivate these employees and meet business needs. Explains Jill Smart, Accenture's chief human resources officer, "We can no longer survive like we have in years past with a single employee value proposition. Attracting, retaining, and improving employee performance means ensuring that HR practices can flex enough to be relevant to all."[25] Today, Accenture has four distinct workforces—consulting, outsourcing, IT solutions, and corporate support roles, with highly distinctive talent strategies and value propositions for each.

Instead of getting more granular, some organizations are grouping employees broadly by role into categories like "knowledge worker" or "the creative class."[26] Artists and writers at advertising company TBWA\Chiat\Day, for example, are rewarded based on intellectual contribution, not just bottom-line results, and they have different work spaces customized to accommodate their unique needs (for example, rather than working in cubicles, an artist and a writer working on the same project share an office with flexible workstations that can be moved to enhance collaborative creativity). Explains Lee Clow, chairman and worldwide creative director and the person responsible for people practices, "Creative people tend to have more insecurity and more ego at the same time . . . The most frustrating thing for them is when they encounter barriers to their ideas—like when people don't understand their ideas, or when they don't have time to develop them. We now work hard to recognize and reward the intellectual contribution from our creative people. Managing creatives is like managing a baseball team—you have all these star players, and you need to find a way of building a culture that enhances their assets and allows them to work together as a team. By customizing our practices to the creative types, we've been able to maximize their performance."[27]

The Extended Workforce. There's another type of workforce to consider when using segmentation to craft customized people practices: all of the people who work and create value for an organization but who aren't employees at all. These are the contractors, business partners, outsourcing providers, temps, and even perhaps you and I or other people in the general public. Human resources policies tend to address only formal company employees, but these people can be segmented in their own right, either as differentiated segments by virtue of their relationship with the company, or by extending any of the segmentation schemes covered in this chapter to include them. Leading organizations are pushing talent management beyond the confines of the enterprise wall to ensure that people who temporarily lend companies their skills and talents are just as motivated and high performing as employees—and that the company can continue to attract and retain the best extended workforce.

For example, a company might tailor certain rewards to appeal to its outsourced call center employees who are primarily Eastern European Millennials. Or performance management could be specially applied to the extended workforce; talent management software company SuccessFactors, for example, built a prototype Web application that allows employees and nonemployees alike to clearly understand their relationship with one another. This helps them align with each other based on common goals rather than by department or business unit.[28] And training can be extended too; the auto parts and logistics services company Unipart, for example, doesn't offer training to just its own employees; it extends it to its business partners across its supply chain.[29]

Many companies are getting very creative when it comes to identifying the most effective workers in the extended workforce. Some companies are starting to leverage former employees who already know the ins and outs of the company and who have a proven track record and relationships built on trust. Instead of contracting out HR, legal, tax, or basic manufacturing to outsiders, for example, Brazilian conglomerate Semco has been known to help its workers set up their own companies, transforming them from employees to partners.[30] And The Aerospace Corporation (a U.S. defense contractor) and Principal Financial have designed talent programs where retirees can work on a project-consulting basis.[31] Other companies are finding highly talented workers all over the globe by tapping Web-based talent profiles of prescreened people available for work, where test scores, experience, ratings, and referrals from other users à la Amazon and Facebook style help them make a strong match for a particular need, and where screen shots of what an individual is working on can be captured several times per hour to ensure that unknown talent is on track.

Probably the most innovative development in customizing practices for nonemployees has been made by companies finding ways to motivate the general public to perform highly specific pieces of work. It's an emerging dynamic called by various names, including *mass collaboration*, *peer production*, or *crowdsourcing*. People find many of these tasks fun and highly motivating; for companies, they get to tap into a vast storehouse of people's creativity or extra time and execute work more effectively and inexpensively. New idea markets like InnoCentive and Kluster allow companies to pose unsolved R&D or product design challenges to a broad and diverse community; if they are solved, individuals win cash prizes. In part by tapping into such markets, half of P&G's product development portfolio now has key elements that were discovered by nonemployees, and it has brought to market hundreds of successful products such as Swiffer Dusters, Crest SpinBrush, and Olay Regenerist.[32] Stanford University uses online gamers in addition to pathologists to view real medical scans inside the game to find signs of cancer.[33] And medical supply maker NationsHealth farms out piecemeal telesales calls to thousands of individuals rather than to employees; a sophisticated monitoring system allows the company to route calls to those who have handled similar calls well in the past.[34]

Value

Recently, companies have been segmenting employees based on either their current or perceived future value to the organization, or based on their performance. Proponents of this strategy argue that just as organizational investments, product lines, functions, and strategies are not all equally important to the company, not all employees are of equal value and therefore do not warrant the same level of investment.

A common form of such value-based segmentation that many companies, such as GE, have used is a forced ranking system to segment employees based on performance, placing them into A, B, and C tiers.[35] These companies then offer different reward structures and development opportunities for each. Another form is to identify high-potential employees and offer them differentiated treatment to ensure they develop fully. Campbell Soup Company does this by giving only high-potential and promotable employees access to certain programs, such as formal mentoring. And only the highest performers can be nominated to participate in a selective two-year leadership development program led by CEO Doug Conant.

Most recently, companies have shifted their emphasis from individual top-performing players to broader roles deemed most critical to the organization. Even one of the authors of the best-selling book *The War for Talent* now concedes there are really *multiple* wars for talent that should be fought in very different ways based on the value the employee brings to the organization.[36] Whether they're called *talent-intensive workers, pivotal employees,* or *A players*, these people are generally considered to be both strategically important to the organization and highly variable in their performance (i.e., there is substantial variability between the best-performing and worst-performing people in these roles).[37]

Companies are beginning to take these messages to heart; one study of twenty high-performing U.S. organizations showed that many, for example, are now investing more of their training budgets in their critical workforces.[38] Limited Brands, for example, creates tailored people practices and deliberately invests in two workforces it deems critical to its business success: its merchants and merchandise planners and allocators. These are the people responsible for merchandise assortment, demand planning, and achieving financial targets for particular merchandise categories like swim wear. Merchants, for example, determine the general direction of the category and figure out how to effectively sell and promote the products based on detailed market research, a financial plan, a well-honed fashion radar, and a deep understanding of competitors and customers. Explains one HR representative at Limited Brands we interviewed, "We believe that the emphasis we put on tailored HR practices for these workforces gives us a competitive advantage. We have invested specifically in customized development programs for these workforces and have created customized career paths for them."

Sometimes, the people most critical to organizational success may not be the likely suspects. At Disney, street sweepers who greet customers and provide helpful advice like directions are seen as having one of the most important roles in fulfilling the company's strategy of creating a delightful customer experience.[39] An Accenture study of 251 organizations showed that such strategies pay off; 43 percent of companies considered to be leaders tailor their HR support to how important they deem segments of their workforces to the company's success, as compared with only 31 percent of companies considered to be laggards.[40]

Variants of value-based segmentation continue to be invented. One interesting variant that might be the trend of the future is to place a value on the skills that employees acquire and to pay each individual in a customized way based on those new skills.[41] Another variant used by many companies (such as Travelers and Limited Brands) is what we call *market-based* segmentation, in which a company identifies employees whose expertise is crucial and in short supply; many companies pay premiums and offer other advantages to such employees.[42]

Learning Style, Personality, Strengths, and Networking Type

Scientists have long shown that people have distinct learning and thinking styles—visual versus verbal, for example, or converging versus diverging.[43] That's why companies like Hallmark Cards now tailor many of their management training programs based on learning style.[44] Technology makes this easier; companies can now provide an online assessment of learning style that employees can take on their learning portal; the portal can then guide employees to learning options based on their preferred learning type.

Companies can also segment a workforce based on individual temperament or personality characteristics. By some estimates, at least twenty-five hundred U.S. companies, from Starbucks to Apple, now assess their employees on personality-based characteristics.[45] And when hiring, companies are increasingly assessing personality and other noncognitive factors to produce statistics that segment potential employees. Explains one hiring manager we interviewed at a financial services company, "You can always train for skill gaps; but you can't change the way a person fundamentally is. It's made a big difference to hire based on personality and by viewing the whole person, rather than hiring based just on skills."

Organizations have widely adopted personality-based segmentation schemes such as the Myers-Briggs Type Indicator to help managers tailor their styles to the people they supervise based on personality type.[46] Tom Hennigan, chief operating officer of Victorinox Swiss Army, Inc., reports that when managers use such indicators to segment their people, it's had an enormous impact on performance. "If you are analytical, then sometimes you need to reorient your communication and management approach to fit someone who isn't analytical, for example," he says. "This also helps managers match people with the right roles."[47]

New schemes related to people's interests, strengths, and passions are being developed and applied in companies. Consultant and author Marcus Buckingham, for example, now advocates that people identify themselves as having one or more of thirty-four different strengths; he then helps companies develop people practices that capitalize on the unique strengths of each individual.[48] At P&G, training and assessment revealed that many employees weren't aware of their strengths. Expanded training is provided now to both employees and their managers on how to better understand and play to their unique capabilities.

An R&D group at U.S. network test-equipment maker Acterna came up with its own personality segmentation scheme to refine job descriptions. The group created separate roles for each engineer to leverage the personality-based strengths of each one. Some engineers were defined as "parachutists" (experts who drop into projects and offer short-term help), some were defined as "ambassadors" (engineers who represent the firm's work to the outside world), and others were defined as those who perform heads-down, concentrated work on one project at a time.[49]

Some companies are even categorizing employees based on their unique communication and networking styles. Steelcase, a corporate furniture firm, has experimented with tailoring seating arrangements according to individual personality. Its "floorcasting" approach categorizes individuals into "hubs," "gatekeepers," and "pulsetakers," who when strategically mapped and placed, may enable an organization to improve communication flow and even employees' concentration and creativity.[50] Accenture has likewise developed a technology that divides employees into networking types—central connectors, peripheral players, boundary spanners, and information brokers. Using the software, companies can identify which individuals, groups, and relationships are critical to collaboration and executing the business strategy; model the impact of losing specific people in a network; and identify key people for carrying out certain strategies.

Health and Well-Being

Clearly, a person's physical and mental health greatly affects his performance, yet until now, companies have largely steered clear of intervening in this very private and personal domain. But companies today are increasingly interested in employees' health and well-being, such as whether a person is depressed or optimistic, a couch potato or a fitness enthusiast. These companies know that energy—not time—is the true currency of high-performance business results. And as work intensifies and more people work extreme jobs with long hours and little boundary between personal and private lives, more companies feel responsible for helping employees manage stress and perform at their best.

To encourage healthy behaviors and well-being, companies have long given discounts on health insurance to nonsmokers or to those who join weight loss organizations. Some companies, like P&G and PepsiCo, have developed "corporate athlete programs."[51] These programs often segment employees based on whether they've accomplished certain activities in several health and well-being domains. PepsiCo employees are also encouraged to take health assessment surveys that identify health risks based on health type. Personalized suggestions are then provided regarding healthful activities like exercise and eating well, and employees are rewarded for participating in the program.

But many companies are getting more innovative in segmenting their workforce by health and well-being profiles. University Health Care System of Augusta, Georgia, for example, segments its people into three categories: the healthy, the at-risk, and the ill. It then targets the at-risk with wellness coaches and assigns "wellness case managers" to all.[52] Intel replaced its health risk assessments with on-site objective checkups and a health profile database of employees. By using analytics, Intel gets an accurate picture of its workers' health and then develops a highly personalized approach to disease management tailored to the specific needs of the company and those who work for it.[53]

In one innovative segmentation scheme, Accenture segments employees based on indications of their overall well-being, including data such as the number of vacation days an individual has taken, length of time on the same project, or whether an employee didn't receive a promotion he or she was working toward. The company may then alert a manager about employees who may be at risk for leaving the company or for stress-related issues such as health problems or job dissatisfaction. Explains Sharon Klun, manager of work/life initiatives in the U.S. for Accenture, "We've created a system to help our employees and leaders recognize an individual's level of resiliency and give them tools to intervene. Lost productivity because of health concerns or the risk of employees leaving have both personal and bottom line impacts. If we intervene early and offer tools and assistance to help employees manage through critical career stages, we can help our people balance work/life responsibilities and keep our high performers healthy and engaged."[54]

Management researchers are now even analyzing brain scans to determine the optimal brain functioning patterns for certain types of jobs; visionary leaders can be identified by wave patterns that are different from those of nonvisionary leaders, for example.[55] Scientists are also hard at work developing technologies and methods to improve brain functioning—ranging from biological techniques that boost memory to electronic implants.[56] As one recent *BusinessWeek* article provocatively pointed out, considering the impact such enhancements could have on business performance, "Brain enhancements may become as available—and compulsory—as software updates."[57]

Behaviors and Values

Segmentation schemes based on demographic characteristics, such as geography or role, although useful, are often really just proxies for employees' deeper-seated behaviors and values. Leading companies, therefore, are tackling behaviors and values head-on in an even more meaningful way and segmenting their workforce accordingly.

We heard of one restaurant chain, for example, that segmented employees based on career values and aspirations: those who are second wage earners, those who are working only to have more money or fun, and those desiring a long-term career in the industry. They then catered to these particular segments; the fun-lovers, for example, could indulge their wanderlust by working at any of the company's restaurants throughout the country, jumping from restaurant to restaurant as they chose.

Companies can create their own schemes based on why and how their employees like to work, and create tailored motivation, compensation, learning, recruiting, and other processes accordingly. In fact, management writer and researcher Tamara Erickson and her colleague Ken Dychtwald propose categorizing workers into six segments they have found to be statistically valid and distinct: self-empowered motivators (work is about building lasting value beyond themselves), fair and square traditionalists (work is about a steady, predictable path to success), accomplished contributors (work is an opportunity to be a valuable part of a winning team), maverick morphers (work is an opportunity for change and adventure), stalled survivors (work is a source of livelihood but not particularly satisfying), and demanding disconnects (work is frustrating and is about short-term economic gain).[58]

In addition to segmenting based on values, many companies are segmenting based on observed employee behaviors. Sun Microsystems, for example, tracks employee work patterns and the behavior of its employees in using physical work spaces (e.g., through an online reservation system of workspace and conference rooms as well as physical walk-throughs performed by facilities management) to help it determine optimal work spaces for different types of employees based on their mobility patterns. Employee badge data that allows for visibility into where employees are located is even being analyzed by some companies for the same purpose.

One high-tech company in our study instead relied on extensive anthropological-style research to determine the unique behaviors of eight different types of teams based on factors like degree of interdependence and mobility; it then designed corresponding workplaces for each. And an eWorkforce group at Intel ran a pilot that likewise segmented its employees based on their physical and technical work patterns; it divided its workforce into teamers, nomads, and sitters, each of whom might be tied more or less to one location by equipment or their type of work. The group later refined this scheme into six different profiles of people to take into account not only mobility but attitudes toward technology as well, to develop customized physical and technical work environments.[59]

Another behavioral scheme growing in popularity is to segment based on those employees most likely to leave. Telecommunications provider Sprint Nextel, for example, found that employees were most likely to leave within the first forty-five days of being hired and were more likely to leave if they hadn't signed up for the company's 401(k) plan. After HR began spending more time with these employees on career development, salary review, and whether the company was a good match for them or not, turnover dropped dramatically.[60]

Companies like Harrah's Entertainment (a gaming company that operates several casinos) have even determined through rigorous data analysis that certain employee behavior—namely, the display of an upbeat, positive attitude—is the single biggest service delivery factor customers value most (beating out other employee behaviors like smiling and eye contact, for example). In fact, this attribute is statistically correlated with customers' perception of waiting time—long recognized by many as an important factor in customer satisfaction, which can in turn drive revenues and growth. Harrah's has thus started segmenting and rewarding employees based on their ability to demonstrate an upbeat, positive attitude. John Bruns, Harrah's director of customer service, explains, "We know how to describe what it looks and sounds like and we train to it. We certify observers to measure it, we score it in real time, and we give employees ongoing feedback."[61] Such behavioral and values-based segmentation is still in its infancy, however. Just as marketers are learning how to segment customers based on past and predicted shopping behavior, we predict leading companies will eventually learn to segment employees based on past and predicted work behavior.

Using Multiple Segmentation Schemes at Once

With so many different ways to segment a workforce, executives can quickly get overwhelmed. But because many schemes may in fact relate to one another, organizations need not use all. By segmenting based on values and behaviors, for example, you may not need to segment based on generation.

Some organizations, like the U.S. Office of Personnel Management (OPM), have simplified segmentation by identifying common profiles of groups of individuals that vary across multiple segmentation schemes. The organization identified five distinct career dimensions: time spent in career (closely related to generation); need for flexible arrangements; degree of

Segmenting Employees *Before* You Hire Them

Some companies segment "their people" before they even become employees. For example, when Lee Vikre, vice president of HR at marketing communications firm McMurry, or one of her hiring managers meets someone with an interesting skill set and the right attitude at a conference, she enters the person's information (and even scans in hard-copy materials like a business card or résumé) into her company's database. Soon after, these high-promise folks start receiving targeted e-mails from McMurry, tailored to their careers: quarterly newsletters about relevant company developments, relevant job openings, or even birthday gifts of the company's product.[62]

"Candidate relationship databases" like McMurry uses, offered by software companies like Taleo and Authoria, work much like customer relationship databases. Instead of collecting static résumés that become quickly outdated and that contain only limited information, many leading companies are now using these databases to build relationships with candidates over time, rather than simply gather and store documents. The software allows companies to gather information on an unlimited number of variables that rarely come to light in interviews or résumés—things such as career interests, work location desires, willingness to travel, career aspirations, ideal jobs, personality characteristics, and more.

Based on segmentation of these types of criteria, the database can be mined to create automated, customized, and meaningful communications between a corporation and its pool of potential hires. In one pilot done by Intel, the company segments potential candidates based on work preferences, creating a better fit between the individual's passion and company needs.[63] Travelers likewise uses a candidate relationship database to send targeted communications based on an individual's aspirations and skills. By using sophisticated segmentation techniques, these relationship databases keep candidates interested and engaged until you need them, and increase the likelihood of a good match between individual and position.

permanence (e.g., contractor, long-term, seasonal); values (broadly public-service driven or driven by profession of choice); and mobility (among geographies or agencies, or between public and private sectors). Using these criteria, executives at the organization then crafted ten distinct segments, each based on where employees fall in the range along each of the five dimensions—with one dimension taking prominence over others. In the "student" segment, for example, the prominent characteristic is that these people are early in their careers. But they also tend to value more flexible arrangements, be more short-term and more mobile, and have either a public-service or a profession-driven orientation toward work. For each segment, the U.S. OPM has identified unique work attractors, HR policies and programs, and recruiting and retention strategies.[64]

Royal Bank of Scotland also uses this approach for some of its practices; to segment employees based on preferred rewards and to tailor communications accordingly, the bank segments its people based on earnings (which gives some indication of net disposable income), generation (which indicates broad lifestyle preference), and tenure (which indicates people's trust in the organization—for example, the longer a person's tenure, the longer the time frame she might accept for her rewards plan; say, five years versus three) to arrive at a handful of classification schemes that vary on each of these dimensions.

Although these types of "collapsed" segmentation schemes can simplify things a bit, they also tend to overgeneralize people. An alternative to managing multiple schemes at once is to get even more granular. Royal Bank of Scotland often doesn't just segment based on generation, gender, or geography; it sometimes analyzes data in such fine detail that it strives to find what motivates people on all three dimensions at once—younger white females in the northeastern part of the United States, for example.

But no matter what your strategy for segmenting your workforce—whether you pick a few schemes most relevant to you, collapse the schemes into one overall scheme, or get so granular that you have dozens of employee categories to tailor practices to—segmentation is a viable and proven path to customizing an organization's people practices. Even so, in the next section, we'll look at some of the advantages and disadvantages you'll want to weigh when considering the segmentation approach to customizing for your workforce.

When Should You Use a Segmentation Approach?

Like all four workforce of one customization approaches, segmentation will likely reduce turnover costs and improve workforce engagement, performance, and business results. But among our four approaches, segmentation has certain strengths both for employees and for organizations over the other three (each of which we'll explore in detail in the coming chapters). Segmentation allows an organization to provide a limited, manageable set of viable variations in people practices while avoiding the additional complexity inherent in some of the other approaches, where people practices can have substantially more variability. Senior managers maintain the highest degree of control, compared with the other customization approaches: they decide what form of segmentation to use, and which practices and policies will be tailored accordingly and, often, for whom. Executives can thus generally see exactly how talent is being managed with an extremely high degree of transparency.

Moreover, if your organization operates in a highly regulated environment—such as in a union environment or a country with lots of labor regulations, which charges HR with defining the details of people practices—you will find segmentation a very useful approach. Segmentation will allow you to provide customization but can still accommodate meeting regulation requirements that often require organizations to centrally define specific practices or rules. For example, through segmentation, an organization could still limit work hours to thirty-five hours a week for certain groups in its population, whereas other approaches we'll examine (such as broad and simple rules) would be more difficult to conform to stringent labor requirements.

The segmentation approach can also be useful when you're just getting started with customization efforts, since it usually requires the least amount of organizational change. It can also be helpful when an organization is in flux, either growing quickly or experiencing high turnover: segmentation will help you maintain the control needed to quickly and easily add a large number of new employees to the organization.

And there are other advantages to this approach: because people practices are centrally defined and communicated by HR, employees can easily understand the principles behind the practices and the logical reasons regarding why variations exist. Organizations with employees who thrive when being told what to do in clear, detailed, and logical terms may prefer this approach. Because specific groups of employees are identified with unique needs and interests, segmentation also creates an excellent opportunity for employees and managers to craft shared meanings about different types of workers. Employees are likely to react positively to segmentation efforts because they signal that the organization cares enough to learn about what differentiates one employee from another.

Of course, segmentation also comes with certain drawbacks, which you'll want to weigh when deciding to what extent to segment your workforce. (See "Segmentation: Weighing the Pros and Cons" for a summary of these points.) Creating predefined categories of employees may offer less fit than other, even more personalized, approaches. An organization is sure to risk oversimplification and even stereotyping when it assigns people to large, generalized segments based on statistical averages or logical assumptions; there will always be employees who don't fit neatly into any of the available classifications. One employee we interviewed explained, "The idea that organizations should develop strategies around employee classifications like generation is to me dangerous and shortsighted. The reality is that there are a lot of age fifty-five-plus people who use BlackBerrys and iPods just as heavily as the twenty-five-year-olds!"

Segmentation: Weighing the Pros and Cons

W*hat it is:* Grouping employees based on shared characteristics, such as performance, geography, learning style, role, or any other germane factor, and developing practices customized for each category.

Advantages	Disadvantages
• Affords the greatest degree of control	• Offers the least degree of customization; some employees may not fit easily into any category
• High transparency: executives can see exactly how talent is being managed	• May require substantial resources to manage and administer multiple programs and practices
• May require less change management and organizational change compared with other approaches	• Of the four customization approaches, segmentation is most likely to be perceived as unfair
• Opportunity to create shared meanings and appreciation of difference for different types of workers	• Inappropriate implementation may lead to privacy concerns
• Employees can easily understand the principles behind the practices and why specific people have differentiated work experiences	• May be difficult to change segmentation schemes once set up, or recategorize people from one group to another
• Analytics and data-driven approach to talent management lends itself well to companies with these types of cultures	• May require advanced HR infrastructure and analytics capability to support segmentation; companies that have a standard HR platform are most easily able to support segmentation efforts
• Accommodates businesses whose employees tend to thrive with more direction	• Companies with employees who value autonomy and self-direction may find it too controlled
• Easily accommodates high-growth companies with lots of new employees	• May be tricky to segment by legally protected segments; requires care and attention to ensure that differentiation does not become discrimination
• Still allows companies in highly regulated environments to centrally define the details of a people practice (e.g., limiting work hours to thirty-five hours a week for certain segments) while also achieving the benefits of customization	

Sometimes, too, it is hard to classify someone accurately because of the simplifying constraints of a segmentation scheme itself. We once witnessed an executive complain, "But he's a high B!" only to be told by another, "That doesn't exist! Either he's a plain, solid B or he's not!" Microsoft recently gave up its forced ranking of employees based on performance, because it failed to accurately reflect someone's true performance—if everyone on a team performed well, for example, it forced a manager to inaccurately relegate some to poor-performer status. Other times, it is difficult to classify someone accurately because employees learn the system and try to game it; research done on those taking personality tests, for example, shows that about 30 percent of people change their answers to what they think the test giver is looking for.[65]

As we mentioned earlier in this chapter, fairness and even legal issues may also come up if employees feel that segmentation decisions are subjective or that other segments receive greater benefits than their own. When the Hartford Financial Services Group started treating its employees from top MBA programs visibly differently by offering them special networking and development opportunities, for example, a cultural backlash ensued. One of the company's executives explains, "Employees want to be treated equally; we've had difficulties communicating the message that we must treat people fairly, but not necessarily equally."[66] Some companies deal with fairness issues by letting employees segment themselves under some schemes (like strengths or personality), or by making sure that their segmentation schemes are fact-based as much as possible (like basing performance judgments on objective, measurable outcomes). Other companies deal with fairness and legal issues by making sure that all legally protected segments get the same overall benefit, just in slightly different ways. Ultimately, successful segmentation may require careful communication and cultural change.

Segmentation is also somewhat less flexible than other workforce of one approaches. As workforces change, the defining characteristics of segments may become outdated, forcing organizations to redo their segmentation approaches and practices. And once employees are placed in a segment, it may be hard to resegment them. When one company in our study segmented its high-potential employees, for example, it often included not only those who were ready for the challenge of a new position but also those who were simply good at their jobs—and once those employees were so classified, it was hard to remove them from the list.

Finally, segmentation is likely to require more resources up front than a one-size-fits-all plan would. Like marketing segmentation, workforce segmentation relies on extensive data gathering and analysis—building the technology-enabled analytics capability to perform segmentation alone can require more up-front resources than are traditionally required with a standard people management approach. Organizations that have standardized employee data across businesses and geographies will find it easier to implement segmentation. A common HR platform and integrated computer systems help enormously with this, as well as with effectively rolling out new segments in a systematic and rapid way. Imagine the pain you might feel rolling out differentiated practices for a new segment in forty-two different computer systems, as compared with just one!

Yet consider, too, that gathering extensive data on employees in order to segment them appropriately may make some employees feel that their privacy is being breached, a topic we'll address in more detail later in the book. And managing multiple practices for multiple segments will most certainly add complexity to an organization's systems, processes, and the roles and responsibilities of the HR function. Providing multiple variations of performance appraisals, for example, will require a system to support different variations, as well as people to design the different variations. The amount of resources required will vary, however, depending on how many segments are created and the degree of difference in policies and practices that go along with each segment. But despite this list of challenges that come with segmentation, we nevertheless have found this approach a manageable and useful way for organizations to address the varied needs of their employees. We offer these caveats simply as a way to help you weigh whether—and to what degree—your organization might use segmentation to customize its people practices.

Although many companies today segment their workforce based on organizational structure (e.g., business unit, geography, rank, or function) or administrative or legal segments like exempt versus nonexempt, *this is not what workforce of one is all about*. To really drive improved workforce and business performance, leading workforce of one companies are taking a page from their marketing colleagues' playbooks by segmenting their people based on *their employees'* needs and desires: by geography or role only when employees truly differ on these dimensions; by dimensions such as generation, gender, and value; and increasingly by highly sophisticated dimensions like employee behavior, personality, wellness, values, and more. This unlocks the power of diversity and allows it to flourish—a quality many companies see as a true competitive advantage.

In the future, we expect to see organizations develop even more sophisticated and innovative segmentation schemes based on a data-based understanding of true employee differences—ranging from how employees approach and use technology to differing ways people's brains process information and their differing energy and work patterns. We hope that the many employee-driven segmentation schemes we examined in this chapter will help you determine which ones might work for your organization, and help you think of creative new ways to segment your workforce to drive true business value and help your employees be the best they can be. (See "Recommendations for Customizing Through Segmentation.")

In the next chapter, we'll examine another way to customize your people practices—by offering modular choices—a method that companies can use either alone or in combination with segmentation or either (or both) of the additional customization approaches we'll explore in subsequent chapters.

Recommendations for Customizing Through Segmentation

- Be transparent with all employees regarding what the segmentation schemes are and why they exist, to help instill a sense of fairness and shared understanding of diversity in your organization.

- Use an empirical, data-based approach to determining key segments of your workforce; this will help you create the most relevant segments (which will likely vary from other companies, depending on the composition of your workforce), help you choose among segmentation schemes that may overlap with one another (e.g., generation and preferred learning style), and help your employees understand and embrace differing people practices for different groups of employees.

- Respect employees' privacy by gathering data about them (to decide on segmentation schemes) in compliance with all applicable data privacy laws.

- To avoid stereotyping, make sure segments are defined based on data regarding true differences rather than making assumptions; segment employees directly based on norms, behaviors, and values rather than proxies for them such as generation or gender; or else try letting employees self-segment.

- To simplify, try collapsing multiple segmentation schemes into one; to get really sophisticated, go the opposite direction and segment on multiple schemes at once (e.g., pinpointing the needs of young males who value play more than work and who live in Scotland).

- Don't turn segmentation into discrimination—for legally protected segments, for example, make sure you comply with applicable labor laws when considering how to segment.

- Balance the ease of administering differing people practices for lots of narrow segments with the actual needs of your workforce and how different employees really are; doing so will help you make careful decisions about how many categories of employees you will define for each segmentation scheme.

- Build the infrastructure to support variety—companies that build a common HR process and technology platform first will have an easier time segmenting their workforce than those that do not.

Offer Modular Choices

People have different expectations of work and feel engaged by it based on a number of different criteria—like life stage, business unit, geography. So why would you do the same thing for everyone? This doesn't maximize productivity or performance.

—Greig Aitken, group head of employee engagement, The Royal Bank of Scotland Group[1]

W E ALL LIKE HAVING CHOICES in our lives—to decide whether we'd prefer a computer with a digital fingerprint reader or one with a webcam; to choose between a lazy day at the beach or learning a new sport during our tropical vacation; to decide whether we'd rather eat a plate of organically grown bulgur and lentils or a more indulgent cheeseburger and fries. Choice empowers us, lets us express our unique individuality, and, most important, allows us to pick options that are most in tune with precisely what we need to be effective and happy in both our work and our lives.

People's desire for choice came up again and again during our interviews with employees. But choice has its challenges; employees also told us that too much choice—unlimited, undefined choice—could in fact decrease their ability to perform well. They said they did not have time to identify the perfect option; having a limited but highly relevant set of options to choose from would keep them from feeling overwhelmed and frustrated. The good news is that having a range of choices might no longer be paralyzing, but manageable—that is, when employees are allowed to select from a menu of modular options to make choices that best fit their needs, preferences, and stage of their career or life.

Limited, relevant choice is good for organizations too. By limiting employees' options to a predefined list of organizationally defined and sanctioned alternatives, offering choices becomes manageable, affordable, and controllable. This menu-based approach has long been used to customize products; by breaking down products into more granular component parts, or standardized modules, they can be dynamically configured on demand, based on an individual's unique preferences. This is how Dell delivers customized computers and how packaged tour companies create customized trips. Companies like Capital One are getting increasingly sophisticated at helping their customers make trade-offs between choices, dynamically presenting only the options available based on choices they've already made (e.g., presenting only certain interest rate options available based on choices already made regarding annual fee), and allowing customers to model various scenarios.[2] In this chapter, we'll see how organizations now are creatively applying these approaches in innovative ways to effectively manage their people.

Modular Choices in Practice

Today, leading companies aren't offering just benefits choices. We'll now look at how offering limited, modular choices can transform nearly every people practice domain, including learning, work activities and projects, rewards and recognition, performance appraisals, work space, work time, career development, compensation, and benefits. (See "Possible Ways to Offer Modular Choices.")

Choice in Learning

Organizations have a long history of assembling learners in the same room at the same time and force-feeding them information as though each had identical prior knowledge, learning styles, and knowledge needs. But a modular choice approach to learning starts with a very different premise: that everyone has different prior knowledge, different learning styles, and different rates and timetables for learning. Modular choice applied to learning gives people a defined set of choices regarding how and what to learn; by doing so, learning structure is no longer built around the provider, but rather around learners and their unique needs and preferences.

By breaking down learning content into much smaller, modular components, learning paths need no longer be specified at a macro level (typically by workforce or skill family), but instead can be mass configured at the highly granular level of the individual employee. Just as we create custom playlists of music on our iPods, learners at the news service Reuters can custom configure learning on the fly, based on their individual needs and preferences, by choosing among a vast array of ten- to twenty-minute bite-size learning components.[3] Accordingly, companies might create small components like short videos, simulations, games, traditional e-learning, podcasts, virtual classrooms, and more, based on how an individual learns best and what she needs to learn most—and these can be delivered on an employee's platform of choice. Such modularizing when it comes to learning makes good business sense: people tend to digest information better when it is delivered in smaller quantities at a time, and can be consumed at a point when it is needed and can be immediately applied.

To help employees navigate an often overwhelming sea of learning choices, new technologies that make use of collaborative filtering (algorithms that automatically predict the interests of a user by collecting taste information from many users) and smart push (algorithms that push relevant content to users based on intelligence embedded in a computer system) promise to help learners make even smarter, faster choices by presenting them with the most relevant learning options, based on previous learning choices, skills inventories, and more. The U.S. Navy, for example, developed an interactive system that allows sailors to take a pretest that will give them credit for what they already know, and presents options for creating a personalized learning plan based only on what they don't know.[4] Other technologies allow a subscription service that pushes content based on the interests and learning gaps revealed by an employee's past inputs into the system, while still other technologies use powerful search engines, knowledge maps, indexes to databases, and inference and collaborative technologies, together with a constantly changing profile of an employee and his previous choices and documented development plans, to push only relevant content choices to him.

Companies are also offering employees a choice of learning channels to help them tailor content delivery to how they learn best. For example, employees at Unisys, the information systems consulting company, can input their style preference in the learning portal to help them search for choices based on their individual learning style.[5] Similarly, call center employees at Coventry Building Society, a U.K.-based financial services institution, can choose from classroom training, self-development activities, computer-based training, structured visits to other key customer-facing departments, and more. After the company offered these varied learning modes as part of its plan to reinvigorate training, call center capture rates improved from 78 percent to 94 percent, the average number of sales leads and calls answered increased, and staff turnover decreased.[6]

Possible Ways to Offer Modular Choices

This chapter covers many domains in which companies can offer their employees modular choices, but not all. For example, Sun Microsystems provides a menu of technology options (both hardware and software) from which employees can choose.[7] Here's a checklist of possible ways you can introduce modular choices that your organization may want to consider:

- *Rewards and recognition:* Menu of choices
- Learning
    - Modular chunks to be configured at will
    - Choices in learning channels
- Place
    - In the office, at home, at a satellite center, or on the road
    - Menu of place choices within the office
- Time
    - Daily and weekly options (e.g., part-time, job shares)
    - Monthly options (e.g., seasonal work, cycle between work and nonwork)

Choice in Work Activities and Projects

After years of managing people and experimenting with ways to improve their performance, Tom Hennigan, chief operating officer of Victorinox Swiss Army, Inc., had a lightbulb go off. He explains, "I finally figured out that if you truly want to maximize people's performance, you change the job to fit the person rather than change the person to fit the job."[8] To do this, Hennigan no longer thinks of jobs as standard, monolithic entities, but rather as a series of small, discrete assignments that can be mixed and matched, configured based on individual needs, strengths, and preferences. For example, Hennigan once assigned a warehouse supervisor temporary responsibility for a cross-organizational product fulfillment project. This harnessed the supervisor's innate strategic visioning skills, which she might otherwise have had to wait to use until she'd advanced several career levels.

- – Career break options
- – Pace of promotion options
- *Performance appraisals:* Assessment criteria options
- Work activities
  - – Disaggregation of monolithic jobs into smaller, modular tasks that can be reconfigured at will
  - – Menu of optional assignments
- Career development
  - – Dual career paths
  - – Finite set of next job choices
  - – Paths through multiple functional areas to the same destination
  - – Choice of starting over on a new career path
- *Compensation:* Menu of choices regarding compensation mix and delivery timing
- Benefits
  - – Cafeteria-style benefits plans
  - – Build-your-own health plans
  - – Total rewards plans with flexible dollars
- *Technology:* Menu of hardware and software choices

Companies are now experimenting with adopting such strategies at an organization-wide level. Instead of trying to force fit individuals into a standard job description, these companies are now breaking apart whole job descriptions into smaller, discrete tasks and activities to allow employees to modularly configure their own custom jobs. Consulting company Booz Allen Hamilton, for example, took apart the standard series of job tasks in some consulting jobs, identifying smaller, discrete chunks of work that can be modularly configured based on interest and skill, and completed by working at home or in brief visits to the office.[9] We've also seen some companies use internal temporary staffing agencies to allow employees to mass configure their jobs by choosing specific assignments best suited to them.[10] Such internal agencies can draw on skills databases that send only relevant assignment choices to employees based on their skill and interest profiles.

Marriott's information resources group has taken yet another mix-and-match approach to assignments. Senior managers are offered opportunities to take on tasks and assignments from a second, lateral role, while moving some of their current responsibilities to others to pick up. For example, the vice president of guest services has now added on assignments from a secondary role as regional vice president for information resources of Marriott Canada.[11]

A more common option growing in popularity is to offer people the choice of doing volunteer work, or other assignments outside their job descriptions, which can temporarily be performed on company time. At PNC Financial Services Group, for example, employees are offered predefined volunteering choices based on partnerships with two hundred nonprofits nationwide; employees can choose between skills-based assignments and projects unrelated to their jobs.[12] Volunteer assignments typically range from days to a year (depending on the company), and afford the opportunity for individuals to configure their own work for a time by choosing from a list of assignments that can tap into their unique skills, career goals, interests, and a growing value of corporate social responsibility and meaningful work—especially on the part of Millennials and women.

One management consultant we interviewed, for example, chose an assignment of developing a learning strategy for a nonprofit savings and loan in Africa. His choice in assignment promoted his personal interest to "give back," to travel in second and third world countries, to work with an innovative international nonprofit business model, and to experience extraordinarily high levels of autonomy and impact. All of these were opportunities he wouldn't have had during the course of his regular job. As a result of being able to customize his job through such an assignment, he reports that he feels more engaged with and committed to his company. He's also improved his performance—he credits his experience with helping him develop skills faster than the usual route that he can now use on future consulting jobs, including effective cross-cultural communication skills, the ability to understand the context of local cultures, and the ability to link organizations together. Our findings echo his experience: companies that offer such programs get a leg up in attracting and retaining top talent, good publicity, more motivated and rejuvenated employees, a valuable development opportunity, and the ability to help their employees customize their activities at work.

Choice in Rewards and Recognition

Everyone knows that a motivated worker is a more productive worker. Wouldn't we all be more motivated at work if our supervisors could tap into our deep-seated desires by offering personally meaningful rewards? Research has shown the standard awards of cash or a service plaque rarely do the trick; employees often view these as impersonal, insincere, or just plain forgettable.[13]

To get personal, many companies are radically expanding the range of reward options from which employees and their managers can choose to fit any lifestyle, demographic, or value system. The Carlson Companies (owner of T.G.I. Friday's), for example, established a list of predefined reward choices from which employees can select for immediate, on-the-spot recognition, and at Unreal Marketing, workers get to choose their own end-of-year bonuses.[14] Depending on the company, reward or bonus options may include a personalized electronic thank-you certificate, more time off, a night at a Ritz-Carlton hotel, a new kitchen, a safari through Tanzania, a big-screen TV, movie tickets, a Harley-Davidson motorcycle, or just plain cash. One employee we interviewed selected his dream incentive: a horse trailer and saddle for his beloved horse Apache; another, more time off to accomplish his dream of running a marathon. Increasingly, rewards include not only lifestyle awards but work-life options such as flextime, child care, and elderly care.

Companies can support such efforts with leadership training programs to help managers deliver personalized recognition or by offering tools and exercises to help supervisors know what kind of behaviors an employee would like recognized, and how. Disney and Baptist Health of Florida, for example, have new hires complete a questionnaire detailing how they wish to be rewarded and recognized; managers can later refer back to this to find the best ways to motivate each of their people.[15] Computer systems can also assist managers in recommending award options; Thanks.com provides suggestions based on interest and price category, and provides managers with tips on how best to give the reward.[16]

The benefits of a personalized rewards strategy? Carlson Companies attributes its highest levels of retention ever to implementing a choice-based rewards program.[17] At staffing company Kelly Services, participants in the personalized reward program generate three times more revenue than employees who don't participate, and according to a Watson Wyatt study, companies that provide customized rewards have a median three-year total return to shareholders nearly double that of organizations that don't provide such rewards (9.4 percent versus 4.9 percent).[18]

Choice in Performance Appraisals

Recall Helen and Jill, whom we introduced near the beginning of this book. Both had the same job but performed very different tasks. Their supervisor, frustrated that the generic performance criteria he was given didn't reflect the nature of what they actually did in their jobs, ignored it and wrote, "See attached."

To avoid such problems, some companies are applying the idea of modular choice to performance appraisals. At Accenture, for example, broadly defined assessment criteria—like the extent to which an employee is a people developer, business operator, and value creator—are defined and applied to all, but under each a modular menu of choices based on level and workforce is then provided to supervisors from which they can flexibly select. A supervisor could select from characteristics such as "contributes to knowledge capital," "provides new solutions or services," "establishes self as an expert," or "makes improvements to work products," for example, when assessing whether a junior consulting employee is an effective value creator. In this way, standard ratings are still collected, but the ratings are based on the unique work the employee performs rather than on ill-suited assessment criteria.

Choice in Work Space

Some people prefer to work in a quiet, closed office without hearing the radio or cell phone conversations of the colleague next to them, while others rather enjoy the hubbub and sense of camaraderie they feel working side by side with colleagues and team members. Still other people would do their best work at home—and save commuting time to do extra work or spend time with family. Recognizing that people vary in the types of environments they need to be effective at work, and that these environments may need to fluidly change to meet the changing nature of people's work tasks, many companies are offering a menu of options for where employees can choose to work.

Some of the most innovative developments in workplace design combine elements of both modular choice and segmentation. For example, Microsoft is now introducing customized work spaces by combining the two approaches. Instead of the perk of standardized private offices that Microsoft famously offered in the past to most employees, the company now suggests certain environments for business groups based on a segmentation scheme that takes into account worker mobility and work type: there are providers (desk-centered employees who provide support to teams), travelers (the types who work anywhere but work), concentrators (head-down, always-at-work types), and orchestrators (internally mobile and highly collaborative individuals).

Once Microsoft workplace design professionals suggest a work setting based on type, Microsoft teams can then mass configure their designated setting. They can choose between a setting designed for privacy versus collaboration, for example, by moving walls or sliding doors to create open or closed spaces based on the needs of their team or their task at hand. This way, the space adapts to its users, instead of forcing its users to adapt to it. Managers and teams can also provide input on choosing from a list of component parts certain aspects of the work space—down to carpeting that doubles as a golf green, Xbox lounges, or luxury kitchens—that work best for them.[19] Work teams also get to provide input regarding the selection of their own modern furniture from a vast range of choices.[20]

Apart from their own individual work settings, Microsoft employees can choose to work (or play) in a vast array of other spaces too—from living-room-like gathering spaces, touch-down spaces to check e-mail while waiting for a meeting, media rooms, lounges, "agile project rooms" that support Microsoft's approach to flexible and rapid product development, informal huddle rooms, and even nap stations. The result? Microsoft's work setting feels less like an office and more like a house, or perhaps a town: many Microsoft employees can even go to the post office, a spa, a bookstore, or one of a dozen restaurants without feeling like they left campus, thereby integrating work with life as they see fit. Employees can also choose to work from home, their car, or the road when they want—many employees have smartphones loaded with Microsoft's own software that gives people anywhere, anytime access to their calendars, tasks, contacts, and mail.

Similarly, Capital One's Flexible Work Solutions environment initiative combines segmentation with modular choice to customize its work environment, although in a slightly different way.[21] There are defined work settings for executives (who sit at narrow tables in open space with about four managers at each), anchors (administrative and executive assistants who create a sense of continuity for teams by staying in one place), mobile workers (who have no defined work space and leverage various activity settings depending on the work they need to accomplish), residents (who have the same work space each day), and teleworkers (who work largely offsite). Executives and anchors are assigned their work spaces in a segmentation approach, but other employees choose among the additional categories offered in a modular choice approach.

The payoff? Employee satisfaction has risen 41 percent at Capital One as a result of the initial pilot, and surveys continue to reveal that employees feel their groups are more productive, the work atmosphere is more creative, and they get faster feedback from peers and managers.[22] Microsoft is sure that resulting improvements in employee productivity will quickly make up for the greater expense of offering choice in work spaces; it estimates that a 1 percent gain in employee productivity covers a 10 percent increase in construction costs. So while there may be some up-front costs to such initiatives, a smart, holistic business case can reveal some often hidden but very powerful benefits that far outweigh the costs.

Choice in Work Time

For most people, life calls on us to take temporary pit stops—to have children, to go to graduate school, to care for aging parents, or to take that around-the-world tour we've put on our "top ten things to do before we die" list. In some phases of life, we need to downshift our work responsibilities; in others, we want to work full steam ahead. Increasingly, organizations are engineering a much wider range of modular choices so that individuals can arrange their workday, their workweek, their work year, or even their work decade according to their unique work and personal demands, and to suit their very different stages of career and life that cycle and change over time. The business benefits of offering such a range of choices regarding time are well documented: lower turnover rates, less absenteeism, and more motivated and engaged employees.

Organizations like Royal Bank of Scotland, Microsoft, Travelers, and some divisions of PepsiCo now offer a mix-and-match menu of time options, including job shares, part-time work, work-from-home options, and compressed workweeks. After Royal Bank of Scotland introduced its Yourtime program (offering four-day compressed workweeks), productivity and morale significantly improved, short-time sickness absences decreased by 3 percent, and expensive overtime decreased by 7 percent. Others, like an oil and gas company in our study, offer options like nine-hour days for nine days, with the tenth working day off. Still others offer the option of seasonal work or on-again, off-again schedules: at tax firm Ernst & Young, tax professionals can work full-time part of the year and part-time the rest of the year.[23] (See also "Crafting Choice for Hourly Workers.")

What's new in offering choices about when people work? Scaling the idea of flexibility to include options for longer-term career breaks. Too often, employees who take career breaks return to lower-status jobs or work for less pay, often for a different company. And when companies do offer career breaks, few also offer support or resources while an employee is out. Some companies are working to change this. IBM, for example, offers employees the choice to leave for certain time periods while keeping in touch with them through an active alumni network. These employees then go through formal reentry programs to support their transition back to work.[24] Other companies, like Microsoft and Nike, offer paid sabbaticals (something that only 5 percent of U.S. companies do, given how expensive that option can be).[25]

Crafting Choice for Hourly Workers

When Macy's department store leaders learned that the area of dissatisfaction among its workforce was scheduling, they knew they had to act. After all, here was a workforce comprised primarily of Millennials—young people known to value choice and flexibility above all. Macy's is therefore experimenting with a software system that generates multiple predefined shift choices from which an employee can choose each week, based on an algorithm that optimizes schedule options for the employee—*and* the business.

Such software programs are good news for retailers who want to satisfy employees. In an industry where increasingly sophisticated schedule-optimization software has meant that employee work time often depends on variables like customer traffic and spending forecasts, new solutions are emerging. Rather than companies dictating the time when employees work based solely on their own needs (resulting in a backlash of disengaged employees and higher employee turnover, all ultimately quite costly), companies like Macy's are creating a unique differentiator that will help them attract, retain, and motivate employees by offering more choices for when they perform their work.

An innovative alternative is Accenture's Future Leave program, which gives employees the option of funding a sabbatical by contributing a portion of their salary to a specific fund. They then draw the amount they contributed to that fund over the course of their leave. Participation in the program does not affect an employee's long-term career potential, and, in fact, provides assurance that participants can return to work. While gone, employees still receive health-care and other insurance coverage at standard employee premium rates.

Many companies would like to offer such breaks and cyclical work, but feel these would disrupt business too much. One solution is to do what PricewaterhouseCoopers is trying: a work-design pilot program that groups employees into teams that share responsibility for a group of clients. If one employee is away, another easily steps in; it all depends on careful coordination and information sharing.[26] Even doctors, who are notoriously on call and find it difficult to break away from their patients, are experimenting with such shared responsibilities and thereby creating a cultural revolution in the world of medicine.[27]

Leading companies make sure that employees who take such work-time options suffer no stigma in the organization as a result: they still receive rewards, are seen as active and valued contributors, are promotable (though at perhaps a slower pace than workers putting in more time), and don't languish on a dead-end "mommy track." Stop-the-clock programs common in university settings now are being applied in many companies, where people are not penalized for taking time out. And for people who want to step up their pace of time and effort, we imagine a future in which employees could structure the timing of their own advancement by taking GMAT-style challenges (the MBA program entrance exam, where questions become progressively harder or easier based on how well an individual has answered previous questions, to determine a final score).[28] In such a scenario, employees would be doled out certain challenges, like a project or an activity, and if they succeed, they would be given other challenges of increasing difficulty, enabling them to climb the ladder more quickly than they otherwise might.

Choice in Career Development

Most people want a lot of freedom and choice to determine what jobs to take along a flexible career path, but many also prefer structure and clearly laid-out career plans. In a survey of 1,025 middle managers, for example, 35 percent felt frustrated at having no clear career path.[29] The middle ground that many organizations prefer provides people with a few well-defined options in a modular choice approach; this offers clarity and some predictability, but also some choice and flexibility. Options may include more and varied ladders to the top, choices for lateral movement in a career "web" rather than a career ladder, or the option of starting whole new careers in the same organization.

Take the Singapore Armed Forces, for example. The organization found that to best attract and retain young people, it needed to provide more varied career choices. The organization offers a choice of multiple, clearly defined career paths, so people can enter different functional areas if desired. The U.S. Army also found it needed to offer more choice to help stem an officer shortage; in exchange for three additional years of active duty, it now offers a menu of job choices or assignment locations from which an officer can choose.[30]

Many organizations are now creating modular career path options that allow people to increase their earnings and level in the organization without ever assuming managerial responsibilities they may not like or for which they may not be well suited. Research shows that such options reduce turnover and improve engagement, probably because they allow people to build on their strengths.[31] Microsoft, for example, offers the choice of a technical-specialist and management-focused career track. This allows high-performing technical experts to have increasingly higher levels of pay and perks without ever becoming managers. Unlike most companies with such tracks, however, Microsoft allows its developers the freedom to laterally move back and forth as they desire, with no stigma attached. These choices are packaged as part of a greater career stage profile presented to each Microsoft employee that defines what is appropriate progression in each stage on a given career path, and what potential paths are available from any given point.

Some companies like truck maker Navistar are even allowing multiple entry points so that people can gain new experiences and thereby start new careers if they desire by moving any direction in the organization. Fran Smith, manager of leader resources (leadership development) at Navistar, explains, "We believe in giving people the opportunity to try various things within the organization in order to obtain certain skills and competencies. We have developmental assignments people can apply for where somebody can go up, down, or sideways in level to familiarize themselves with something in the organization that they might need to know. To make it easier for them to change roles, we even grandfather their salary and level for two years so they can do it without penalty or consequence."[32] Since companies often pay one and a half to two times a person's salary to replace them, such initiatives—though they may sound costly—can in the long run save a company significant sums of money.

Finally, companies can leverage technology to provide relevant sets of choices for different people to consider; talent management software company SuccessFactors built a prototype, for example, that provides a few well-defined options regarding next positions—both lateral and vertical—that each employee may consider based on competencies and experience, and computes the person's readiness for each opportunity.[33]

Choice in Compensation

Most of us are paid in the form of wages based on market rates, with perhaps an additional equity plan thrown in, like the ability to buy limited quantities of a company's stock at a reduced rate. But different people have different needs and circumstances: a young new employee might want to take as much of his compensation as possible in the form of wages to pay off student loans, whereas someone who's ten years into her career might prefer high-risk equity options. Today, nearly all organizations have similar compensation structures. The few that offer employees the ability to configure their own customized compensation structures have created a unique advantage that can be difficult for competitors to duplicate.

Eighty-three percent of Best Buy long-term-incentive-eligible employees surveyed, for example, said that the introduction of a choice-based long-term incentive plan made them more likely to stay with the company. In the program (offered to managers and executives only), employees are given a menu of four options, each with a different degree of risk and time horizon. Choices include various combinations of stock options, performance shares based on different performance criteria, and restricted stock, with various vesting schedules and based on the performance of the company over various time frames.

Another company that recently introduced modular compensation options is Skyline Construction Inc., a San Francisco–based construction firm. Eligible employees can now pick their own salaries (within a certain range), choosing between lower salaries and a shot at a larger bonus, or higher salaries and the possibility of a smaller bonus. Bonus factors include commission targets (bigger bonuses are provided for exceeding targets), customer satisfaction, and timely project completion; no bonuses are paid if the company doesn't generate an operating profit. Skyline employees say the pick-your-own salary plan offers flexibility and motivates them to succeed; CEO David Hayes says the plan is a success, noting that Skyline's revenue grew to $76 million in 2007, from $42 million in 2004.[34]

Choice in Benefits

Most companies today offer at least a few options in health plans, insurance, or retirement funding. Leading organizations, however, are getting increasingly personal with their perks. Take Dell's Build Your Own health plan. On the basis of personal factors such as tolerance for risk, health care needs, and the prior year's health expenses, employees can draw from a plethora of menu items, including benefit levels, network options, and contribution rates. After introducing the plan, Dell has reduced its health care cost by 14 percent, or $6 million.[35]

Microsoft employees can now choose not only from a range of health and insurance options, but also from a vast array of lifestyle benefits that give them substantial discounts of up to 25 percent on such things as hybrid cars and services like housekeeping, yard and pet care, auto repair, grocery delivery, financial planning and banking services, and even doctors that come to their home in case of an emergency.

But how can providing such benefits be cost-effective? First, companies provide options that cost the organization less (through discounts obtained due to purchasing power) than the value individuals place on them. Second, using what is called a *flex benefits* scheme, they may give their employees a set of predefined benefits choices that they can choose from, as long as they stay within the predetermined budget of the cash equivalent of their employee deal. Royal Bank of Scotland is an early adopter of such an approach. It allows employees to select from more cash, more time off, subsidized bicycles, child care vouchers, pension contributions, and more as long as they stay within their defined compensation amount, which lumps base pay and benefits funding together. Explains director of reward Trevor Blackman, "There aren't any limits of how many benefits a person can choose—employees can drive right down into what is traditionally considered salary if they want to obtain as many benefits from the list as they desire, or they can take it all in cash and have no benefits at all."[36]

In the future, experts imagine that trade-offs could be made based on just about any desired attribute at work, including development opportunities, flextime, work spaces, promotions, or more. For example, people might choose an office at work or receive additional cash for saving the company money because they work from home. Or they might use the employer contribution toward retirement to pay off their student loans instead. To help people allocate their budget wisely, companies like pharmaceutical company AstraZeneca are helping employees model scenarios regarding how their choices might play out using Web-based technology, and be warned by built-in triggers of the risks associated with their choices.[37] (See "Benefits That Truly Benefit Your Varied Workforce.")

Offering Multiple Interrelated Modular Choices at Once

Some modular choices that a company might offer employees can affect other dimensions of work life. How much time you put in at work, for example, may determine how quickly you get promoted. And the type of work activities or career path you choose—such as whether you are managing people or working on your own—will most certainly influence the location and schedule choices you can pursue. It makes sense, then, to couple interrelated choices together, so employees can clearly see the implications and trade-offs of each choice they make.

To help people understand exactly how a choice in one domain may affect a selection in another, some companies are combining interrelated choices across multiple dimensions in a single model. Some divisions of Deloitte Touche Tohmatsu, for example, offer many of their employees a definite set of options across four interrelated domains (pace, workload, location, and role) as part of a single model the company calls Mass Career

Benefits That Truly Benefit Your Varied Workforce

Imagine the challenge facing HR executives at Wal-Mart who hope to offer meaningful benefits options. Here is an organization that employs people from both ends of the age spectrum, with workers ranging from seniors who work as greeters to sixteen-year-old teens bagging your groceries![38] That's why Wal-Mart is now working to include benefits options that will appeal to this wide cross-section of employees. It offers more than one hundred discounts on everything from new cars to movie tickets, and now has more than fifty ways for employees to customize their health coverage by selecting from a menu of deductibles, health care coverage options, and health credits and premiums.[39]

To be sure, determining the right set of benefit choices has many companies analyzing their workforce to ensure that various groups' needs and values are covered in choices offered. But don't confuse this with segmentation; these leading companies are performing sophisticated analyses of their employees to group them into workforce segments—not to offer specific, tailored practices for each (as they would in a segmentation approach to customization), but rather to help them offer the most relevant set of choices to all.

For example, U.K.-based Tesco, the world's third-largest grocer, offers a wide variety of predefined benefits and compensation choices based on a rigorous statistical analysis of its workforce needs, broken into five distinct employee groups: pleasure seekers (mostly highly mobile single men who enjoy their leisure time; they have the least

Customization™.[40] Pilots of the program at Deloitte have shown improved employee productivity and increased satisfaction. Dimensions include:

- *Pace:* Options regarding how quickly a person will be promoted and take on more responsibility (ranging from accelerated to decelerated)

- *Workload:* Options regarding the quantity of the work output (ranging from full to reduced)

- *Location/schedule:* Options regarding when and where work is performed (ranging from restricted—for example, specific commitment to Tesco); want-it-alls (employees who desire promotions and money, and want their work to be challenging and varied); work-life balancers (employees who want to work flexible hours or part-time, and want stimulating work but aren't so interested in promotions); live-to-work employees (highly loyal employees who want to work long hours and who desire promotions and challenging jobs); and work-to-live employees (employees who aren't interested in long hours or promotions and who don't mind working on repetitive tasks).

These groupings were based on extensive research and analysis by its employee insight unit (EIU). EIU interviewed more than one thousand people outside Tesco, held twenty focus groups with representative employees, and surveyed sixteen hundred employees to determine what employees valued in work and their motivations, people's perception of Tesco as an employer, and the trade-offs employees make between the two. The analysis also incorporated results from previous and ongoing employee surveys.

As a result of this in-depth understanding of its workforce, Tesco offers a relevant set of choices for all. Options cover the needs of all five segments; a want-it-all might choose share options; a work-life balancer, child care vouchers; and a pleasure seeker, an eight-month career break option so that he can travel the world. Following the trend of the future, Tesco is now expanding the array of choice into areas such as training and development.[41] One can imagine, for example, that work-life balancers would appreciate options to work from home, flexible hours, or part-time arrangements for periods of time. Live-to-workers, on the other hand, may be more likely to embrace options that would help their career advancement.

conditions related to working remotely, compressed workweeks, and inability to travel—to unrestricted)

- *Role:* Options regarding position, responsibilities, work assignments, and span of management (ranging from individual contributor to leader, or line versus staff)

By presenting interrelated options in a common structure, companies can easily show employees how one choice may have an impact on another, thereby helping them responsibly make the most informed decisions best for them.

When Should You Use Modular Choice?

Compared with the other three workforce of one approaches that we're examining in this book, modular choice offers several specific advantages— for either employees or organizations, and often for both. First, it combines flexibility with manageability and control by offering all employees a limited array of organizationally sanctioned choices. Because HR is centrally defining the specific people practice options, companies will retain a relatively high degree of control—although not as much as they would have by using the segmentation approach. Unlike segmentation, modular choice doesn't necessarily control exactly how many and which particular people use a specific people practice. Rather, it is up to employees to determine which people practice they want to choose from the organization's approved list of menu options. This makes modular choice a bit more employee driven than the segmentation approach, enabling employees to get in the driver's seat by allowing them to custom configure their own people practices from a predefined list.

Yet modular choice is still very much an HR-driven approach; it is much more centralized and run in a more top-down fashion than more employee-driven approaches like broad and simple rules and employee-defined personalization. This allows for more transparency in how it's used and more organizational control. That's why the approach provides a good way for traditional organizations to introduce customization into their people management strategies, without requiring huge shifts in conventional HR ideology.

The control the approach affords also means it can be useful when an organization has acquired a lot of new employees, as it doesn't require the kind of extensive support, such as education, coaching, and change management, that more employee-driven customization approaches need. Likewise, the high degree of control lends itself well to organizations in highly regulated environments. Using modular choice, these organizations can still centrally define their people practices in detail to meet regulation requirements.

Perhaps one of the biggest advantages of the modular choice customization approach is that employees perceive it as quite fair. Having the same set of options spelled out in detail by HR means that employees can easily understand why specific people might have a differing work experience from their own; they have merely chosen different options from exactly the same list.

Even so, employees may have trouble making decisions about which option to choose, and then fail to take responsibility for the consequences when they do. Consider the scandals that ensued, for example, when companies gave employees options in how to allocate their retirement savings, only to hear gripes from employees when they lost significant sums of money. Or consider the complaints we often hear from people who have failed to advance as quickly as colleagues when they've made career-limiting changes or choices to accommodate life changes. For this reason, many companies are concerned about giving employees too much choice. Others assume responsibility for helping employees choose the right options and for educating them about the consequences of their choices. To help people navigate their sea of options, companies may invest in modeling technologies.

Alternatively, companies may combine the modular choice and segmentation approaches by offering only certain sets of choices to certain segments—just as McDonald's offers different menu choices to people in different countries based on eating habits and cultural behavior. At P&G's Beauty division, for example, since employees are given a great deal of predefined choices in learning, the division's learning portal suggests choices based on the individual—such as their length of service, general type of role (administrative, manager, function head, etc.), skills they'd like to attain, and other criteria.

Another advantage to modular choice is that it lends itself quite well to analytics and therefore is a good choice for companies with a data-driven orientation. Data analysis is crucial for determining the most relevant set of options for employees. And as employees choose among the options provided, data analysis will be critical in helping the organization gain insight into which are most valued. This information can then be used to further refine the list. Companies may also start to build data-based profiles of each employee based on the options they choose. Having standard employee data already and a common HR platform can greatly enhance an organization's ability to offer modular choices in most people practice domains.

Finally, modular choice can often be a more flexible approach to customization than segmentation can be. Generating new lists of choices whenever conditions change is usually easier than recategorizing employees or dealing with segments that are no longer relevant. And depending on the particular people practice area, employees can easily change their choices whenever they desire. Still, adding new choices, such as new places to work in a company's building, an additional benefit option, or new learning options, may still take substantial time; the approach is thus not as flexible to change as more employee-driven approaches to customization.

As with each of our four approaches, you should also consider the drawbacks when it comes to offering modular choices. (See "Modular Choices: Weighing the Pros and Cons.")

For instance, compared with more employee-driven approaches, modular choice may not offer as great a fit between individual and practice; employees may still feel constrained by the limited array of choices, especially if the list doesn't include the choice they desire most.

Modular Choices: Weighing the Pros and Cons

W*hat it is:* Providing employees with a standard set of menu options from which they can choose to enable them to custom configure their own schedules, jobs, rewards, benefits, or more.

Advantages	Disadvantages
• Affords a high degree of control since the organization determines the final set of detailed options offered (however, the approach affords less control than segmentation does)	• Offers less customization than employee-driven approaches; choices may be too limited to be relevant for a particular individual
• Relatively high degree of transparency: executives can see how talent is being managed, especially if they track which options are chosen by which individuals	• May require substantial resources to manage and administer multiple programs and practices
• May require less change management and organizational change compared with more employee-driven approaches	• Some organizational support may be needed to help inform employees of choices and help them make the best decisions
• Most likely approach of all the four customization approaches to be perceived as fair and egalitarian, since everyone is offered the same set of options	• May be difficult to change modular choice options frequently to adapt to changing conditions (though modular choices may be easier to change than segmentation schemes)
• Employees can easily understand why specific people have differentiated work experiences	• Employees may not take responsibility for the consequences of their choices
• Analytics and data-driven approach to talent management lends itself well to companies with these types of cultures	• May require advanced HR infrastructure and analytics capability to support modular choices; companies that have a standard HR platform can most easily support modular choice efforts
• Puts employees in the driver's seat and gives them some degree of control compared with the segmentation approach	• Companies with employees who value autonomy and self-direction may find it too controlled and the choices too limiting
• Easily accommodates high-growth companies with lots of new employees	
• Can accommodate highly regulated environments by still allowing the organization to centrally define the details of a people practice	

Modular choice also requires more effort and more resources than traditional one-size-fits-all practices. When Best Buy offered its choice-based long-term incentive plan, for example, it spent months surveying employees to determine the right set of options—and then more effort and time to make sure people understood the choices by sending out e-mails and work-sheets, holding webinars, and offering one-on-one counseling. Still, modular choice may require less communication and change management than more employee-driven approaches will (by their nature, such approaches often require companies to teach people how to define their own people practices appropriately).

Managing multiple options also often ups the administrative burden on a company. For example, tracking compensation by individual employees based on the choices they've made, rather than by job level, is quite a bit more complex and requires more sophisticated technology and administrative support. What's more, cost savings created by economies of scale may sometimes be sacrificed when splintering a company's offering into multiple options. But offering choice need not always be expensive; companies often offset costs because they're not paying for benefits or other practices that employees don't choose—and that these companies might have paid for automatically in the past.

To be sure, most companies will find that the modest degree of effort they make to introduce a modular choice customization approach is well worth it. We have seen that, time and time again, companies have been paid back through an order of magnitude in improvement in reduced turnover costs and, more important, in the improved business results created when people practices support the specific things that every employee needs to reach peak performance.

Companies have long offered modular choices when it comes to benefits options or even schedule choices. But a workforce of one approach to modular choice creatively unleashes the concept: with it, companies can offer customized people practices in revolutionary new ways across the whole spectrum of people practices—transforming everything from learning to jobs, to workplace, to career paths. Just as customizing products and services through providing modular choices revolutionized the consumer experience, so can creatively customizing people practices through giving employees modular choices revolutionize the employment experience. Throughout this chapter, we've provided examples of many ways companies are creatively offering employees highly relevant options—and we hope that we've challenged you to consider doing the same in your own organization. (See "Recommendations for Customizing Through Modular Choice.")

In the next chapter, we'll explore a third way to customize your workforce, by using broad and simple rules. Again, organizations can choose to use this and all of the workforce of one approaches singly or else in combination with one or all of the others.

Recommendations for Customizing Through Modular Choice

- Focus on the quality of options and how well they suit the specific needs of your workforce rather than the sheer quantity of options provided.

- Use analytics to determine the best set of options to offer (based on a data-based analysis of your workforce), track the options chosen to further refine the list, and build a better understanding of your workforce through data-based profiles of options chosen by each employee.

- When appropriate, combine segmentation with modular choice to offer only some options to some workforce segments—thereby preventing employees from being overwhelmed by a sea of choices and encouraging even greater fit between people practice and individual.

- Keep options fresh by continually analyzing whether they are still relevant, and replacing them when they are not.

- Build a thorough business case for modular choice by showing that the cost incurred by not pursuing economies of scale can be overcome: companies often offset them because they're not paying for practices that employees don't choose. Companies also save on workforce turnover costs and benefit from more engaged, better-performing employees.

- Build the infrastructure to support choice through using a common HR platform upon which to build choice and more easily manage and administrate it.

- Support employees in making informed choices, and encourage them to take responsibility for choices made.

- Consider offering interrelated modular choices in one common modular choice scheme.

Define Broad and Simple Rules

To really improve people's performance, HR needs to develop a philosophy of helping individuals perform at their personal best. And this means providing different support for different people—to truly achieve superior performance, we need to contextualize our talent practices based on each and every individual's unique needs and circumstances.

—Charlie Bresler, former president of Men's Wearhouse
and current executive vice president of human
development and marketing[1]

ANYONE WHO WATCHES *The Amazing Race*, a reality TV show that airs in many countries, has seen a clear example of how many different kinds of routes can take people to the same end destination. In the show, teams compete in a race around the world—by any means they can get there. For example, in a race from the ruins of Rio, Greece, to a desert in Jabreen, Oman, teams may choose different forms of transportation (camel or jeep?) that journey at different times (the 10 a.m. or the 12 p.m. flight?) and through different routes (a pit stop in Jordan or Qatar?). Some teams may be led by a dominant leader; others might navigate their journey through teamwork. But they all get to the same place, drawing on their unique strengths and individual set of circumstances and dealing with the roadblocks along the way.

Similarly, by defining the end, and letting individuals and their managers customize the route or the means based on an employee's unique strengths, preferences, and needs, organizations can create customized people practices while still retaining control and consistency. We call this approach to customization *broad and simple rules* because people practices are so widely defined that individuals can interpret and apply them in myriad ways. Instead of rigidly and narrowly defining the one best way (e.g., prescribing exactly how to get to the Jabreen desert), rules are abstract and general enough (e.g., get to the Jabreen desert) that employees have some freedom in interpreting and implementing the rules to uniquely suit themselves.

Unlike with modular choice, the organization doesn't predefine selections for how to achieve a particular outcome. Rather, broad and simple rules work because they constrain freedom through organizationally sanctioned limits—such as limiting activities to only those that help achieve a specified outcome or strategy (see "'Structured' Freedom"). Limits act as wide parameters within which people can operate. For the organization, limits enable it to retain some degree of consistency and control, essentially "widening the guardrails" of what they offer the workforce. For the individual, research confirms that limits are good too; without them, people have trouble making decisions.[2]

Broad and simple rules make use of a technique commonly used in strategy formulation—*upframing*, or generalizing to higher levels of abstraction to get at the essence of what an organization really wants. Business strategies can then be *downframed* and applied in more concrete ways to suit local business needs.[3] Broad and simple rules also have been used in customizing for customers—Nordstrom, for example, customizes clients' shopping experiences by giving sales associates general, high-level sales guidelines only, allowing a great deal of freedom to tailor their sales approach to each customer. Says one Nordstrom representative, "The more rules you have, the farther and farther you get from the customer."[4]

Accordingly, many organizations are adopting broad and simple rules in their people practices. Explains Debra Hunter Johnson, American Airlines' vice president of HR, "We feel that as an employer of the twenty-first century, we should be trying to define culture and broad guidelines instead of writing rules and rigid policies."[5] Some organizations, such as The Container Store, have abandoned lengthy employee manuals altogether in favor of a few simple HR guidelines.[6] In this chapter, we'll see how The Container Store and other organizations, like Best Buy, Google, Men's Wearhouse, and W. L. Gore, have become leaders in rewriting their people practices across a variety of domains using a broad and simple rules approach.

"Structured" Freedom

The broad and simple rules approach allows employees or their managers to customize people practices by granting them structured freedom that is constrained by clear, organizationally determined and sanctioned boundaries and limits. Different types of constraining boundaries include:

- *Strategic boundaries.* These describe the organization's broad mission and direction to help clarify how an individual must act within the bigger picture.

- *Values-based boundaries.* These spell out the critical behaviors based on organizational values to which an employee must adhere.

- *Time or money boundaries.* These define a specific time frame, amount of resources, or budget allocation to which an employee must conform.

- *Results or outcome boundaries.* These are determined by the outcomes deemed successful for a given task or responsibility.

- *Abilities boundaries.* These define a person's broader abilities or potential (e.g., her capacity to learn languages), as opposed to narrow skills or experience (e.g., how many years of French she studied in school).

- *Organizational scope boundaries.* These define a specific domain in an organization within which an individual may work—such as career paths that are constrained within a particular functional area or jobs constrained by a particular scope of activities performed in the organization or function.

Companies can set different kinds of constraining boundaries independently or in conjunction with one another, or they may even invent new types of boundaries altogether. No matter what kind of constraints organizations choose, however, they'll be offering their workforces a great deal of freedom while both maintaining control and providing guidance and structure so that their people can make wise and informed choices.

Broad and Simple Rules in Practice

In the following sections, we'll explore seven different areas for customizing people practices using broad and simple rules: namely, define results, not time or place; broadly define jobs and careers; hire the whole

Possible Ways to Introduce Broad and Simple Rules

Traditional, narrow people management practices and strategies can be made broader and simpler across multiple domains. Here's a checklist to help you consider whether your organization has narrow and specific rules or broad and simple ones. The list can also help generate ideas for the various kinds of broad and simple rules your organization might consider.

	Narrow and detailed	Broad and simple
Work place and time	Specify hours and location of work.	Specify work to be done.
Jobs	Detail all the tasks and responsibilities of a job.	Define a job by outcomes, mission, or broad area of scope.
Career development	Define specific career paths and the precise skills and knowledge it takes to get promoted.	Broadly define career trajectories in terms of general organizational area; base promotions on contribution.
Hiring	Hire solely based on specific skills or experience.	Hire based on abilities, potential, and cultural fit, along with considering skills and experience.
Compensation	Determine pay using narrow pay scale associated with job or position only.	Determine pay using broadband pay schemes or by contribution to the business.
Time off	Define sick and vacation days separately.	Define *paid time off*.
Travel	Pay for travel expenses between the business site and home only.	Pay for travel anywhere when gone on business, when of equal or less expense to the cost of travel between the business site and home.
Benefits eligibility	Provide benefits for employees and immediate nuclear family only.	Provide benefits for employees and any individual dependent on the employee.
Rewards	Reward based on narrow scales associated with role and performance.	Distribute rewards at managers' discretion.
Performance appraisals	Assess specific attributes and skills.	Assess achievement of end goals.
Competency management	Create competencies based on specific skills and knowledge.	Create competencies based on values or outcomes.

person; broadly define pay and benefits; cascade your performance goals; let the manager allocate rewards; and finally, define competencies by values or outcomes. (For more on how to make traditional people practices broader, see "Possible Ways to Introduce Broad and Simple Rules.")

Define Results, Not Time or Place

Imagine being able to define when and where you work—as long as you get the job done. If you were an employee with twenty-five years of experience and a broad perspective, you might work thirty hours to accomplish the same amount of work that a newer employee, who gets sidetracked by the details, might accomplish in fifty. You could pop out to enjoy your son's Little League game in the middle of the afternoon or take a spur-of-the-moment shopping trip to clear your head, and then make up for it by working that evening—without ever feeling you were playing hooky or not putting in the required face time. And if the type of work you do permits it, you could even work from a rented cottage on the coast of Greece for a few weeks, enjoying the sea breezes and view while pounding away at your laptop.

At Best Buy, more than 60 percent of the four thousand employees who work at Best Buy's Minneapolis headquarters have an opportunity to customize their work arrangements in such a way, as long as they get their work done. Working fewer hours in a given month or year—or not attending meetings at all, for that matter—isn't a problem as long as people achieve quality results. Hourly corporate employees also enjoy customization to some degree; as long as they work a set number of hours to comply with federal labor regulations and scheduled operations, they get to choose when they work. Explains one employee, "It used to be that I had to schedule my life around my work. Now, I schedule my work around my life."[7] One Best Buy worker, for example, wrote training modules while following a traveling rock band around the country.[8]

Although the new broad and simple rule that defines work by results rather than by time or place has required a big cultural change at Best Buy, employees say they are more loyal, have better relationships with family and friends, and are more focused and energetic thanks to the approach. Best Buy's procurement department, for example, attributed increased savings by 50 percent compared with the previous year to better employee focus and energy. Productivity increased by 35 percent, and voluntary turnover dropped between 52 percent and 90 percent in the three divisions that first adopted the rule.[9] Employees even report that the new structure is spurring them to find ways to become more efficient; in one department, for example, they gave up creating unnecessary PowerPoint decks for equally unnecessary meetings.

Broadly Define Jobs and Careers

As a member of the Best Buy Geek Squad, Moira Hardek had core job duties that had once involved fixing customers' technical computer problems, often by roving around in her Volkswagen making house calls. After a while she made a discovery: customers really resonated with her personal style and expertise. This discovery fueled a highly personal passion and interest for Moira—to get more females interested in technology careers, such as Best Buy's Geek Squad jobs. Because Best Buy broadly defined her job in terms of one simple outcome—helping Best Buy deliver superior customer service—she was able to customize her job and get creative. Her project? To create a technology summer camp with unique hands-on experiences and to demystify technology for a younger generation—specifically young women. She hoped this would spark their interest in technology as both an area of study and as a potential future career. The project was so successful that the following year she was able to conduct several Summer Academies across the country, reaching over eleven hundred young students and engaging over three hundred Geek Squad and Best Buy employees.

Like Best Buy, a number of organizations have thrown out their detailed lists of tasks associated with each job and more broadly defined jobs in terms of results. These organizations no longer require the employees to mold to the job; they let the job mold to the employee. Explains Joe Kalkman, leader of Best Buy's HR centers of excellence, "Our big 'aha' moment was when we realized that people's strengths and passions were different, and that we should thereby allow people to take different avenues in performing the same role."[10] While most organizations base job tasks and who does them solely on what will further business strategy, Kalkman says, "We decided to more broadly define jobs to still achieve our business goals, but to also enable individuals to achieve their personal goals. In the extreme, our strategy sometimes even shifts precisely because of the individuals who are here. By capitalizing on the differences between individuals, rather than trying to squash them, we believe we have a more motivated, committed, and high-performing workforce."

Academic studies confirm this—they've shown that better fit between a person and his or her work can affect an applicant's attraction to the job, job acceptance, and performance.[11] At Best Buy, data analysis performed jointly with Gallup reveals that helping people play to their strengths effectively doubles the rate of increase of employee engagement. This makes a dramatic difference in Best Buy's financials, since a 0.10 increase in engagement (on a 5-point scale) is worth an estimated $100,000 in incremental profit per store, per year. And since the strengths-based approach has some direct impacts on sales and profit growth in addition to those it has on engagement, the total financial gains from the combined strengths and engagement work are estimated to be 1.5 times the gains of engagement alone.

Perhaps that's why Best Buy also encouraged Jeff Appelquist, an HR generalist at corporate, to infuse his passion for military history into a leadership development program he created. Drawing on leadership lessons learned from the Battle of the Little Bighorn in Montana and the Battle of Gettysburg, for example, he developed a leadership program that takes leaders on-site in Montana or Pennsylvania where the battles took place to drive his lessons home. Early success led Best Buy to angel-invest in a for-profit model of this work and, ultimately, in spinning off Appelquist and his program into a start-up named "Blue Knight Battlefield Seminars."

When defining a broad and simple rule for a job, many organizations still mandate a set of required job activities, leaving other activities and tasks open to be customized as long as they stay within a defined boundary. Some organizations limit the required core job activities to a certain amount of time: at 3M, researchers only need spend 85 percent of their time on their core job, and at Google, engineers need only spend 80 percent. The rest of their job may be customized as long as they stay within the strategic boundary of working on projects they feel have the greatest potential to create value for their organizations. Both companies point to the benefits of customization—at 3M, the highly successful Post-it note resulted from one person's broadly defined time parameters, and at Google, job customization produced the e-mail system Gmail and new search engine products like Google News and Google Suggest.[12]

Instead of using outcome or strategic boundaries in defining broad and simple rules for jobs, other companies use organizational scope boundaries. The U.S. Navy, for example, reduced and consolidated the number of jobs in favor of broader, more generic job descriptions, freeing sailors to customize their jobs and to serve in more varied positions within a career track. For example, a sailor with a job of submarine electronics specialist might now be deemed a more broadly defined "electronics technician" who could work on an aircraft carrier, an installation ashore, or a submarine, as he chooses. The training consolidation associated with the move alone is expected to save the navy $200 million.[13] After Acxiom, a data-mining company, similarly broadened and reduced the number of its job descriptions, it experienced much greater employee productivity and launched an era of phenomenal growth for the company. After the change, three-quarters of Acxiom employees said they had the opportunity to do what they do best every day.[14]

A few organizations broaden the scope of a job to such an extent that they no longer have job titles locking them into specific tasks at all. This is the case at W. L. Gore (maker of the famous GORE-TEX® clothing, among other products), where employees determine their own roles and tasks on each project, working within the loose limits of general functional or broad work areas only—crunching numbers, for example, or running machinery.[15] Employees are expected to commit to projects that match their skills and interests, but they are still hired to fill certain set expectations and meet business needs—what Gore calls the *core commitment*. Beyond that, jobs may be customized. People are encouraged to move around in a wide variety of job functions or projects; a person in sales, for example, could pick up some assignments in a different but related discipline, such as marketing. W. L. Gore thus welcomes overlaps in different work areas and has no defined career paths. Leaders (who naturally evolve, rather than being centrally appointed) help employees decide when they are ready to tackle a new work area and help them develop missing skills when starting new projects.[16] Though such an approach may feel organic and laissez-faire, there is in fact a lot of organizational support required to make it successful—such as recruiting the kinds of people who thrive in such an environment, and finding supporting managers to take an active role in developing others.

Hire the Whole Person, Not Just Their Job-Related Skills or Experience

People have a lot to offer their companies beyond the specific skills, knowledge, or experience that shows up on a résumé. An employee may not know French, for example, but she may enjoy a broader ability and passion for quickly learning languages; another may not have experience as a sales rep, but he may have an unusually persuasive manner and love to work with people. By broadening the criteria you look at when hiring individuals for a job to encompass abilities, potential, attitude, values, and related nonprofessional experiences, you have a better chance of achieving a good fit between company needs and the range of abilities that a person has to offer. Specialty contractor TDIndustries' Jessie McCain calls this "the ability to look at the whole person, not just the professional self that might mask the other parts he left behind in the car."[17]

Microsoft, for example, places a premium on hiring bright and creative individuals above hiring for specific skills and experience. Bill Gates once quipped that Goldman Sachs was the competitor that worried him most, since to remain competitive, Microsoft must win the IQ war.[18] Microsoft recruiters have, in the past, been known to ask questions like "How would you design a cell phone for a five-year-old?" Competitor Google likewise asks questions such as "If you were a flower, what kind would you be?" in an effort to understand broader values and attitudes.[19] Google has also been known to use a billboard puzzle, "first 10-digit prime found in consecutive digits of e.com," to attract and filter candidates based on broader numerical capabilities.[20] The company even gives applicants an elaborate survey that includes a far-ranging set of questions about attitudes, behaviors, personality, and biographical data to determine how well they'll fit Google's culture.[21] Marriott likewise uses a quantitative, predictive model that combines a job skills assessment with an evaluation of candidates' mind-sets and values. "We can teach people the job," explains COO Bill Shaw, "but you can't teach people to be friendly, for example, if they aren't that way already."[22]

Hiring on broader attributes can be done when hiring internally as well. Companies like Men's Wearhouse and Microsoft encourage managers to hire people from other areas of the company even though they might not yet have all the skills and knowledge to perform the job. Lisa Brummel, head of HR at Microsoft, for example, had no prior formal experience in HR at all—she was a former product manager with an interest in HR issues and a strong track record of managing projects and people well. At Men's Wearhouse, employees are often accepted for jobs where they have only a 60 percent skill fit, and sometimes even less. Charlie Bresler, former president and current executive vice president of human development and marketing at Men's Wearhouse, offers this example: "I saw a natural talent in a salesperson in one of our stores and we hired her as an assistant buyer—even though she didn't have most of the formal qualifications." Such practices keep employees happy and challenged with jobs that fit their broader abilities, values, and interests—and help organizations that adopt them to remain at the top of their industries.

Broadly Define Pay and Benefits

Perhaps the most common application of broad and simple rules is in pay and benefits. Broadband compensation schemes, which collapse an organization's salary hierarchy into fewer, wider bands, for example, has been a widely recognized HR practice since around 1990 and is now used by many companies, such as Men's Wearhouse and Nike. Broader financial parameters allow a manager more freedom to customize pay based on an employee's unique situation. We spoke to one manager who was able to hire people in a start-up division and quickly escalate their salaries as their responsibilities grew under a broadband pay scheme; another manager was able to reward a high-performing employee with a significant salary increase—and kept her from leaving the company altogether. Salary bands can even be designed to overlap, so that the top end of pay for a lower-level role overlaps the bottom end for the role above it.

Some companies place no upper limit on employees' salaries at all. At The Container Store, salaries are broadly defined in terms of employees' contributions to revenues.[23] At W. L. Gore, pay is defined broadly by outcomes or strategic contribution rather than with limits on specific money amounts. In fact, Gore employees are paid based on a poll of fellow colleagues within their team and function who rank each other in terms of their contribution to the group. Pay raises are calculated in proportion to the individual's effort and contribution, and on the basis of the quantity, quality, and financial outcomes of their work. Using general guidelines based on external salary data, the company pays employees at the top of the list more than those at the bottom.[24] The company is careful to take the whole context of a situation into account when making such pay decisions, however; explains HR associate Jackie Brinton, "People can be involved with projects that weren't successful, but still can be ranked high from a contribution standpoint. When you're an entrepreneurial organization, you're going to be taking some risks . . . We're valuing people who take smart risks."[25]

Companies can apply broad and simple rules to other areas in this domain as well. Instead of narrowly defining an employee's number of vacation days and sick days, many organizations now lump them together and more broadly define them as *paid time off*, allowing employees to customize how they use their time off. Accenture has applied a broad and simple approach to its travel policies by instituting a program it calls "flexible trips"; instead of a narrow policy that pays for an employee to fly home from a business trip (e.g., from Madrid to London), the company now enables an employee to fly to any destination (e.g., from Madrid to Rome), as long as the cost is equal to the average cost of a return ticket home. We've even heard of rules regarding who can receive the benefits on an employee's policy being more broadly and simply defined. For example, Time Warner, recognizing that many employees now care for people outside their immediate nuclear families, has broadened its employee assistance program to include not just dependents but anyone who relies on the employee.[26]

Cascade Your Performance Goals

Another broad and simple rule that has become quite popular in organizations is to broadly define a person's performance goal based on broader divisional or corporate-level goals, thereby tying individual objectives to group, division, and corporate objectives in a cascading hierarchy. Variations of this system—like hoshin planning, management by objective, or cascading performance goals—broadly define *what* an individual is to accomplish, but not *how* they must accomplish it by dictating a detailed road map to the desired result (think *The Amazing Race*).[27] As long as the employee stays within the prescribed limits of the broader business goal, she and her manager can customize her own performance targets, leaving her free to draw on her unique strengths and interests when it comes to how she accomplishes the job and ensuring that the assessment criteria on performance appraisals are relevant and customized to her work.

Men's Wearhouse, for example, establishes sales targets for its stores, but doesn't dictate how employees should reach them. Some individuals may be "wardrobe consultants" who excel at individual selling, for instance, while other consultants may prefer to sell in teams. "Individuals in stores hit their goals in different ways, and that is not only tolerated but encouraged," says Charlie Bresler. "It's no different than training for tennis—someone with a great forehand often doesn't develop a great backhand. So the trainer works with the player to set goals for continually improving the forehand so the person plays the best game of tennis he can."

Note that while most broad corporate goals are related to company objectives like profits, revenues, and customer satisfaction, some divisions at PepsiCo have cascaded down to every employee what might be considered a softer, albeit critical, corporate people priority—*balance*. PepsiCo's One Simple Thing program makes sure that every employee sets an individualized goal related to the corporate goal of ensuring that employees have work-life balance. The goal must be documented as an objective for the year. One employee may commit to working from home on Fridays, and another, to leave work by 5 p.m.—it all depends on what works best for individuals and their managers.

Explains Beverly Tarulli, vice president of organization and management development at PepsiCo, "We knew a one-size-fits-all program (e.g., child care) could never meet the needs of all employees, since each employee has unique challenges with respect to achieving an appropriate balance. And we didn't want to create another complicated 'program' that would require paperwork, policies, or approvals. We creatively solved the problem by introducing a broad and simple rule with respect to balance instead."[28] The program has been so successful that employee survey results with respect to how effectively they feel supported by the company in their efforts to balance work with personal life are 11 percentage points higher in the division that piloted the initiative (the corporate division) than results for PepsiCo's other divisions.

Technology vendors are now making software much more flexible to accommodate broad and simple rules through cascading of goals. Software made by Saba, for example, allows organizations to specify and automatically populate the broader standard goals for different roles to allow for consistency and comparisons between individuals. It then allows workers to set customized goals and development opportunities based on their broader standard assignments, and helps them assign weights to indicate the importance of each.[29] Technology can make goals transparent and easily visualized in relationship to one another throughout the organization and produce real-time dashboards to help employees track progress toward specific goals. With the aid of technology, alerts can even be sent to people with lower-level goals that they must update them to stay within the limits of the new boundary.

Our research confirms that organizations in which managers and employees jointly establish customized performance criteria perform much better than those that do not.[30] But with just 20 percent of executives saying that more than three-quarters of their employees understand the company's strategy, it seems that few companies have succeeded at helping their people understand the broader context within which they can set relevant goals.[31] Doing so can have a big payoff; Hewlett-Packard's founder David Hewlett once remarked, "No operating policy has contributed more to Hewlett-Packard's success than the policy of management by objective."[32]

Let the Manager Allocate Rewards

Other than an employee himself, no one understands his performance potential and best ways to motivate him better than his manager. That's why some organizations give a defined budget to managers to allocate rewards among employees as they see fit: Avis Budget Group, for example, allows department managers to control their rewards budgets within preset limits, with the explicit goal of keeping the best talent—even if that means a manager rewards one employee with a big chunk of that money.[33]

When the parameters are broadly defined, managers can get quite creative in how they reward their people. Explains Lina Echeverría, Corning's vice president of science and technology and director of exploratory markets and technologies, "I once supervised an employee who has a difficult time in winter with depression. For two years in a row I gave her extra vacation time during the winter to go to a sunny place as a reward for great work. More than anything else, I think this created a sense of loyalty, engagement, and motivation for her at work."[34]

Define Competencies by Values or Outcomes

A common best practice in many companies today is to define competencies, or a detailed checklist of all the knowledge, skills, and behaviors associated with top performance in a job. A broad and simple rules approach radically redefines such competencies—from detailed lists legislating exactly what an individual is to know and do, step by step, to broad and simple rules that free workers from complying with a single, narrow standard and instead allow them to customize their work based on their unique talents and interests.

One method is to redefine competencies in terms of broader values. Coventry Building Society, for example, moved from rigid, organization-wide, skill-based competencies to flexible, customizable, value-based competencies. The previous framework, in which any job could be described in terms of a list of ten competencies and four levels, was deemed simultaneously too rigid and too generic. Coventry employees felt that the company's competencies list didn't reflect the skills they actually used for their jobs. The new approach is broader and more adaptable, and allows managers and employees to customize the system contextually, in a relevant way, to a large variety of jobs and to workers' unique attributes. According to head of HR Julian Atkins, "If people live and understand values, then behavior and skills take care of themselves. Out of the core value of reliability, for example, might come specific skills, knowledge, and behavior that help you operate more reliably with a customer, but that will vary based on your role and how you as a person can best accomplish reliability."[35] So while one person might achieve reliability by acquiring skills in a particular computer technology, another might do this by learning the general skill of organizing. That way, the value of "reliability" comes first, over a specific manifestation of that value. Adds Atkins, "Just because you have skills in organizing doesn't mean that you will be more reliable. You have to take into account the context and the details of unique jobs and people; that's where the rubber hits the road in terms of performance and how well these systems translate into effective tools."

Best Buy chooses to focus its competencies on broader outcomes. (The company depends on widely embraced companywide values; they just aren't directly embedded in its competency descriptions.) An outcome, for example, might be achieving a certain level of local growth in a store, or having a target level of customer satisfaction. This broad and simple rule is important to Brad Anderson (CEO of Best Buy from 2002 until 2009), and is partly why he has dedicated his career to the company. When he started selling stereo systems at Sound of Music, a store that later became Best Buy, he was so bad at traditional selling strategies that he almost quit. But because he was allowed to accomplish results in his own way, he got the attention of the store's founder, Dick Schulze, who promoted him to store manager and ultimately to CEO. For example, to make a sale, Anderson once offered a customer something previously unheard-of: to deliver a set of speakers 80 miles away, install them, and make sure they were working, before getting the sale.[36] Without a broad and simple rules approach to competencies, Best Buy might have lost one of its most successful leaders today; since Anderson took over as CEO in 2002, Best Buy stock has skyrocketed, it has gained significant market share from competitors, and it was named *Forbes'* "company of the year" in 2004.[37]

When Should You Use Broad and Simple Rules?

Broad and simple rules help organizations focus on what they really want, rather than on the narrow rules they can only hope will get them there. Employees we interviewed generally favor broad and simple rules, since they provide both structure and guidance, as well as discretion and freedom. Many organizations in our study, such as Best Buy and Men's Wearhouse, report that they believe adopting this approach has boosted employee retention, engagement, and performance.

To be sure, for employees or their organizations, and often for both, this approach to customization has certain advantages over our other approaches. One of the strongest advantages of having broad and simple rules is the high degree of customization that results, compared with more HR-driven approaches. For example, with segmentation and modular choice, HR decides on the details. With broad and simple rules, workers and/or their managers make these decisions within wide limits, resulting in a wider range of customization and increased fit between a worker and a particular people practice.

In particular, organizations in fast-moving, turbulent business environments should consider the broad and simple rules approach, since it more easily accommodates change. When using broadly defined salary bands and more generalized job descriptions and competencies, you don't have to continually reclassify a job based on changing business conditions, for example. W. L. Gore has credited this approach to helping it cope with change; one Gore employee remarked, "Our workforce is like an amoeba, a single-cell organism that continuously adapts and changes shapes in response to an altering environment."[38] Likewise, a broad and simple rules approach can help an organization more flexibly respond to changing customer needs. By being given the latitude to customize her job at Best Buy, for example, Moira Hardek was able to respond to one Best Buy customer need: to have more women in the Geek Squad.

Broad and simple rules are also often chosen by organizations because employees perceive them as fair and egalitarian, since a single set of consistent, transparent, and easily understandable rules are applied to everyone. Having the same set of rules for all can also help unite an organization. Explains Men's Wearhouse's Charlie Bresler, "They strike a healthy balance between egalitarianism and unity on the one hand and individualism and embracing difference on the other."

But employees may not always be comfortable with how broad and simple rules are implemented, and they may at first challenge the rules' fairness. When two people are paid differently for the same jobs while under the same band of compensation, based on different decisions by different supervisors, or when one worker puts in fewer hours than another even though they get the same results, employees might complain. Crystal clear results metrics or other clearly defined boundaries are thus crucial to implementing rules appropriately and ensuring fairness (refer back to "'Structured' Freedom," at the beginning of this chapter).

Because broad and simple rules rely on a single set of simple, organizationally consistent guidelines, they may often be easier for HR and other people management executives to manage and may require less HR resources and infrastructure than segmentation and modular choice would (which require executives to define, implement, and manage multiple detailed options in menu-based form or for multiple segments of their employee population). Often, the same set of boundaries can even be threaded through multiple talent management domains, making talent management extremely simple and understandable. A pillar of P&G's broad and simple rules approach, for example, are P&G's nine success drivers—broadly defined capabilities and values like the ability to embrace change, innovate, and build diverse, collaborative relationships, that are required for all employees to be successful at P&G. These broader capabilities are threaded through the hiring, performance appraisal, and competency management processes. With broad and simple rules, executives must only predefine and clearly communicate the general rule, paying careful attention to the type of boundary they use and how broadly they define it.

This is a harder task than it sounds, however, and that brings us to some of the disadvantages to consider when deciding whether a broad and simple rules approach is right for your company. (See "Broad and Simple Rules: Weighing the Pros and Cons.") Our experience is that most people have a great deal of difficulty generalizing and abstracting enough to identify the ultimate objective they want to serve; most people prefer to think in terms of tangible, narrow, concrete rules instead. Explains Tom Hennigan, chief operating officer of Victorinox Swiss Army, Inc., "I experimented with a new style of management [what we call broad and simple rules] by telling everyone the main goal and letting them figure out how to get to it by the shortest route possible. It worked wonders for some—it really unleashed their performance. But for others it was a disaster; they want to be told exactly what to do. So I think this only works for

Broad and Simple Rules: Weighing the Pros and Cons

What it is: Rules with clear boundaries that are simple, broad, and flexible enough that they can be interpreted and applied in a variety of specific ways to accommodate individual needs and circumstances.

Advantages	Disadvantages
• Offers a greater degree of customization and fit between individual and practice than segmentation or modular choice approaches	• Offers less control than more HR-driven customization approaches
• Allows employees or their managers more power and autonomy than HR-driven approaches, but still with some structure and guidance	• Rules may be inappropriately interpreted or applied by individuals
• May require fewer HR administrative resources than more HR-driven approaches	• May require substantial change management and support to help individuals best interpret a broad and simple rule
• A single set of consistent guidelines and rules is easier to administer and manage than more HR-driven approaches	• Lower transparency: executives may not always be able to see exactly how talent is being managed (though they can use technology to remedy this)
• Does not require a sophisticated analytics capability or HR infrastructure to implement (although having these often improves the approach's effectiveness)	• Requires more employee involvement and responsibility; some employees may find it difficult to interpret a rule using their own judgment
• Easily accommodates change and highly turbulent business environments where people practices must change frequently	• May not suit organizations in high-growth mode that hire lots of new employees or organizations with very high turnover
• Unites the organization with a single set of consistent rules for all	• May not be suitable for employees who need lots of direction and things spelled out for them in detail
• Generally perceived to be fair, since all employees and/or managers are provided with exactly the same rules	• Employees may question the fairness of how a broad and simple rule is interpreted, especially when different managers interpret a rule in different ways among their subordinates
• Helps an organization flexibly respond to changing customer needs	• May not be suitable for organizations seeking to make work as predictable and structured as possible through centrally defining competencies, career paths, learning, and more
	• May be difficult to use in highly regulated environments where people practices must be centrally defined

a certain type of employee, and for others, they need substantial organizational help and support to learn how to do this effectively."[39]

Indeed, such an approach is often not easy for employees; they must learn to be comfortable with broadly defined boundaries and learn how to use their own judgment in interpreting them so that they are aligned with both their own needs and the organization's. Employees uncomfortable with this will often ask their HR representatives for specific rules to help guide them in making their decisions, and often HR will comply—resulting in broad and simple rules that gradually become narrower over time. Extensive change management is thus almost always necessary to implement this approach and ensure that rules remain broad and simple. At Best Buy, for example, converting to its Results-Only Work Environment was roughly a six-month process involving leadership, managerial, and team training, extensive role-playing, and simulation of the environment for six weeks. In general, HR must be actively involved to ensure that rules are appropriately and fairly customized, and that a customization practice results in the desired benefits. But costly activities associated with tracking and ensuring that employees are conforming to narrow standards—like time-keeping policies, rules, and procedures—often evaporate.

Although broad and simple rules can often simplify the management and administrative burden for HR, they can complicate it for those who must do the customization: the employees and their managers. Implementing broad and simple rules puts line managers and employees close to the action; they become highly active participants in people development and management. But with greater authority to decide how to tailor people practices comes increased responsibility and sometimes a heavier workload: when managers and employees must agree on customized goals, for example, it can become more time-consuming. Not all managers may want more responsibility and decision-making power. In a workaholic era when we can work twenty-four hours a day seven days a week, some people may prefer having someone telling them to go home at 6 p.m., for instance.

With broad and simple rules, organizations must also give up some degree of control, compared with more HR-driven customization approaches. Since organizations cannot control exactly how a broad and simple rule will be interpreted by a worker, and thus cannot define the exact details of each people practice for individuals, companies have considerably less control with this approach. Organizations needing more control because they work in highly regulated environments, or because they have a large number of new employees to onboard and acculturate, may therefore not want to rely on a broad and simple rules approach.

As with any approach that involves subjective decision making, a reduction of policing, and a dispersion of power, there is always the risk that broad and simple rules will be inappropriately interpreted or applied. For example, one survey revealed that as a result of so many companies implementing broad-based pay schemes, about 60 percent of employees said they had a salary mismatch—either they were underpaid or overpaid for their work.[40] Setting clear boundaries for the rule and supporting employees with sound decision logic guidelines, changing management initiatives, and coaching from HR business partners to help employees hone their own judgment will help address this concern. Without this support, many organizations find that what was originally intended as a broad and simple rule quickly becomes lots of narrow rules once again as an organization attempts to regain control. Our experience has been that in organizations with strong support systems, however, rarely are rules inappropriately interpreted.

One consequence of broad and simple rules, even when appropriately applied, is a great deal of variation and lack of consistency in the detailed implementation. In some cases, it may be hard to track exactly how an employee has interpreted a rule; Best Buy doesn't centrally track the number of hours each headquarters' exempt employee puts into his job, for example, or how each interprets his job (but neither does it feel the need to). This approach therefore doesn't lend itself as well to an analytics or data-driven approach to management as segmentation and modular choice do. But although analytics are not always necessary to use this approach, they can significantly enhance and improve its effectiveness. Best Buy does use extensive analytics and data analysis to track the effectiveness and results of its broad and simple rules practices, like its Results-Only Work Environment. What's more, organizations can often collect data on exactly how an individual is interpreting a broad and simple rule, to check for appropriateness and gain some transparency about exactly how its people practices are being implemented. For example, technology can track exactly how managers allocate rewards and exactly what employees are paid within a broadband pay scheme.

Workforce practices that treat people like replaceable components by ensuring that they conform to narrow rules and standards may seem as if they reduce an organization's risk level. And many organizations—because of their unique business models or cultures—may still choose to make work as predictable and structured as possible by centrally defining the details of competencies, performance goals, jobs, skills, and experience they seek when hiring a new employee, and more. Yet in an age when component-based production of tangible goods has rapidly given way to a knowledge-based economy where learning, decision making, and people's performance can make or break organizations, it may be time to unleash the power of the individual over the power of a rigid system. With a broad and simple rules approach, companies can do so without sacrificing the need for control, manageability, and the ability to harness the unique strengths of every employee in helping their organizations reach their full potential. (See "Recommendations for Customizing Through Broad and Simple Rules.")

In the next chapter, we'll look at our fourth and final approach to customizing your workforce: employee-defined personalization, which can be used alone or else in combination with one or all of the other workforce of one approaches we describe in this book.

Recommendations for Customizing Through Broad and Simple Rules

- Embrace rather than resist the fact that employees will now have more power to define their own people practices (within organizationally sanctioned boundaries you establish); as long as they remain within the limits of the broad and simple rules, refrain from telling them what to do, and learn to trust (and support) your employees' good judgment.

- Do track how employees are interpreting broad and simple rules, when possible and appropriate, to gain corporate-level visibility into how your talent management practices are being interpreted, to ensure that employees are not going outside of the rules' boundaries, and to share successful practices among employees regarding different interpretations that work for them—but *don't* track them to pass judgment or police how each employee chooses to interpret a rule.

- Support employees in honing their own good judgment in interpreting a broad and simple rule with sound decision logic guidelines, data and information, education, examples of other ways employees have interpreted a broad and simple rule, coaching from HR business partners, and other means.

- Avoid the specificity creep that often occurs when HR managers inadvertently create more narrow rules to address specific situations or when employees request more specific guidelines; continually check to make sure rules remain broad and simple.

- Build a culture and change program that supports employees in helping them get comfortable with using their own judgment to interpret a broad and simple rule. Employees who thrive in such environments will learn of your culture and be attracted to your organization; employees who still insist on narrow rules (despite your best efforts to support these people) will eventually self-select out.

- Use the opportunity of driving culture change through broad and simple rules to closely engage with the CEO—the role most often responsible for culture change—and elevate HR to a truly strategic, C-suite-level agenda item.

- Choose the boundaries of your broad and simple rules carefully based on what works for you and your employees; not all companies will want to use the same scope and type of boundaries for each people practice domain.

- Make the boundaries of a broad and simple rule crystal clear, and spend significant time and effort communicating these; doing so will ensure that the company maintains control, increase the likelihood that employees will feel their organization is treating them fairly, and help employees feel more comfortable with increased responsibility.

- To help employees learn how to effectively use broad and simple rules and gain some momentum and quick wins, consider broadening rules in areas where you can afford less control, broadening them at first for certain segments of the workforce accustomed to more autonomy before extending them to other segments, or starting with more narrow boundaries that gradually get broader over time.

5

Foster Employee-Defined Personalization

If companies can figure out a way to acknowledge and respect the uniqueness of each person—and then figure out how to do that in a reliable and scalable way—we will make an enormous impact on individual employees' success and on our companies' collective success. The paradox is that we need to establish a norm that is itself abnormal.

—Joe Kalkman, leader of HR centers of excellence, Best Buy[1]

J UST AS CONSUMERS TODAY can define and create their own content using the video-sharing site YouTube or the volunteer-written reference site Wikipedia, employees today can define and create their own people practices using an employee-defined personalization approach to customization. Think of Linux, the operating system developed by thousands of its users; or the fact that Google, Yahoo!, and other search engines now produce results based on mining billions of links of Web site owners like you and me. Or think of online markets like eBay, where consumers can trade directly with one another with no intermediary and where peer-contributed feedback on one another helps buyers and sellers make more informed decisions. Indeed, much of the impetus for employee-defined personalization has come from what has variously been dubbed mass collaboration, peer production, Web 2.0, or crowdsourcing, where consumer content is created by end users instead of by centrally appointed experts or organizations.

These innovations in the consumer sphere are gradually making their way into the organizational sphere. In fact, of all the four workforce of one customization approaches, employee-defined personalization has probably yielded the most innovation in the last few years. Technology has made huge strides in enabling employees to define people practices organically—making these practices more accurate, relevant, customized, and, ultimately, more valuable than those defined by a central body that's a step removed from employees' immediate, fast-changing needs.

More than any of our other workforce of one approaches, employee-defined personalization places people management directly in the hands of the people whom the practices are meant to serve. With employee-defined personalization, employees define specifics like how and when to get feedback, or how and when to learn from one another. Customization takes place without any centrally defined limits, choices, or practices designed to serve particular employee segments.

Savvy organizations, however, don't take a laissez-faire approach to letting this type of personalization happen; they deliberately decide which practices to foster. They also monitor and support these with processes, technology, and incentives to help them bloom and grow. Employee-defined personalization, therefore, is not some kind of ad hoc scheme, nor is it completely uncontrollable or unscalable.

As the next generation of workers increasingly expects to be able to define their own content alone or in collaboration with one another, we expect employee-defined personalization to continue to be a growing area of innovation in talent management. In this chapter we'll profile many of the new developments under way when it comes to this approach, and conclude with a brief discussion of the benefits of employee-defined personalization versus the challenges and issues it raises.

Employee-Defined Personalization in Practice

When employees begin defining their own people practices, almost every conceivable domain becomes fair game. In this section we'll look at such customization in the following areas: schedules and timing of work; learning; recruiting; hiring; development through mentoring and coaching; performance feedback; jobs; careers; and even compensation. Some of these practices are completely new. And although other employee-defined personalization practices have been around for a long time—such as coaching and mentoring or informal performance feedback—we'll see how companies are applying new technologies and creative new methods in these areas to radically transform the way they are performed to achieve even greater organizational benefits and organization-wide consistency. (See "Possible Ways to Introduce Employee-Defined Personalization.")

Time Trading

Can you imagine enabling your company's employees to dynamically trade blocks of time with fellow workers, creating customized schedules that reflect when they want and need to work? Many companies are now pursuing such a strategy. Certain employees at Accenture, for example, are now able to donate and/or receive donations of accrued paid time off for critical personal situations and family emergencies by taking advantage of a recently adopted policy that allows employees to donate their paid-time-off days to one another. When one Accenture employee lost her husband to cancer, for example, friends and colleagues all donated so much paid time off to her that she was able to take three full months off to grieve her loss and resolve his final affairs.

Other companies, like Tesco and JetBlue Airways, have created shift-trading markets where employees broker changes in their schedule with others without ever having to consult their manager.[2] After instituting an online community board where call center employees can trade shifts, Jet-Blue experienced a 30 percent increase in agent productivity and a 38 percent improvement in customer-service levels.[3]

Time trading is only beginning to take off; we expect innovations in this area to continue to rapidly advance. Already, in the newest, most sophisticated versions of shift-swapping schemes, employees are only allowed to trade with others who have similar performance ratings, productivity rates, skill sets, and experience in certain tasks and functions—thereby enabling businesses to continue creating the best schedules based on specific business needs and forecasts while still meeting employee needs for customization.

Peer-to-Peer Learning and Innovation

Instead of defining a one-size-fits-all linear learning curriculum from on high, organizations encouraging employee-defined personalization allow employees themselves to create learning content and dynamically pull and push it to one another on an as-needed, highly customized, and collaborative basis. Instead of turning to a book or a course if there's a tech problem, for example, an employee may look up friends on a corporate version of Facebook, locate a friend of a friend who has knowledge or experience in that area, and instant message him with a question—using a few key pieces of information, such as the fact that they went to the same college, to establish common ground. Or he may post it on an online threaded discussion group of like-minded people in a community of practice, post it on a blog or wiki, or initiate a chat group. Alternatively, he may search for a video online that captured a person working to solve that particular technology problem, or troll for knowledge that has been codified and

Possible Ways to Introduce Employee-Defined Personalization

This chapter explores many domains in which companies can foster employee-defined personalization—but not all. For example, companies like design firm IDEO enable their employees to create their own workplace design by decorating their offices as they want—accessories brought in by IDEO employees have included a classic model motorcycle, colorful umbrellas, a sailboat sail, an airplane wing, and bicycles (for commuting) to hang from the ceiling.[4] Here's a checklist of possible ways you can foster employee-defined personalization in your organization:

- Time
  - Shift trading
  - Paid-time-off donations
- Learning and innovation
  - Blogs, wikis, YouTube, and other peer-to-peer learning technologies
  - Information and knowledge markets
  - Social networks facilitated by technology, physical space, or other means
  - Experience-based learning through observation, structured assignments, or simulations and games
- Recruiting
  - Employee referrals, social networks, and relationship recruiting
- Hiring
  - Trying a candidate out through trials, simulations, or competitions

posted by another employee and ranked in terms of usefulness by others in an online knowledge marketplace.

Such peer-to-peer learning ends up being much more customized and therefore more relevant because content created by employees themselves is generally closer to the frontline needs of the workforce. As one employee put it, it allows employees to "get behind PR to the real story." What's more, such learning is more timely; friends and colleagues can provide immediate alerts to new and important information in the field before a class or book is ever rolled out on the topic. Finally, with peer-to-peer

- Mentoring and coaching
  - Encouraging employees to mentor or coach one another
  - Enabling "self-coaching" through technology that delivers personalized feedback
- Performance feedback and recognition
  - Informal, confidential feedback or praise from manager to subordinate or from peer to peer
- Jobs and careers
  - Job descriptions or career paths that are defined bottom-up through technology that tracks employee communications or transfer and promotion histories
  - Letting employees define their own job titles
  - Open talent market listing both jobs and people
  - Encouraging managers to discuss specific employees with one another to suggest where their employees might move next in customized career paths
  - Horizontal networks that facilitate job movement and customized career paths
  - Job rotations
  - Job swapping
- Compensation
  - Job auctions
- Workplace design
  - Letting workers bring in their own furniture or accessories

learning, people can easily condense or expand information to the level of detail the peer may need, and they can screen out irrelevant or redundant information.

Many companies are now working hard to facilitate this kind of informal, peer-to-peer learning. Microsoft gives many of its employees the tools to create, capture, and share their own learning content with one another using blogs, wikis, online bulletin boards, SharePoint, and YouTube- and Facebook-like applications that can be delivered on a device of choice, such as a smartphone. Other applications, like Second Life, a three-dimensional online virtual world created by users that mimics real life, are also used to help people make the informal connections with one another that facilitate impromptu learning. These are the kinds of connections that are difficult to achieve with teleconferences or other technologies traditionally used by virtual teams. To facilitate finding others who know what you need to know, Microsoft has also developed technology that mines sources of content (e.g., e-mail, content repositories, tags on Web pages, blogs, instant messages) to dynamically and organically uncover and highlight individuals with particular areas of interest or expertise. The technology analyzes who is communicating with whom and how many degrees of separation lie between you and that person, thereby facilitating an introduction.

At Best Buy, peer-to-peer learning is a business imperative, since its tech-savvy employees have demanded it—even creating such opportunities on their own with no corporate permission. Although Best Buy maintains corporate peer-to-peer learning sites, like its online Watercooler, employees also extensively use Blue Shirt Nation, an internal social network created by two marketing employees, which is not maintained by corporate communications and resides outside the company's firewall (although only employees can access it). Explains Best Buy's Joe Kalkman, "It's happening with our employees, whether we like it or whether we join it or not. If we can be proactive by helping facilitate, sponsor, and reward such peer-to-peer learning, and most important, listen and respectfully respond to it when appropriate instead of ignoring or squashing it, we'll make Best Buy a much better place to work." For example, the company sponsored a contest to create the best video promoting retirement savings. Stores with the most improved enrollment received a cash prize, and the creators of the winning video received a free trip. Thirty-two entries were submitted, and the humorous winning video was then posted on Blue Shirt Nation—with the result of an enormous uptick in retirement plan participation rates (rates improved from 18 percent participation to 47 percent).

At a few companies, peer-to-peer learning even occurs across organizational boundaries, such as at Wieden+Kennedy, the advertising company known for its award-winning campaigns like Nike's "Just Do It." Wieden+Kennedy encourages learning and innovation with a highly unusual "open source" approach that facilitates employee interaction with artistic peers across organizational boundaries. For example, the firm brings in a diverse array of design professionals and artists—poets, writers, dancers, and performance artists—to share its space in Portland, Oregon. It invited a contemporary art institute and gallery, a lectures-series sponsor, and carefully chosen design-oriented retail stores to occupy the first floor of the building. And it's not uncommon for institute artists-in-residence like the dancers of the Bebe Miller Company to have preperformance practice in Wieden+Kennedy's space during work hours or for the advertising firm's staff to frequent the institute's gallery space. Most important, artists like comic book writer Art Spiegelman and radio host Ira Glass are often invited to share their work with employees (and even the general public sometimes) in what Dan Wieden, president and creative director of the firm, refers to as the agency's "heart and soul"—its four hundred–seat, four-story amphitheater.

By conceiving of its building as a semipublic space—at least in aspiration, if not in ownership—Wieden+Kennedy represents a bold new idea in both workplace design and in the use of open, cross-organizational peer-to-peer networks to spur the kind of creativity and learning the organization needs to thrive. Explains Wieden, "I wanted our space to be a gathering place not just for us, but for the city. By cutting a hole in the middle of the building (the amphitheater), we let the rest of the world come in and share what they are doing with us. Now, not only are we in the city, but the city is in us."[5]

Experience-Based Learning and Simulations

Winston Churchill once said, "I am always ready to learn, although I do not always like being taught."[6] To be sure, studies by the U.S. Department of Labor and others have shown that many people share that sentiment: an estimated 70–80 percent of workplace learning occurs informally.[7] Yet many companies still spend most of their learning budget on formally structured courses or make facilitated experience-based learning, like carefully chosen assignments or "after-action reviews," the sole prerogative of leadership candidates.[8]

Fortunately, things are starting to change, with some companies enabling employees to custom define their own learning by helping them learn from their own experience. Many companies, for example, have now adopted a "10-20-70" learning model: 10 percent of learning comes from formal training, 20 percent from coaching and mentoring, and 70 percent from on-the-job developmental activities. "Formal training is great for a quick foundation, but the most important learning is on the job because it is customized to what you need to know," says one product marketing engineer at a high-tech company we interviewed. At another company in our study, for example, managers draw on a list of HR-recommended development activities; a manager may ask an employee to write a business case or to provide a presentation on some relevant matter—and then the manager gives the employee feedback. On a different level, managers at Avis Budget Group guide new hires through a list of structured experiences—including cleaning a car and operating a filling station island safely—before the new hires receive any formal classroom training.[9]

Informal learning can also occur through direct observation. In work environments such as Men's Wearhouse, where sales associates and their managers are completely visible to one another, learning through direct observation is fairly easy. Men's Wearhouse has successfully relied almost entirely on an apprenticeship model to train associates in sales; managers will demonstrate effective sales approaches and then coach employees in a highly personalized way. At Toyota, learning through observation is embedded into the very fabric of its culture: observation of everything from mechanical processes to business practices is encouraged, proposed changes are then structured as experiments from which employees can learn, and managers are encouraged only to coach, not fix, to encourage continuous learning by all.[10]

In office-based organizations, however, it can be harder to have employees learn through observation. Tom Hennigan, chief operating officer of Victorinox Swiss Army, Inc., gets around this limitation by pairing people up and assigning them joint responsibility for a project or role; that way, they are forced to learn from one another. At the technology research firm Forrester, novice researchers not only pair up with experienced researchers; everyone also works in a completely open, transparent physical work environment, with no office or cubicle walls to hinder the shadowing and learning process.[11]

Today, experience can just as easily (and sometimes more cheaply and safely) occur in cyberspace, through virtual worlds or simulated games. The U.S. Department of Homeland Security, for example, offers experience-based learning through private online virtual worlds where the goal is to kill and avoid being killed. Avatars include soldiers, medical personnel, police officers, firefighters, first responders, and corporate staffers.[12] Similarly, Ford built a virtual factory to facilitate learning for its production leaders. Explains Hossein Nivi, one of the factory's principal designers, "Typical teaching techniques create disengaged students who are eager to escape an instructor reciting canned material. In the virtual factory, students learn by discovering the material through simulation and they develop the mental muscles needed to apply their discoveries."[13]

Relationship Recruiting

Instead of having HR drive recruiting, why not leverage the power of every employee—and their respective networks of friends and colleagues—to find and attract the best job candidates? Instead of placing one-way, impersonal ads oriented toward the masses, why not let current or potential employees help define the recruiting experience—and make it an information-rich, two-way, highly collaborative and personal process that ensures a custom fit between the individual and the position or organization? After years of companies turning recruiting over to professionals, we are increasingly seeing a trend toward using employees to help define the recruiting experience.

The Container Store, for example, rarely, if ever, runs classified employment ads or uses recruiters. Instead, the company relies on each employee—from sales staff to executives—to champion the company. Anyone employees run across in the course of their everyday lives is considered fair game—especially customers who are already engaged with the brand. A Saturday kids' soccer game, for example, is considered as good a place to discuss a job at The Container Store (with other parents hanging around the sidelines) as is the Dallas headquarters offices. Employees are trained to recognize the sort of people the company is looking for and to make recruiting part of their jobs. Monetary awards are given to those who make successful referrals. Sales staff even carry employment handouts in their aprons so that they can give them to customers they think might make good employees, or slip them into their bags with their purchases. Over 40 percent of new hires come from employee referrals.

The Container Store's success as a leader in its industry and its amazingly low turnover rates of 10–12 percent, in an industry where 100 percent turnover is common, attest to the power of this practice.[14] But there's a whole list of very good business reasons that lie behind relationship recruiting. For example, it:

- Provides a personalized introduction and experience. It engages candidates in a meaningful, two-way dialogue with an actual person rather than losing them with a mass-produced e-mail from an unknown source. Not only will the candidate be compelled to answer because he knows the person or is a friend of a friend, but the referring employee can easily tailor the messaging (and even work with the hiring manager to tailor the offer) based on his knowledge of the candidate's unique desires and strengths.

- Improves the "fit" between the individual and the job or organization. Employees can get to know potential candidates in a far richer and more personalized way than HR ever could by looking at a résumé—thereby increasing the likelihood of a custom fit. On the other side of the equation, candidates can get to know the company in a far richer way through communicating with actual employees than they could by reading carefully vetted information from HR.

- Allows more wide-ranging reach in attracting top talent. Skilled, able staff is likely to associate with, and bring in, a like-minded cohort—an individual presented by a respected colleague has far more potential, due to prescreening, than a cold lead coming from an external database. Referrals also offer candidates multiple routes into the company rather than a single official, HR-driven route, and can easily reach people in faraway lands, for example, who would be otherwise hard to know. Finally, referrals easily penetrate top performers in other companies who aren't actively looking for jobs.

- Enables candidates to hit the ground running. If hired, the candidate will already have a built-in network to help her get started. Research shows that referrals are initially more productive and are able to make an impact more quickly.[15]

- Often results in longer tenure for the referring employee. Employees will likely think twice about leaving a company when they have referred their friends there. It's called the *checkout line phenomenon*, where you'll be less likely to move if you know there is someone (especially a friend) waiting in line behind you.

Indeed, relationship recruiting has always been used by top managers and successful companies. Google managers, for example, keep in touch with professors at major universities to make sure they know who the best students are—doing so can help a company forge ongoing, personalized relationships with them.[16] Corning's vice president of science and technology Lina Echeverría likewise identifies potential candidates in schools and in positions both inside and outside the company. She keeps up with their work and gets to know them as individuals through informal contact, even when she has no specific hiring need. She explains, "Hiring is one of the most important things, but you cannot do it through the central HR channels only."[17] Other research confirms this; in one survey of executives, 88 percent said the best job candidates came through referrals, yet fewer than one in five candidates was referred.[18]

The advent of digitized social networks may change all that. Technologies can help employees stay in touch with passive candidates and follow them more easily online. And businesses can now post jobs and ask employees to share them with their friends and networks on social network sites like Facebook or LinkedIn—thereby using technology to scale and more easily manage the informal networks that The Container Store has been successfully relying on for years. Ernst & Young, for example, uses Facebook to let prospective employees talk freely with real ones and answer any questions they have about the company.[19] And through the online recruiting and social-networking site Jobster, hiring managers in any company can track and categorize job candidate leads generated through networks by using criteria such as skill level and referral source; members gain status by contributing the most valuable information and by making the most successful referrals. Since top workers are often happily employed, Jobster's "dream job" feature lets users pen their ideal job descriptions that would lure them away. Use of such sites has dramatically increased relationship-based recruiting; after using Jobster, for example, some divisions at payroll and tax-filing processor Automatic Data Processing (ADP) went from one-half to two-thirds of its new employees coming from referrals.[20]

Other information-rich sources about employment from employees themselves may include blogs, such as the ones Best Buy and Microsoft have, where employees post their experiences at the company and engage in dialogues with interested candidates. Some companies are getting creative by offering everything from employee-made rap videos to documentaries about office life to give potential hires a realistic view of the organization. Companies may also use employee-generated online webinars, case studies, or simulations.

Still, people need to remember that all of this incredibly transparent information cuts both ways. In an age where a rich amount of information about a company—everything from salaries to culture—is available to individuals through virtual sources, a rich amount of information about potential hires is likewise now very transparent to a hiring company. By networking with people who know candidates or browsing Web sites that contain information about an individual, employers can now collect far richer information than ever before regarding strengths, interests, personality, and values, to help make more informed hiring decisions as well. Not surprisingly, "reputation management" companies like ZoomInfo have popped up to help people verify and correct the accuracy of information about themselves that is floating out there in cyberspace.

Try-Before-You-Buy Hiring

An even more radical employee-defined personalization recruiting practice is to actually try out candidates in real or simulated work conditions and perhaps even with their actual potential colleagues and boss. That way, companies can ensure that each party is happy with the match before making a mutual commitment. Internships are a well-known try-before-you-buy approach, but they tend to be restricted to people fresh out of school.

A few leading companies, however, are experimenting with requiring hourly employees to work on a temporary basis first so that hiring managers can get to know them in a real work setting. We heard of one high-tech company, for example, in which each applicant for a permanent job in one of the company's major plants must work for ten months as a temporary contractor; the employee reports to the company manager even though the temp agency is his or her legal employer. During the trial, company management is able to become closely acquainted with the temporary hire's strengths, opportunities, personality, and career goals, and the information thus gleaned is then used to make informed decisions about the temporary hire's employment track, job fit, and more. At Whole Foods, employees must undergo a four-week trial so that both candidates and potential colleagues can first get to know one another personally. Team members then get to decide whether the person stays or goes through a vote; a two-thirds yes majority is required for the potential employee to stay.[21]

Although jobs for white-collar knowledge workers have largely been exempt from such trials and tests, increasingly, companies are asking potential senior-level, white-collar employees to participate in simulated work experiences, mock assignments, or role-playing exercises so the company can better understand them as individuals.[22] Forrester Research, for example, asks potential analysts to produce a research report and then to address the comments a line manager makes in response to the report. Not only does this help the hiring manager understand the candidate's ability to write and analyze, but it also tells him a great deal about how the candidate relates to people and takes criticism and feedback.[23] Likewise, a plant that makes a joint-venture engine for DaimlerChrysler, Mitsubishi Motors, and Hyundai asked about fifty salaried professionals, including operations managers and plant engineers, to participate in work simulations that included talking to employees about poor performance and sifting through memos and phone calls to determine the day's priorities. Plant executives believe that the practice has led to reduced turnover and higher-quality employees.[24]

Another innovative way of extending a try-before-you-buy approach to a larger number of people in a highly meritocratic—albeit one-sided—way is to sponsor a competition for a piece of work, thereby enabling anyone who wants to try out the work itself to do so. Google, for example, drew more than fourteen thousand applicants for Google India Code Jam, a coding contest designed to find the most brilliant coder in South and Southeast Asia; all finalists were offered jobs.[25]

Mentoring and Coaching

Employees who coach and mentor one another can dramatically raise the performance bar as well as significantly improve motivation and retention.[26]

At Sun Microsystems, for example, people who are mentored receive four times the promotions and double the number of top performance ratings as the average Sun employee.[27] Unlike most business processes, which tend to reduce information to abstractions, mentoring and coaching encourages employees to engage with one another in highly customized ways—by lending one another relevant, personal advice, for example, or by delivering highly personalized feedback to unlock a person's abilities in a particular area. Although these practices have been historically reserved only for potential leadership candidates, many companies are extending them to every employee.

At Microsoft, for example, many people at all levels of the organization have mentors. HR facilitates mentoring by giving employees a Web-based matching tool that provides them with potential mentors (using blinded profiles) every five to six months. The practice is structured and encouraged centrally, but is optional and driven and performed by employees themselves. Studies confirm that such an employee-driven—rather than HR-driven—approach works; one study found that 90 percent of formal mentoring programs fail, but those that succeed support employees in taking their own initiative to create mentoring opportunities.[28]

Coaching is also no longer reserved just for executives; companies like Best Buy and Men's Wearhouse support their employees across a variety of levels in coaching one another for high performance. Men's Wearhouse's Charlie Bresler calls it "developing a culture of personal best," where manager coaches listen, observe, and customize a coaching session to improve the individual's performance relative to her own best record, rather than relative to the record of others.[29]

But if your concept of a coach is an expert who designs a plan to help you reach your goal and gives you regular feedback to inspire and guide you, think again—in the future, that "coach" may be your mobile phone or any other electronic device. Data has long been collected and mined on athletes for such coaching, so why not for employees? For example, at elite Italian soccer club AC Milan, more than sixty thousand data points overall on every player, from physical to psychological makeup, have been recorded. Players are continuously tested against the data to "coach" for any bad habits they may develop.[30] One can easily imagine data like this being automatically collected on employees through technology-enabled monitoring of people's bodies and environments, with smart algorithms comparing their observed behaviors with their goals or best practice, and coaching provided in real time for when they diverge.

Companies are increasingly experimenting with self-coaching applications. Partners HealthCare (owner and operator of several hospitals in Massachusetts), for example, developed an electronic coaching system for its health care workers—every time a doctor orders a test, a drug, or a referral electronically, the system checks it out and reports back as to whether it is consistent with medical best practice.[31] And Accenture has developed a prototype cell phone that monitors conversations and "whispers" in a person's ear or indicates by graphics when he is interrupting or talking too much. The application can coach you by reporting on how loudly you are talking, whether meetings ran longer than planned, tardiness or missed appointments, and even your use of a sarcastic tone or frequency of negative versus positive remarks.

One Accenture manager, for example, used Accenture's technology to meet a goal of spending a few hours each week with his staff. A Wi-Fi network for indoor locations kept a record of how much time he spent with each staff member and prompted him when he needed to spend more. The technology also can help people track patterns, correlations, and trends—down to the tiniest nuances, such as whether an employee tends to interrupt others' conversations more during morning or afternoon. Using the same principles of biofeedback, which has helped millions of people reduce blood pressure or heart rates through feeding back information in real time, employees can learn to "self-coach"—thereby placing development and learning directly in the hands of every individual in a highly customized way to help them reach peak performance.

Frequent, Informal Performance Feedback and Recognition

As work becomes more team and project based, standard sets of job requirements, evaluated through HR-directed performance reviews, are falling by the wayside. And as the youngest generation of workers—famous for expecting constant, customized feedback—enters the workplace, companies that support traditional once- or twice-yearly feedback systems will likely fall out of favor.

Many companies, therefore, are already supplementing traditional performance reviews with ongoing discussions with employees about goals and progress. Not only can problems be caught earlier on and feedback be made more specific and relevant with this method, but also employees are more likely to learn from timely feedback received in the context of their regular workday. And after all, isn't relevance the whole point of feedback? As one R&D manager told us, "What goes on the form and what I tell you as an employee is different. Formal performance appraisals then become an exercise in compliance. The true value is in the honest, informal feedback that is given at the point it is needed rather than in a standardized yearly review."

Microsoft supports and encourages this kind of feedback with an information system that lets managers and employees record informal feedback confidentially. The information isn't reported to human resources and doesn't follow the employee from job to job. Instead, employees and managers use the information for their own reference—making it far more likely that managers will say what they really think.

And at Hewlett-Packard and Intel, people are encouraged to seek feedback proactively from those they work with and then to synthesize and reflect on this feedback on their own (without it going through HR).[32] Other companies help this process by encouraging employees to maintain year-round feedback logs that enable employees, peers, and managers to post comments that capture feedback that traditionally gets lost in e-mails or quickly forgotten hallway conversations. As the practice is driven and maintained by employees, performance management becomes completely customized as well as integrated into the fabric of everyday business.

Employee-Defined Jobs and Careers

Instead of defining the details of a career path or a job—or even a broad and simple rule for one—organizations can let employees define them in a highly fluid, organic, and bottom-up approach. Imagine, for example, that competencies and job descriptions were defined not a priori from on high, but rather in a bottom-up fashion by employees themselves. New technologies now enable this; by scanning résumés, e-mail, and other electronic communications, systems can organically tell the organization what skills, experience, and knowledge each employee has.[33] Organizations could thereby understand what each employee actually *does* in their job, rather than what they supposedly do based on their HR-defined job title or their location on a predefined organizational chart. Technology can analyze patterns and trends to create common, dynamic, and ever-evolving bottom-up job profiles, and it can alert executives when an unusual exception pops up, enabling them to maintain a degree of control. It's only one step further to imagine that employees could then create their own more relevant and customized job titles to reflect the work they actually do; at Yahoo!, this is already a common practice. Fun and more relevant employee-defined (but still company approved) Yahoo! titles include "Ambassador Plenipotentiary to Madison Avenue" (instead of vice president of trade marketing), "Yahoo Evangelist," and "Party Princess."[34]

Companies can take a similar approach to organically create employee-defined career paths. Software company Taleo, for example, is currently developing software that will enable companies to analyze employee transfer and promotion histories captured in the system to determine common (or uncommon) career paths taken by these employees. Other employees will then be able to view the actual career paths others have taken who have similar skills, preferences, and roles, and then network with these people to learn more through social networking technology. Technology like Taleo's will help provide some degree of structure and guidance for employees in complex organizations with no clear career paths.

Of course, such technology won't work unless an organization already enables people to create customized career paths by promoting fluid, internal mobility between positions and functions. (To see how customized career journeys have helped some highly successful people reach their full potential, see "Famous Customized Career Journeys.") This can be nurtured by ensuring that job changes aren't blocked with excessive rules about when and where an employee can move—such as restricting movement based on a manager's approval or minimum time in the position or to high performers only. A culture where managers don't hoard their best performers helps, as does one where managers work with employees to create individualized plans to reach their ideal jobs. Companies can also encourage internal mobility with promote-from-within policies and a transparent global talent marketplace that allows employees anywhere in the organization to sell their skills for short- and long-term engagements to others who have a need. At Hewlett-Packard, for example, anyone with a new project idea can propose it to a board of senior managers; approved projects are then posted on an internal talent market network, and anyone interested in the project is encouraged to volunteer for the team.[35]

Not only can positions or projects be posted in an open talent market, but the other half of the equation—the individuals who might match them—are increasingly being posted in an open-market format as well. Talent databases enable employees to list their skills, abilities, goals, development plans, interests, up-to-the-minute availability, and any other pertinent information, and then allow computer systems or hiring managers to continuously cull them for highly customized matches between talent and task. Deloitte Touche Tohmatsu's Career Value Map, for example, helps individuals get clear on their interests and ambitions, records them, and then matches them with relevant openings in new or ongoing client projects.[36] At some companies, project or job opportunities are even ranked by how closely they match an individual's "dream job." On the other side of the equation, a hiring manager could search for someone—say, with digital experience in Argentina—and that person would show up as a pushpin in the center of a bull's eye, with surrounding pushpins representing other people who closely fit the bill. At IBM, dedicated managers or "networkers" monitor databases and serve as matchmakers between jobs and people. The result? These databases have cut the average time to assemble a team by 20 percent and have saved the company $500 million overall.[37]

Famous Customized Career Journeys

Some of the most successful people today took highly unusual and customized career journeys. The kinds of customized career practices described in this chapter can allow your company to support a budding potential that otherwise might not be unleashed, by allowing employees to try on different roles before arriving at one (or two, or three) for which they are best suited. Here are some examples:

- Tom Freston, former Viacom CEO. Freston worked in advertising and then in Afghanistan and India at a company manufacturing and exporting women's clothing. After making a lot of money and losing it all, he bought a copy of *What Color Is Your Parachute?* and landed a marketing job at MTV in 1980 before it went on the air, rising to become its CEO in 1987.[38] After leaving Viacom in 2006, he has been busy helping Oprah start a new TV network and Bono to save the world.[39]

- Mitchell Kapor, founder of Lotus Development. The Yale graduate had been a disc jockey and transcendental meditation teacher before founding the software company.[40]

- Geraldine Laybourne, founder of Oxygen Media and former Nickelodeon president. After trying her hand at architecture, Laybourne went back to school to get an education degree and taught school before founding a nonprofit group that researched kids' media opinions and created curricula. With her animator husband, she then created a few shows for cable TV station Nickelodeon, which she later joined as a program manager, eventually becoming its president.[41]

- Carly Fiorina, former CEO of Hewlett-Packard. After dropping out of law school, she worked as a receptionist, teacher, and AT&T sales rep, which eventually led her to become president of a division at AT&T's spin-off company Lucent Technologies and, eventually, CEO of Hewlett-Packard.[42]

- David Ogilvy, advertising legend. Ogilvy was a chef, a door-to-door salesman, a farmer, and a member of the British intelligence services before starting a career in advertising at age thirty-eight.[43]

Being able to systematically document individual interests, strengths, and skills—often done in a trading card–like format with photos of the individual and their relationships among others mapped in a Facebook-style internal social network—has also enabled the high-touch, largely word-of-mouth customized practice of succession planning to be extended across an organization to every employee. Documented employee profiles and the ability to easily call mutual colleagues for references enable managers to intimately know a large number of employees. When a position opens up at a company, for example, hiring managers can look at employee profiles and contact possible candidates' colleagues who have worked with them before to discuss their strengths and where they might best move in their next job. At Nike, many divisions facilitate this with biyearly meetings where managers discuss employees' personal strengths, weaknesses, and interests as well as what new opportunities in other parts of the organization might best suit their employees (a process know as HRP).

Nike has another highly unique way of facilitating cross-organizational job movement and highly customized career paths: sports activities and events. During any given lunch period on the company campus, rugby, basketball, soccer, and just about any sports activity you can imagine take place. According to many Nike employees we interviewed, these sports activities have fostered such a strong horizontal network (crossing every organizational boundary but geography) that they are a highly effective conduit by which people (and ideas) traverse the organization.

For organizations that prefer more structure while they help employees choose different positions to customize their career paths, job rotations may fit the bill. New engineers at Trilogy Software, for example, work on various projects before choosing the position that will let them make the best contribution to their company.[44] Perhaps the most radical work rotation practice is done by Brazilian conglomerate Semco, where some new recruits are allowed to roam through the company for a year, searching for the place that best suits their individual strengths and interests.[45] With these approaches, decisions regarding employees' career paths aren't made a priori; instead, they are informed by the insights employees gain as they observe or rotate through positions. Research suggests that job rotations increase employee satisfaction, motivation, involvement, commitment, and personal development.[46]

Job swapping provides another innovative way to help employees build customized career paths. At Semco, within any given year, up to 25 percent of managers have changed jobs with one another—and it's completely up to the employees to decide when and where to do this. It doesn't matter what they have on their résumés or the kind of education they have; anyone can swap with anyone. A sales manager once swapped jobs with a comptroller, for example. Once someone identifies a fellow employee who would like to swap jobs with them, they start planning a year or two in advance so that they can teach each other the job duties. Once swapped, the fellow employee is only a phone call away to lend assistance.[47]

Employee-Defined Compensation

You might have trouble imagining how employees could set their own salaries with no organizationally imposed limits. But that's exactly what people do in the U.S. Navy. The navy has an online job-auction site where employees can bid on hard-to-fill jobs; whoever offers the lowest salary and meets the qualifications gets the job. Sometimes, this results in much higher salaries than the organization normally would define, and sometimes much lower ones. But the navy has found that the system works well to correct a long-standing problem in the service—what sailors call *slamming*—where personnel specialists send sailors wherever needed with organizationally defined pay, regardless of whether they want to go.

The result? This democratic, market-based system means that the navy's top performers who seek extra education and a broader range of assignments will have the opportunity to be paid more and advance more quickly on their own timetable, based on their own custom-designed career paths—not the navy's. (Of course, the reverse is also true: sailors with mediocre work records or limited training will find themselves without chances for promotion.) The navy is considering eventually posting all jobs on its online job-auction site to allow all personnel to define their own pay and career paths using a market-based system.[48]

When Should You Use Employee-Defined Personalization?

As with our other three approaches to customizing people practices, employee-defined personalization presents certain advantages—for employees or for organizations, and often for both. Of all the approaches, it best realizes the workforce of one ideal of customization. Employee-defined personalization allows people to fully tailor the company's workforce practices to their individual needs, generally free from organizationally imposed constraints. And the greater the degree of fit between people and practice, the more likely performance will improve. Employee-defined personalization may be particularly suitable for organizations with a lot of young people, since they'll likely already be comfortable using Facebook-like applications, wikis, blogs, online trading applications, simulations, and other employee-defined practices.

But the approach also allows organizations to be highly responsive to changes in the business environment and to customer needs, and it requires fewer HR resources than segmentation and modular choice typically do. The details of a practice are handed off to employees to fluidly define, based on their own unique needs, preferences, and the specific business environment at the time—rather than requiring HR to define and administer these details (like the content and timing of a particular learning session). HR may thus spend fewer resources on HR administration. And HR then becomes free to be more of a facilitator, enabler, and encourager of the general practice only, and, that way, becomes more of a cultural change agent (either directly or as a coach to senior leaders) or a function that encourages certain general work environments. Think of the work environment established by Nike, for example, when it encouraged networking through sports activities, the work environment established by Forrester Research when it set up work space to encourage learning through observation, or the one that Microsoft established when it encouraged frequent informal feedback among employees.

Employee-defined personalization practices do, however, still require substantial change management, education, or supporting technology. Technology, in fact, is one of the key drivers behind this approach; a tech-savvy organization will be able to most fully realize the approach's benefits. That said, many technologies that support these practices (like systems to collect and track informal feedback, or blogs or social network sites) can stand alone and don't require expensive integration into a core HR system. This is another reason why the approach may require fewer HR administrative resources than more HR-driven approaches. It also means that employee-defined personalization often doesn't require as sophisticated an HR infrastructure.

The fact that employee-defined personalization does usually require significant organizational change and support for employees is one disadvantage of the employee-defined personalization approach. But there are others as well that you should consider when deciding whether the approach is right for your company. (See "Employee-Defined Personalization: Weighing the Pros and Cons.")

For example, employees may sometimes shun the added responsibility of defining and customizing their own people practices. Some may not want to coach, mentor, recruit, give informal feedback, or share their gems of wisdom and knowledge with one another. Or they may feel overwhelmed and even paralyzed when given full responsibility to define their own learning or career paths. Like broad and simple rules, employee-defined personalization practices require employees to demonstrate a high level of commitment, activity, and good judgment.

Because employee-defined personalization practices place so much responsibility in the hands of employees, this customization approach runs a greater risk that people practices may be misused or applied inappropriately or inaccurately. When using such democratic media as wikis and blogs, how do you know the information that employees contribute is

Employee-Defined Personalization: Weighing the Pros and Cons

W *hat it is:* People practices that are fully defined and customized by employees themselves alone or in collaboration with one another.

Advantages	Disadvantages
• Provides the greatest degree of customization and fit between individual and practice—thereby offering the greatest chance of performance improvement	• Offers less control and consistency than other customization approaches do
• Allows employees or their managers substantial power and autonomy to define their own people practices	• Greater chance that people practices may be misused or applied in an inappropriate or inaccurate fashion compared with other approaches
• May require fewer HR administrative resources than more HR-driven approaches would	• May require substantial change management and support to help individuals define their own best people practices
• Does not require a sophisticated analytics capability or HR infrastructure to implement (although having these will often improve the approach's effectiveness)	• Potential for lower transparency: executives may not always be able to see exactly how talent is being managed (though advances in technology are working to change this)
• Talent management truly becomes a line responsibility and is fully integrated into the very fabric of everyday business	• Requires more employee involvement and responsibility
• Many (but not all) of the technology applications to support this approach can stand alone and need not be integrated into core HR systems	• Most employee-defined personalization practices require substantial technological support (e.g., time-trading applications, blogs, computer-defined simulated learning, systems to record informal feedback)
• Easily accommodates change and highly turbulent business environments where people practices must shift frequently	• May not be suitable for employees who need lots of direction and things spelled out for them in detail
• Generally perceived to be fair, since all employees and/or managers are provided with the same opportunity to define their own people practices	• Fairness may be questioned sometimes, since different individuals may have very different experiences
• Helps an organization flexibly respond to changing customer needs	• May not be suitable for organizations seeking to make work as predictable and structured as possible through centrally defining competencies, career paths, learning, and more
• Suits younger people, since they are already used to defining their own practices in the consumer sphere through applications like Facebook, wikis, blogs, and simulations	• May be difficult to use in highly regulated environments where people practices must be centrally defined
• Very democratic approach	• May only supplement rather than replace other customization approaches
• Takes the best of what occurs informally in organizations and provides structure and consistency to it	• May raise privacy concerns

accurate, relevant, and fact-based? How do you prevent embarrassing, offensive, or irrelevant content from appearing in an experience-based simulated game? How do you ensure that employees make objective decisions and don't just hire their friends who look and act exactly alike when using relationship or referral-based recruiting? How do you ensure that coaches and mentors are providing timely, helpful, and constructive feedback? When using public forums like Facebook or blogs, how do you ensure that content posted is appropriate and that important intellectual property won't be leaked to competitors? In such a fluid world of open-information sharing, information may be more transparent than ever, but it is also harder to document in a standardized way to enable the kind of transparency and control most companies traditionally favor (for example, knowing that five thousand employees completed twenty hours of training on a particular topic).

Sound like chaos? Think again; great strides have been made that enable organizations to more easily understand and capture exactly how learning, coaching, feedback, or career paths are unfolding in an organization when they've been handed off to individual employees to define. For example, SAP is considering creating software that looks at employees' Microsoft Outlook calendar to see whether any appointments, such as a meeting with a mentor or a coach, constitute a "learning event"; and Plateau Systems tracks any employee searches on external blogs or podcasts to show executives how and what employees are learning.[49] Likewise, new technology can now track results and major themes within electronically recorded coaching sessions. These and other technologies allow organizations to catch exceptions and step in when necessary, as well as to understand common patterns and track usage. A host of other control mechanisms and safeguards can be instituted too, such as filters, approvals, monitoring, and self-policing, as we will discuss later in the book.

To be sure, employee-defined personalization also raises privacy and fairness issues that companies will need to carefully address. When your e-mail is scanned to determine what you do, or when your personal information on the Web is looked at by an organization you hope to work for, many people feel their privacy is being invaded. Fairness may also be challenged. For example, Sharol Tarbini, head of Nike's corporate human resource planning (HRP) process, acknowledges that the fluid job movement made possible in part through informal personal networks established through sports activities "creates a kind of clubiness and a case of glass walls; many people without these networks can't move as easily and feel it is unfair."[50] For example, less able employees or those not interested in sports may feel excluded. She summarizes, "It's a trade-off and a balance—you might get more customization with it being so informal, but you get a greater degree of fairness and consistency with a more structured approach." Although an employee-defined personalization approach gives everyone equal opportunity to define their own people practices, the wide variety of actual experiences people have as a result (such as more frequent or different coaching venues) may make some feel that employee-defined personalization practices are unfair.

In the end, employee-defined personalization practices are only as good as the employees who use them. The jury is still out as to whether organizations can effectively adopt this approach en masse, with no other formal practices to accompany them; the result of other democratic media placed in the hands of individuals, for example, often has included a deluge of conversations about sensational topics such as sex, politics, and violence. Because of this, and for legal and other reasons already presented, many companies strongly believe that employee-defined personalization must supplement, rather than replace, more formal people practices.

For example, most simulated work experiences only supplement traditional interviews, reference checks, and résumé reviews. Nike's HRP process helps match people with work that suits them, but the company could never accomplish job placement using the HRP process alone.[51] Legally, each job must be posted and offered to everyone according to the Equal Opportunity Act. Likewise, most companies that encourage informal feedback still have formal performance appraisals to help with salary administration and to protect themselves against potential lawsuits for unfair dismissal from a job. When leaders have tried to rely on employee-defined personalization practices alone—as Men's Wearhouse's Charlie Bresler did when he tried to eliminate formal performance appraisals in favor of encouraging informal feedback only—they are usually unsuccessful in convincing their more cautious colleagues to follow their lead.

With careful controls, and with carefully vetted and educated employees, however, many organizations are finding ways to successfully adopt this most democratic and revolutionary approach. Employee-defined personalization is at the heart of the informal organization—the bottom-up, organic, unofficial people practices that can be so vital to a company's effectiveness. The approach takes the best of what happens in small companies—knowing one another personally, giving each other informal feedback, coaching, and recognition, or the ability to wear lots of different hats in the same company, for example—and makes it scalable and manageable for larger companies, with the help of technology and consistent management practices. With employee-defined personalization, people practices are no longer solely the domain of HR; they become fully embedded into the very fabric of everyday business. That's why we consider this approach the ultimate form of customization, representing what we believe to be an important and exciting trend of the future. (See "Recommendations for Customizing Through Employee-Defined Personalization.")

The next four chapters of this book (part III) offer some practical tools for building and managing your own workforce of one organization. Let's begin in the following chapter with a guide for determining how to create your own unique path toward a workforce of one—by choosing which customization approach or approaches to emphasize based on your organization's specific business conditions and needs.

Recommendations for Customizing Through Employee-Defined Personalization

- Use technology to accelerate the way you adopt employee-defined personalization practices, improve their value, and gain a window into how your people are defining their own workplace practices. But don't get stuck thinking that without leading-edge technology, you can't pursue employee-defined personalization at all. Many practices, such as coaching, mentoring, experience-based learning, and informal feedback, can still be done without enabling technology, the old-fashioned way.

- Draw on your people's personal lives to mine for the best new and innovative employee-defined personalization practices; online social networks, video games that allow people to customize their own virtual experiences, online auctions and markets, and more all first originated in the consumer sphere (and only later were adopted at work).

- Use younger people in your organization who are most familiar with and accustomed to employee-defined practices, such as online social networks or virtual experience-based learning, as focal points. They can be the first adopters and show others how to effectively use the practices. At the same time, rely on the wisdom and experienced judgment of older employees to help younger ones effectively use such practices to achieve business goals.

- Support employees to appropriately and best define their own people practices through lots of examples, coaching, information, education, change management methods, and other means.

- Don't squash grassroots employee-defined personalization initiatives; support and facilitate them instead.

- Monitor and support employees in defining their own people practices with processes, technology, and incentives; don't fall into the trap of thinking that HR has little to do (or can exert little control) when employees define the people practices themselves.

- Consider supplementing, rather than completely replacing, other, more formal practices with employee-defined personalization practices, at least at first for legal and control reasons, until employees gain comfort with the approach.

- Learn how to facilitate and support rather than directly dictate and control; this will require a very different HR mind-set than traditionally expected in the past.

- Address privacy and fairness issues directly and carefully. Adhere to privacy laws when collecting employee data and do so respectfully and confidentially, and help employees understand that they all have equal opportunity to define their people practices in ways best suited to them.

Part Three

Cultivating a Workforce of One Organization

To thine own self be true.

—William Shakespeare

Designing Your Own Workforce of One

We do what works for us; the same customization approach proba-bly won't work for everyone.[1]

—Charlie Bresler, former president of Men's Wearhouse and current executive vice president of human development and marketing

I F YOU'VE READ this far, you likely have already determined that managing your workforce as a workforce of one could do great things for your organization. You may be looking at many of the customized practices described in the last three chapters as options to help you cope with pressing challenges—everything from an increasingly diverse work-force to your younger workers' expectations for individualized experi-ences, or simply the drive to produce superior business results through improved employee performance. The last four chapters should have given you a solid understanding of the approaches an organization can use to get the best from its people and, ultimately, help propel a company to bet-ter business results.

But the question remains: how do you go about practically cultivating a customized employment experience in your own organization? What does a workforce of one look like in practice? The next three chapters will address these questions, first by presenting a guide to help you determine which approach or approaches your company might favor, and then by looking at how four leading workforce of one pioneers have achieved remarkable results by pursuing customization in the best way for them. The book con-cludes with two chapters that explore how to address the challenges that customization presents, such as fairness and control, and, finally, how orga- nizations can practically advance toward managing a workforce of one through creating a new HR mandate and skill set to support customization.

So, how do you know which of the four customization approaches will fit best with your own organization? Just as employees are different, with unique needs, values, and aspirations, so too are companies different; they vary in their unique strategies, histories, types of employees, values, and cul- tures. In this chapter, we'll help you think through your own company's business conditions and which approaches you might favor. Although most organizations use at least a few practices in each domain of segmentation, modular choice, broad and simple rules, and employee-defined personaliza- tion, they tend to *favor* one or more approaches over others, using them to a greater extent to meet their customization goals. Almost always, this choice is made based on the organization's unique business situation. At the end of this chapter, we'll look at how four workforce of one pioneers—Royal Bank of Scotland, Best Buy, Men's Wearhouse, and Procter & Gamble—have successfully managed their workforces using customized talent management practices in very different ways.

Which Customization Approaches Should Your Company Favor?

Although many factors might push an organization toward emphasizing one customization approach or approaches over others, often one element will emerge as more important than another (see figure 6-1 for a quick guide to when to favor each approach). Let's look at some things to con- sider, including your company's strategic philosophy; culture and values; types of employees; existing HR infrastructure, resources, and capabili- ties; type of regulatory or union environment; and amount of change in your organization.

Strategic Philosophy

Does your company have a particular competitive business strategy that makes it favor greater degrees of control over customization, or greater cus- tomization over control? Although all four customization approaches can generally support and align with any strategy, sometimes a company's par- ticular strategic *philosophy* suggests a preference for either greater degrees of control through more HR-driven customization approaches (segmentation and/or modular choice) or more customization through more employee- driven approaches (broad and simple rules and/or employee-defined personalization).

FIGURE 6-1

The four workforce of one customization approaches compared

	Workforce of one customization approaches	Examples	You may favor this approach when you:
HR-driven customization (*more control, less customization*)	Segment the workforce	HR creates a variety of practices customized for specific groups of individuals	Common group categories • Generation, value, geography, workforce Leading-edge group categories • Values, behavior, health, personality, strengths	• Need more control (e.g., due to regulated environment, business model, or types of employees) • Favor analytics and a data-driven HR approach • Can administratively support multiple variations • Don't face constant and fast change • Seek to create clear, shared meanings of difference
	Offer modular choices	HR creates a variety of options from which all individuals can choose	Common choices offered • Time (e.g., P/T vs. F/T), place (e.g., home vs. office) Leading-edge choices offered • Work activities, compensation, technology	• Have a strong preference for egalitarianism • Need more control (e.g., due to regulated environment, business model, or types of employees) • Favor analytics and a data-driven HR approach • Can administratively support multiple variations • Don't face constant and fast change
	Define broad and simple rules	HR creates a broad and simple rule with clear boundaries that can be interpreted in a variety of ways by each individual	Common broad and simple rules • Cascading performance goals, broad-band pay Leading-edge broad and simple rules • Specify work to be done rather than hours or location of work	• Prefer greater degrees of customization • Have employees who thrive with more discretion • Don't need as much control, and can provide change management and support for increased discretion • Face constant and fast change • Have limited HR resources you can spend
Employee-driven customization (*less control, more customization*)	Foster employee-defined personalization	HR supports individuals in defining their own personalized people practices	Common practices • Learning through blogs and wikis, informal feedback, coaching Leading-edge practices • Job auctions, job swapping, bottom-up career path profiling	• Prefer the greatest degree of customization • Have employees who thrive with more discretion • Don't need as much control, and can provide support to your people to handle more discretion • Face constant and fast change • Are tech savvy and comfortable using new technologies

Accenture's strategy, for example, has been built on a stable business of well-defined work that is as structured, methodical, and predictable as possible. To achieve this goal, the company is increasingly moving toward specialization as a competitive differentiator: centrally defining highly structured career paths that encourage people to specialize in a given industry and business area, competencies that detail the skills needed for a particular role, training practices that teach people how to perform activities predictably and reliably based on best practices, and hiring practices that match people to roles based on specialized skills to ensure that client projects are filled with only the most qualified candidates. Specialization also allows Accenture to fluidly interchange people on projects based on their specialized skills and level. Segmentation and modular choice approaches, therefore, work best since they allow the company to centrally define the details of their people practices. This, coupled with the fact that Accenture has a global workforce with many different workforce segments, has meant that Accenture's business model tends to favor segmentation and modular choice approaches (which tend to have higher degrees of control) over broad and simple rules and employee-defined personalization approaches (which tend to afford higher degrees of customization). Later in the chapter, we'll see a contrasting example of how Best Buy's strategic philosophy of providing highly customized experiences for customers has translated into a preference for more customization in its people practices over more control.

Culture and Values

Does your organization have a particular culture or strong set of values when it comes to fairness, control, or even the use of data to make decisions? Some companies, for example, may strive for an egalitarian culture where every person has exactly the same specific opportunities and options as everyone else. If that describes your company, the modular choice approach to customization may be best, since it clearly provides the exact set of detailed options to everyone. Since segmentation creates different practices for different groups of people with shared characteristics, some employees might view this approach as less egalitarian. Indeed, of all the approaches, segmentation may breed the greatest number of fairness issues. Yet it also provides the greatest opportunity to create shared meanings of difference; everyone can clearly see how various employee segments differ from one another and why they therefore enjoy differentiated people practices.

Broad and simple rules and employee-defined personalization approaches fall somewhere between segmentation and modular choice when it comes to egalitarianism and perceived fairness—everyone is given the same equal opportunity to interpret or define their own people practices, but because HR doesn't centrally define the details, they can vary wildly from one person to another. When two people put in a radically different number of hours at work to perform the same job under a broad and simple rules approach, for example, fairness may be questioned. The egalitarian value is so strong in some cultures and so deeply imprinted by the founders (as is the case at Men's Wearhouse) that it is sometimes the primary driving force behind the customization choice.

To be sure, often it's the founders' personal beliefs that determine the company's approach to customizing people practices, whether that means valuing control most or, alternatively, valuing employees' autonomy and discretion. We've found that many companies prefer segmentation or modular choice, for example, not for strategic reasons, but because of deep-seated assumptions about the need for control that date back to the companies' founders.

Many organizations prefer to centrally determine the details of each people practice for a given segment or for a particular set of choices, giving the company control and transparency when it comes to how people practices are being used. Even highly autocratic cultures can use segmentation. Other organizations deliberately create a culture where individual autonomy is highly valued; these cultures might find employee-driven customization approaches a better fit with their cultural norms and values. Although with more employee-driven approaches, companies often give up some degree of transparency regarding exactly how people practices get used, increasingly technology is helping bridge this gap, allowing organizations at least to understand how their people practices are used, even if they don't control the exact details of how they're implemented.

Finally, some companies, such as Harrah's and Royal Bank of Scotland, have highly data-driven cultures, which value hard facts and use these to make decisions.[2] Although data and analytics certainly play an important part in any of the four customization approaches (at the very least, companies should use analytics to track the results of an organization's customization efforts and to help the company constantly improve), segmentation and modular choice lend themselves most to a highly data-driven, analytics approach to talent management. The very essence of these approaches is to conduct substantial data analysis to determine the appropriate segments or options for employees.

On the other hand, companies can use both broad and simple rules and employee-defined personalization approaches without substantial data analysis, if necessary. For example, the broad and simple rules practice of cascading performance goals can be done without data analysis, as can the employee-defined personalization practices of informal feedback or coaching. In many cases for these approaches, however, data analysis can significantly improve the practice's effectiveness. For example, an organization can improve its coaching practices by collecting data on a person's performance and feed it back to him. Men's Wearhouse chooses customization approaches like broad and simple rules in part because the company doesn't have to employ a lot of data analysis for them to work. Others, like P&G or Royal Bank of Scotland, are so used to making data-based decisions, given the nature of their industries (consumer marketing and banking, respectively), that their existing cultures favor more data-based approaches.

Types of Employees

Any thoughtful workforce of one design will meet the needs of *both* employees and the business, creating a bridge between the two. So when deciding which customization approaches to favor, you should ask questions like these: Are my organization's people highly educated knowledge workers who thrive on autonomy, independence, and discretion (as they might at Google or Microsoft, for example)? Or are they primarily in roles that may require a bit more organizational direction? Are our employees adaptable to change and comfortable defining their own people practices or interpreting a broad and simple rule as they see fit? Or do they tend to seek more predictability and need things spelled out for them in detail through a more HR-driven approach? For a look at which customization approaches employees prefer across a broad spectrum of organizations in our study, see figure 6-2. Note that in our survey, workers largely preferred more employee-driven approaches over HR-driven ones; organizations may consider surveying their own employees to help them determine which approaches to favor based on their own employee preferences.

Although industry can play a role in the types of employees an organization typically has (e.g., more creative industries, like advertising, tend to employ people who thrive best on autonomy), industry isn't always the deciding factor. Even organizations in industries not known for having mostly high-end knowledge workers or creative types (for example, retailers such as Best Buy and manufacturers such as W. L. Gore) can still have employees who work best when granted more discretion under a broad and simple rules or employee-defined personalization approach. These companies tend to attract this type of worker—and employees who don't enjoy the autonomous environment tend to self-select out of the companies.

Another question to consider is whether your employees are here for the long run or for the short run, and whether your company has or will

FIGURE 6-2

Customization approaches preferred by employees

I would prefer my organization to customize our employee practices by using the following approaches (multiple-answer responses accepted):

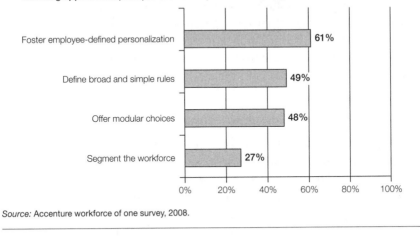

Source: Accenture workforce of one survey, 2008.

have lots of new employees, because of either rapid growth or high turnover. Customization approaches that afford more control—such as segmentation and modular choice—may be easier to use for managing a large number of employees who are new and/or who won't stay long. It often takes time, significant education, and support to help employees learn to appropriately interpret a broad and simple rule or define their own people practices appropriately.

Finally, an organization may also want to consider the average age of its employees. We have found that places with many younger employees often favor employee-defined personalization as at least one preferred customization approach. Younger employees are so accustomed to defining their own content in other areas of their lives that they often demand that their companies help them do so in their work lives too.

Interestingly, grouping your employees into relevant categories can provide a helpful tool for answering all of these questions about just who your employees are—even if you don't choose segmentation as a customization approach. (Segmentation not only groups employees into relevant categories but creates differentiated practices for each.) Doing so can help organizations get to know employees by determining their unique needs and preferences, even as these companies pursue other customization approaches. That's what we saw earlier in the case of Tesco, which defines workers by group type to help determine what kinds of modular choices it offers.

One advantage of looking at your employees in terms of groups is that it forces you to think through which approaches to use for which employees. At Best Buy, a company that favors broad and simple rules and employee-defined personalization, many of these customization practices are applied to only some groups of the workforce. So, for example, only corporate employees, not store employees, are able to set their own work hours using a broad and simple rules approach. Ultimately, companies that first determine whether the customization approach it chooses is appropriate for everyone—or just for certain workforce groups—will make thoughtful decisions about their particular workforce of one configuration.

Existing HR Infrastructure, Resources, and Capabilities

Take a look at the kind of infrastructure your company has in place: has it already gone through the process of standardizing and harmonizing its HR practices? Does the organization have a well-developed analytics capability, or can it afford to support one in the future? Although all customization approaches can benefit from a standard HR platform and advanced HR infrastructure, the segmentation and modular choice approaches depend on it most to track and administer variation in who receives which people practices across the organization. Likewise, these approaches depend on standardized employee data across the organization (often enabled by a standard HR platform) and analytics to effectively segment employees or determine the most relevant set of options.

Many of the more employee-driven practices don't depend nearly as much on a standard HR infrastructure or analytics capability. These include employee-defined personalization practices like coaching and informal feedback, or the broad and simple rules practice of broadly defining a job by outcome rather than with a list of standard tasks. Technology still plays a crucial role here—particularly for many of the employee-defined personalization practices supported by technology, like wikis, blogs, time-trading applications, or computer-aided simulated learning. But in many cases, the applications can stand alone and don't have to be integrated into core HR systems. As we said earlier in the chapter, however, employee-driven approaches can often be greatly enhanced by a common HR infrastructure and analytics: an organization can still have employee-defined career paths without them, for example, but having them allows it to more easily track and analyze promotion histories to determine common career paths in a bottom-up fashion.

What's more, depending on the workforce of one approaches being used, the division of labor between HR and employees will likely differ. More HR administration resources may be called on when favoring segmentation or modular choice approaches; these approaches require HR executives to define, implement, and administer not just one set of detailed talent practices for the organization but multiple ones in either menu-based form or for multiple employee segments. But fewer HR resources may be required when favoring broad and simple rules or employee-defined personalization approaches, since these don't require a company to track and administer multiple detailed variations. Rather, the burden—or privilege—of defining the specifics of a people practice shifts to employees. Managers will have to determine the proper salary in a broadband compensation scheme for their subordinates, for example, and employees at all levels may need to coach or provide informal feedback to one another. With more employee-driven approaches, more HR resources will be devoted to supporting employees in their efforts, and in providing a common set of management practices or tools to help employees best define their own people practices. If your organization decides to pursue these kinds of approaches, it will need strong change-management capabilities and will need to feel comfortable with significant organizational change (compared with more HR-driven approaches that tend to more closely resemble traditional talent management methods).

As Tina Decker, Best Buy's head of HR operations, explains, a company's focus on broad and simple rules and employee-defined personalization doesn't necessarily mean it spends less of its HR resource pie; it just spends it in different ways.[3] Sometimes it expends even more HR resources using the approaches—but executives feel that the benefit they receive pays them back many times over any extra costs incurred. "Sure, we don't spend as much time on defining specific rules and enforcing and policing them, but we do spend significant amounts of time on education, coaching, and helping create the general culture of responsibility that is needed to make this approach successful," Decker says. Best Buy also uses analytics extensively to gauge how much impact its practices have on results. For others, like Men's Wearhouse (as we'll soon see), the organization does indeed spend fewer resources in HR by pursuing a broad and simple rules approach. If your organization operates in a low-margin business, therefore, and can't afford to support things like a vast data warehouse and analytics capability, you'll want to weigh this factor when choosing a customization approach.

Type of Regulatory or Union Environment

Does your organization need to follow specific rules based on regulations set by a country, industry, or union? If so, customization may be more difficult to achieve for some particular people practice areas, but it doesn't necessarily mean you should toss aside customization altogether. The seg-mentation approach to customization in particular works well in heavily regulated environments, since an organization can still centrally define the specifics of a people practice for each employee, thus conforming to strin-gent labor requirements. A country or union that requires manual workers to work no more than thirty-five hours a week without being paid overtime, for example, could easily specify this detailed rule centrally for this particu-lar employee segment. More employee-driven customization approaches that afford less control, however, would rarely work in such an environment: an organization couldn't allow employees to work as many hours as they want as long as they complete the job (using broad and simple rules) or trade a longer six-hour shift on a Saturday for an eight-hour shift on a more coveted Monday that would put them over their thirty-five-hour limit (using employee-defined personalization). But the modular choice approach to customization, like segmentation, may sometimes work in regulated environ-ments: an organization, for example, may still be able to centrally define different benefit plans of equal value, workplace options, or rewards, and still meet labor requirements specified by a union, country, or industry.

Interestingly, since workforce of one is largely about meeting the needs and desires of employees themselves—the very essence of what unions are meant to represent—union regulations may, in fact, someday become much more flexible to accommodate a more customized talent manage-ment approach.

Amount of Change in Your Organization

Does your business need to nimbly adapt to fast-changing business condi-tions, thereby requiring it to constantly adjust jobs, competencies, learning, career paths, and more? Organizations selling a new product or trying to penetrate a new market, for example, will often need employees to rapidly learn new skills and information related to the product, competitors, and the tastes and trends of new customers. Instead of waiting months for the company to centrally define new learning courses on these topics, peer-to-peer learning through wikis, blogs, and other means can help employees adapt to changed conditions at lightning speed, and help the organization nimbly adjust as business conditions warrant. Likewise, if a job is cus-tomized through a broad and simple rules approach (say, a sales job is defined through the outcome of number of sales and satisfied customers), then a salesperson selling new products or penetrating new markets can immediately adjust his selling strategies accordingly—without waiting for corporate to update a detailed list of competencies or job skills, as it might have to when using more HR-driven approaches.

Yet remember that of the more HR-driven approaches, modular choice is usually more flexible than segmentation; generating new lists of choices whenever conditions change is often easier than recategorizing employees or dealing with segments that are no longer relevant. In addition, depending on the particular people practice area, employees can often easily change their choices at will. Even so, adding choices such as new places to work in a company's building, a new benefit option, or new centrally defined learning options may still take substantial time to do; the approach is thus not as flexible to change as more employee-driven approaches to customization.

One final point before we summarize some of the many variables you may want to consider when choosing a customization approach or approaches: should the number of different businesses and geographies your company has factor into the kind of approach you favor? HR executives often assume that an organization with many businesses and geographies requires using segmentation as one customization approach, enabling it to tailor practices for each business and geography. But we don't think segmentation need be the only approach used. You can achieve customization to meet such varying needs just as easily by offering modular choices, defining broad and simple rules, or fostering employee-defined personalization. Of course, we've often seen organizations with an operating philosophy of granting substantial division-level autonomy prefer the segmentation approach, which provides differentiated people practices for each division. But there should be good business reasons for the differentiated people practices, such as the fact that employees in a particular geography really do have very different needs and desires from employees elsewhere. It generally doesn't help people's performance to have divisions pursuing differentiated people practices only because that's what they've always done, or simply as a way for divisions to exert their autonomy.

Rather, carefully thought-out segmentation initiatives from the center, based on data analysis on how employees differ by geography and/or business, can ensure that companies execute differentiated people practices in the most useful way. A less obvious way of adapting people practices to local geographic or business conditions is to administer the same set of modular choices, broad and simple rules, or employee-defined personalization practices across the board. This can provide flexibility and customization based on local needs while allowing some degree of central control and consistency.

Some Questions to Consider

In this section, we'll look at two main questions that HR professionals often raise when deciding which customization approach or approaches to

TABLE 6-1

Workforce of one approaches compared

Workforce of one approach	Degree of customization	Control	Ability to cope with change	Perceived fairness	Resources required (HR/employees)
Segmentation	Medium	Very high	Medium-low	Low	More/fewer
Modular choice	Medium-high	High	Medium	High	More/fewer
Broad and simple rules	High	Medium	High	Medium	Fewer/more
Employee-defined personalization	Very high	Medium-low	Very high	Medium	Fewer/more

favor. We also present here a chart that summarizes the primary variables to consider when deciding on a customization approach or approaches. (See table 6-1. See also "Which Customization Approaches May Best Fit My Organization?" at the end of the chapter.)

How many customization approaches should your company favor, and can you switch between them?

Now that we understand some of the key trade-offs and implications for each customization approach, the question naturally arises: How many customization approaches should I actually favor? Should I favor just one approach, like modular choices; two approaches, like broad and simple rules and employee-defined personalization; or all four approaches simultaneously? Companies that make such deliberate decisions about which approach or combination of approaches to emphasize are more likely to achieve their customization goals in a coordinated, proactive, and well-thought-out way.

Some organizations will have specific conditions that suggest they favor all four customization approaches more or less equally. That's the case at Microsoft as well as at Procter & Gamble. For such companies, the trade-offs between control versus customization, for example, just aren't as important as they are for other organizations. These companies tend not to care about the differences among the approaches; rather, they enable the organization to offer extensive customization by providing employees with a large variety and number of customization practices.

But in our experience studying dozens of organizations, we've found that most tend to favor one or two customization approaches over others. In particular, many organizations favor using segmentation and modular choice approaches together, since they share many qualities. Later in this chapter, we'll see how Royal Bank of Scotland, for example, favors segmentation primarily, with modular choices running a close second. Likewise, since the broad and simple rules and employee-defined personalization approaches share much in common, many organizations favor using these two approaches together. But for some companies, as we'll see in the case of Men's Wearhouse, drawing primarily on a single customization approach works best, and provides a great deal of consistency and common understanding regarding how an organization manages its people as a workforce of one.

Becoming strong in one or a few customization areas (rather than using all four simultaneously) has some advantages. For example, it may help your company develop a compelling, consistent employee brand. It also helps manage expectations; employees who get accustomed to modular choices in some areas, for example, come to expect it in other areas too. And it allows companies to become adept in administering one type of customization. Once the infrastructure and support is built for a particular approach (such as a sophisticated analytics capability to support segmentation), an organization can then use this as a platform from which to offer a whole range of customized practices using that customization approach.

Travelers, for example, started with value-based segmentation and has gradually built up an analytics capability to extend segmentation in a variety of other ways. Because segmentation and modular choice share much in common, Travelers is now easily expanding its customization initiatives into modular choices. For example, employees now can choose the right benefit for themselves, and managers can now tailor the rewards they provide to employees by choosing from a predefined list of rewards. When Travelers tried to introduce some broad and simple rules, however, it proved to be too difficult at once. Cheryl Kozak, vice president of HR, explains, "We'd like to slowly try to build the trust and support needed to use other approaches, like broad and simple rules, that don't allow for as much control, but it's a slow process for us to become comfortable with these other approaches due to our culture. In the past, we tried to give some employees the latitude to work where they wanted, such as at home, for example (using a broad and simple rules approach), but we didn't support it with enough change management (including setting expectations and regular monitoring), so we lost control and leadership decided to stop that initiative. But we have been trying again, gradually introducing approaches that afford less control over time. We think it is smarter for us to master the customization approaches that best fit our culture and capabilities first and then move out in new directions."[4] Often, as is the case with Travelers, it is easier to master a particular customization approach first before trying to expand using other customization approaches if the organization desires.

Sometimes, organizations may want to switch from one customization approach to another. An organization like Travelers may start with segmentation and modular choice for control reasons, but gradually convert to broad and simple rules as trust is established and employees learn to handle more discretion. Or an organization may want to switch from a modular choice approach to segmentation with respect to compensation mix options, for example, to exert more control in a changed environment.

How do you do this? To take the last example, just collect data on the choices that various types of employees select using the modular choice approach, and see whether there's a pattern to which employee types make which choices. For example, upon analyzing the data, you might find that U.S.-based employees may choose only two options out of four, and Chinese-based employees, the other two—thereby allowing you (subject to labor law regulations) to create a highly germane segmentation scheme that provides only the first two options to U.S.-based employees and the other two options to Chinese-based employees (instead of offering all four options to everyone). Or to switch from a broad and simple rules approach to a more HR-driven one, for example, you may collect data on how employees have chosen compensation mixes within the context of a broad and simple rule, and create either modular choices that reflect the most common selections made, or a segmentation scheme based on the choices most commonly picked by certain segments. By analyzing data in this way, an organization can convert from one customization approach to another as values or needs shift.

Should you use only your favored customization approaches for each people practice?

Not necessarily. Deliberately and proactively deciding which customization approach or set of approaches to favor is critical to designing your own workforce of one organization. But ultimately, you'll have to decide, practice by practice, exactly how to apply customization—and though your company may largely favor one approach, it won't necessarily use it in all its people practices. As we mentioned earlier, most organizations do, in fact, use all four customization approaches at one time or another—sometimes using a particular approach for only one people practice, like benefits, while applying their favored customization approaches to most other domains.

A few people practice domains, for example, naturally lend themselves to certain customization approaches. Benefits, for instance, lends itself

FIGURE 6-3

Sample map of need for control versus customization

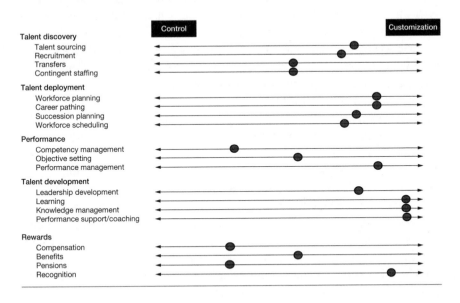

well to a modular choice approach. And some domains, like pay and hiring, may be more sensitive to control or fairness issues than others, suggesting a different approach than what the organization favors overall. For companies in more regulated industries or countries, a company may even be required to centrally spell out certain people practices in detail in some domains, like the number of hours of work, requiring the company to use for that area either a one-size-fits-all approach or one that allows more central control, like segmentation or modular choice. But for the rest of its people practices, such a company could still favor more employee-driven approaches. To help make these decisions, organizations may want to map out where they are willing to grant more customization versus control in each people practice domain. For an example of how an organization might do this, see figure 6-3.

Case Studies: Four Companies' Choices in Customization Approaches

Now that we've explored how to pursue your own way of applying customization based on your company's specific needs, we'll look at four companies we consider workforce of one pioneers—Royal Bank of Scotland, Best Buy, Men's Wearhouse, and Procter & Gamble—and the varying customization approaches they favor. In total, we studied ten companies in high detail regarding the specific customization practices they use—including PepsiCo, Microsoft, Limited Brands, Accenture, Travelers, and a South African petrochemical company. Each company has a unique blueprint for how it achieves customization in its own way, and each is at a different stage in its customization journey. Although we can't share all of their stories, we can provide a high-level overview about which customization approaches some companies we studied favor most, and why.

The companies we'll profile here have all taken different paths to providing highly relevant, tailored work experiences—Royal Bank of Scotland, by focusing primarily on segmentation and modular choice; Best Buy, by focusing primarily on broad and simple rules and employee-defined personalization; Men's Wearhouse, by focusing primarily on one approach only: broad and simple rules; and Procter & Gamble, by focusing on all four customization approaches more or less equally. Using only one approach is not necessarily better than using two or even all four approaches; nor is a particular approach better than another. What counts is that it works for your organization. (To see which approaches other workforce of one pioneers, such as Microsoft, Google, Capital One, and ten others, focus on, see "Thirteen Workforce of One Pioneers" in chapter 1.)

The Segmentation Plus Modular Choice Model: Royal Bank of Scotland

Royal Bank of Scotland is a true leader in managing its workforce of one—primarily by pioneering the use of segmentation to offer its employees highly targeted offerings based on their distinct segment. The company segments its workforce in more than fifteen ways—including by life or professional stage, generation, geography, most likely to leave, type of engagement an individual has with the organization, performance, potential, and gender. Many of its segmentation practices are highly innovative—such as the ability to target highly customized benefits information based on specific workforce segments. The bank stands out especially because of its highly nuanced way of using segmentation: it looks at multiple segments at once to get increasingly granular in its offerings. For example, it determines the specific drivers of engagement based on three or more segments at once—like for young women in China. The company also offers a wide range of modular choices—regarding communication channels, benefits, rewards, and time, for example. (For an overview of Royal Bank of Scotland's approach to customization, see figure 6-4.)

Why does this approach to customization work best for Royal Bank of Scotland? Greig Aitken, the bank's head of employee engagement, says

FIGURE 6-4

Customization at Royal Bank of Scotland

Customization approach	Extent approach used
Segmentation	●
Modular choices	◕
Broad and simple rules	◔
Employee-defined personalization	◑

Note: Although the company focuses most on segmentation and modular choices, it does also use, to a lesser extent, the other two customization approaches.

that segmentation and modular choices fit best with the bank's highly analytic and data-driven management approach that is deeply embedded in its culture and industry. With these two approaches to customizing people practices, he says, the bank "gains insight in a similar way to how our market researchers acquire consumer insight. And we can support this kind of analytics approach because we have done so much work already in standardizing employee data across our businesses. It can be rolled up in a single global view and then sliced and diced every which way you can imagine."[5]

Likewise, explains Aitken, extensively using an approach like broad and simple rules would never work in this organization. "We have to specify most people practices in detail centrally, in part because we are a heavily regulated industry, and in part because we want to maintain the kind of control that this affords. Frankly, many people are nervous that people will make the wrong decisions if given too much discretion; providing people with modular choices, for example, helps us give our employees decision-making power, but in a highly structured and controlled fashion." The fact that 52 percent of the bank's workforce has under five years of experience with the company and that a full 28 percent has a tenure of less than two years also supports a more controlled approach to customization. Approaches that offer more discretion often work best in environments where trust between employees and the organization is built up over time—and where employees stay long enough to learn how to handle more discretion.

Flexibly responding to varying employee needs by segmenting its workforce and providing a range of modular choices is a true business imperative at Royal Bank of Scotland: its incredibly diverse workforce *demanded* that the organization make customization a top priority. Since the late 1990s, the bank has transformed from a medium-size U.K. bank with 35,000 employees to a large, global bank that now employs 170,000 people in fifty countries who support forty brands that span personal, business, corporate, and wealth management businesses. Likewise, with a workforce that's 55 percent female and with the average age of thirty-six, the company had a large portion of employees who needed alternative options, for example, to one-size-fits-all linear, lockstep career paths. The bank's own research revealed that "doing the same thing for everyone in a company as diverse as ours doesn't maximize productivity or performance," Aitken explains. "People have different expectations of work and different drivers of engagement based on any number of different criteria. What works in a call center in Edinburgh might not be so good for bond dealers in New York, for example. Our challenge is to learn how to optimize the contributions each and every one of us makes to the business through a more customized management approach."

Providing highly relevant, tailored HR offerings—begun in earnest in 2004 after the company finished developing its new human capital model and analytics capability to better segment its workforce—has helped it become a widely recognized employer of choice. The company was named Global Bank of the Year for 2007 by the *Banker* magazine, for example, and the Royal Bank of Scotland Retail Network was listed among the top twenty best big companies to work for by the *Sunday Times*.[6] Because of this reputation, the company is now better able to attract and retain top talent—improved retention figures alone have helped build the business case for customization, since, on average, it takes the bank ten months to repay the recruiting and onboarding cost of a new employee. Likewise, the company has found that improved retention leads to better business results; those bank branches with less turnover far outperform those with more.

Most important, by providing tailored HR offerings based on an analysis of the key drivers of engagement and performance for each workforce segment, and by continuously pinpointing employee "hot buttons" where providing customization results in the biggest payoffs, the company has considerably improved employee engagement and productivity—which in turn has been linked statistically to improvements in customer satisfaction and business results. The company now outperforms its banking peers on 13 out of 17 benchmarking measures related to people practices. Between 2004 and 2007, the bank experienced a 19 percent increase in its employee engagement index alone. Engagement leads to better business; contact centers with favorable engagement scores, for example, close 38 percent more customer concerns in less than two days than those with less favorable scores.

Ultimately, the bank's executives believe that improved employee engagement and productivity resulting from its tailored people offerings helped to improve the bank's financial performance between 2004 and 2007. It ranked as the number one High Street bank for customer satisfaction in 2007.[7] And between 2004 and 2007, income grew by 11 percent to 31,115 million pounds, operating profit grew by 9 percent to 10,282 million pounds, and earnings per share increased by 18 percent to 78.7 pence.[8]

In 2008 and 2009, the bank became one of many financial institutions that suffered significant losses in the wake of the global financial crisis. Although its financial performance suffered greatly, it is likely that reasons are systemic and have little to do with its workforce performance. The bank's leaders continue to believe that a customized talent strategy will help them get the best performance from their people and ultimately help the bank improve its business results. High-performing people, they believe, will be key to the bank's ability to weather crises and bounce back ahead of the competition when market conditions grow challenging, as they have in the banking industry's credit crisis during the last years of this decade.

The Broad and Simple Rules Plus Employee-Defined Personalization Model: Best Buy

Best Buy has pursued a different but equally successful path to offering employees highly customized work experiences. Although Best Buy uses all four workforce of one customization approaches, the company's true strength lies in its extensive and often highly innovative use of both the broad and simple rules and employee-defined personalization customization approaches. Employees at Best Buy can shape their own jobs to draw on their unique interests and strengths—store employees are encouraged to use their own words and personality to customize Best Buy's basic selling process, for example. Some corporate-based employees can even define their own schedules and place of work—all by flexibly interpreting rules that broadly specify what results employees are expected to accomplish, rather than exactly how they are expected to accomplish them. (Best Buy calls this its "Results-Only Work Environment.") Best Buy employees also can largely define their own learning experiences through new technologies like blogs, wikis, YouTube, and other peer-to-peer learning technologies, and they enjoy employee-driven recruiting, career paths, coaching, mentoring, informal feedback, and more. For an overview of Best Buy's approach to customization, see figure 6-5.

Why does Best Buy favor the broad and simple rules and employee-defined personalization approaches? The answer lies in the company's

FIGURE 6-5

Customization at Best Buy

Customization approach	Extent approach used
Segmentation	◑
Modular choices	◑
Broad and simple rules	●
Employee-defined personalization	●

Note: Although the company focuses on broad and simple rules and employee-defined personalization, it does also use, to a lesser extent, the other two customization approaches.

fundamental growth and innovation strategy of providing customers with relevant and highly customized experiences. When Brad Anderson (CEO until 2009) took over the company reins in 2002, he led the charge to strategically transform Best Buy's stores from a mass-market, cookie-cutter approach in how they were designed and stocked to a "unique store approach" that would instead focus on serving the specific needs and interests of each customer. Stores would be granted the power to use different store signage, fixtures, lighting, and even uniforms to serve the specific mix of customer segments—like busy suburban moms, young entertainment enthusiasts, or small-business owners—that each store tended to attract.

But most important, under Anderson's new plan, employees would custom tailor their sales and customer-service approaches to every customer, to provide highly relevant experiences that may vary tremendously even within customer segments. This strong preference for extremely high levels of customization—even if it means giving up some of the control that corporate typically likes to exert—directly carries over into Best Buy's talent management strategy. Although the company uses all four customization approaches, it strongly favors those that enable more customization but less control—the broad and simple rules and employee-defined personalization approaches (refer back to figure 6-1). To support its customer-centricity growth initiative, the company has completely transformed its people management approach from centralization and sameness to decentralization and uniqueness by allowing employees leeway not only to define how they serve customers, but also in their own people practices. This places talent at the very heart of Best Buy's strategy.

Explaining why Best Buy addresses individual employee needs primarily using the broad and simple rules and employee-defined personalization approaches, HR operations head Tina Decker says, "If we want our employees to provide a highly individualized experience to our customers using their own judgment in a fairly open-ended way, then our employees need to have that same experience as an employee with respect to their work experiences. This has radically redefined the way HR supports its employees in nearly every respect."

Joe Kalkman, leader of Best Buy's HR centers of excellence, adds, "Our growth strategy emphasizes decentralized value creation and an expectation that ideas and growth can come from anywhere in the system; broad and simple rules and employee-defined personalization customization approaches best fit this strategic philosophy. The challenge we've been working so hard on, of course, is figuring out how to customize based on the individual in a reliable, consistent way—to solve the paradox of establishing a norm that is in itself abnormal. But by doing this, we've found, we can create massive benefits for our customers, our business, and our employees."[9]

Indeed, this unique workforce of one design works for Best Buy precisely because the company has worked so hard to achieve customization in a reliable, consistent way—by clearly defining the boundaries of its broad and simple rules in terms of results; by carefully instilling alternative control mechanisms that ensure that customization is done appropriately; and by establishing a strong culture that supports fairness, diversity, and increased flexibility. Freedom is not granted in a laissez-faire or ad hoc way; managers are held accountable for the performance of their people, employees must still follow important employment rules and policies, and oversight from district and corporate leadership is always strongly maintained.

Adds Gallup's chief scientist, strengths development, Jim Asplund, who has worked closely with Best Buy over a number of years, "Interestingly, our data analysis revealed that one of the most important factors enabling Best Buy to implement broad and simple rules so successfully was the significant amount of hard work Best Buy put into engaging its employees. This work created the kind of culture where broad and simple rules would work as designed. So, for example, we have seen that stores that capitalized most on the customer [and thereby employee] centricity model and engagement work demonstrate significantly greater revenue and profit growth, declining turnover, and superior customer scores. We have over a decade of data on this, so we know that the engagement improvement has to happen first. Once that is in place, employees have enough trust and feel sufficiently connected to Best Buy's mission and strategy to take some risks with their work structures. They also know enough and care enough about each other to invest in development, and individualize their approach to management."[10]

The fact that Best Buy's employees tend to be highly tech-savvy also means that many employees are already used to many employee-defined personalization practices, such as the use of wikis, blogs, social networks, and other supporting technologies, and they have high expectations that their employer will offer them that same kind of choice and flexibility. And although analytics and a data-based approach aren't crucial in implementing the broad and simple rules and employee-defined personalization approaches, Best Buy happens to be a leader in using analytics to measure the impact of its customization practices on results.

Ultimately, Best Buy believes that by pursuing a workforce of one design that favors greater customization over greater control, it will more closely fit people practices with individual needs and thereby achieve better workforce performance and engagement. Even so, Decker has found that she doesn't really need to control employees anyway. "People are still getting their work done [in corporate] without us having to control their hours, for example. In the end, you have to ask yourself from a cost/benefit point of view, is the value being created worth the risk? And at this point in the game, the answer is a resounding yes." Yet Decker acknowledges the risk involved. "Pursuing this approach is riskier, but for us, we believe it is far more valuable. This is a fundamental law: with higher reward comes higher risk. This is why it is hard to do, why other organizations aren't doing it, and why it creates such a strong competitive advantage for our company."

To be sure, Best Buy now enjoys some of the lowest employee turnover rates in its industry. Whereas Best Buy stores had a turnover rate around the industry average of 100 percent in early 2000, most Best Buy stores now have a turnover rate that hovers around 45 percent, and some stores even boast a turnover rate as low as 20 percent. Its corporate employees who have switched to the Results-Only Work Environment using a broad and simple rules approach have 3.2 percent less voluntary turnover than those who haven't switched to the new work environment—and the fact that the per-employee cost of turnover is $102,000 means that when all workers switch to the new environment, the company stands to save an extraordinary $13 million a year in replacement costs alone.[11] Likewise, customization means more productive employees—workers who switched to the broad and simple rules Results-Only Work Environment have improved their productivity by 35 percent.[12]

Engagement scores are also up, reflecting not only the important foundation Best Buy built to help make the implementation of broad and simple rules so successful, but an important outcome of the approach as well. In the late 1990s, Best Buy's employee engagement scores (as measured by Gallup's Q12 index) were in the 50th percentile, or about average compared with other companies. Employee engagement scores are now in the top third of performance as compared to other companies; on a scale of 1–5 (5 meaning most engaged), they have maintained a mean score of 4.0 or better for several years running. Working with Gallup, Best Buy found that a 0.10 increase in engagement (on a 5-point scale) is worth an estimated $100,000 in incremental profit per store, per year.

Indeed, closely tuning in to both customers and employees has paid off, ultimately contributing to stunning financial results by any measure. In the past few years, starting shortly after Anderson took over as CEO and began aggressively pursuing a growth strategy of customization, Best Buy has consistently far outperformed the S&P 500 and its industry peers. Although its financial results are doubtless due to many factors, Best Buy executives believe they are due at least in part to improved employee performance as a result of customized people practices. If you took the same $100 in 2003 and invested it in Best Buy stock, for example, by 2009, you would have had $156.97, compared with only $87.39 if you'd invested it in the S&P 500.[13] Best Buy's market share in the United States increased from 13 percent in 2003 to 21 percent in 2008.[14] From 2003 to 2009, revenues have more than doubled (increasing from $19 billion to over $45 billion), and its diluted earnings per share has increased over 25 percent (from $1.91 to $2.39).[15] Customer satisfaction is also steadily improving; the customer satisfaction index improved from 77.5 to 80.3 from 2007 to 2009, for example. Best Buy's reputation as an outstanding performer and employer of choice—enabled in part through its unique people management approach—is now widely recognized; it was named a *Forbes* Company of the Year in 2004, and it made *Fortune*'s Most Admired Companies list in 2006 and 2009.[16]

The Broad and Simple Rules Only Model: Men's Wearhouse

Men's Wearhouse offers a good example of how a smaller company in a low-margin business can achieve outstanding performance through a customized people management approach. Unlike the other workforce of one pioneers we've featured so far, Men's Wearhouse—the largest U.S. men's dress apparel retailer, employing eighteen thousand people—has achieved stellar workforce and business performance results by focusing primarily on only one customization approach: the broad and simple rules approach (see figure 6-6). The company broadly defines rules for employees to allow latitude for interpretation on nearly every work dimension—including jobs, careers, compensation, timing of work, place of work, performance goals, competencies, rewards, learning, and hiring practices.

FIGURE 6-6

Customization at Men's Wearhouse

Customization approach	Extent approach used
Segmentation	◕
Modular choices	○
Broad and simple rules	●
Employee-defined personalization	◑

Note: Although the company focuses primarily on broad and simple rules, it also uses, to a lesser extent, two of the other customization approaches.

At Men's Wearhouse, such customized practices for employees are profoundly rooted in the culture—in fact, the company began these (then) unusual practices when it first opened its doors, in 1973. Its choice of using a broad and simple rules approach stems from its unique culture and its founders' deeply held beliefs.

Founder George Zimmer (yes, he's the one you've seen in U.S. television ads proclaiming, "I guarantee it!") and initial employees like Charlie Bresler (who became president and now is executive vice president of marketing and human development) wanted to create a company that could express their strong values regarding fairness, but also regarding respect for the individual and his ability to make choices that are best for him. Explains Bresler, "George is an interesting amalgam of two cultures: a small-business, capitalist strain informed by his family—his father owned a coat manufacturing company—combined with a healthy bent towards community values." Both men came of age in the 1960s and shared such beliefs as equality and individual freedom, held by many of that generation. Bresler also had an academic background that gave him insight into what maximizes human performance. He says, "I was hired into Men's Wearhouse directly out of teaching in a PhD program in clinical psychology. So no one at the company had a formal HR background, and we consciously did not listen to traditional HR professionals. This enabled us to pursue an alternative approach to people management which was quite at odds with the retailing industry's preference of strict control over their people."

What made broad and simple rules so appealing to Zimmer and Bresler was that the same rule could be consistently defined and applied to everyone across the board. Yet within the context of applying the same rule to everyone, the company could still "contextually manage"; in other words, the rule could be interpreted in a variety of ways, depending on the specific business circumstances and individual employee needs at hand. Bresler and Zimmer realized that customization through broad and simple rules would not only improve people's performance (since people practices could more closely fit individual and business needs), but it also would help the company deal with an increasingly diverse workforce. Bresler explains that a broad and simple rules approach "provided the balance we were seeking: a healthy tension between egalitarianism on the one hand, and the honoring of the individual and their unique differences on the other hand."

Because of the founders' bent toward egalitarianism, the company doesn't recruit superstars, for example, and often hires people in need; executives receive smaller salaries than those at comparable companies. This underlying philosophy also means that the company eschews most segmentation initiatives, other than very limited and obvious role-based segmentation (salespeople get paid by commissions, whereas others do not, for example; and corporate employees can generally work when or wherever they want as long as they get the job done, while store-based employees cannot).

In particular, Men's Wearhouse avoids any kind of segmentation based on value. Explains Bresler, "We would never do forced ranking based on performance, as it breeds a harsh, negative culture. Our goal is to create positive human energy, because retail work can often be difficult and deadly." The company also shuns segmentation based on most-critical workers, or high potentials. "If someone is not considered a 'high potential,' for example, then it tends to create a cycle of self-fulfillment," Bresler says.

Although providing modular choices would also serve the founders' desire for fairness and egalitarianism, the company does not use this approach. Why? Because its focus on broad and simple rules, supplemented with some employee-defined personalization, requires fewer HR administrative resources than a more structured modular choice approach would entail—a key consideration in a low-margin business that must tightly control costs. Since broad and simple rules and employee-defined personalization require greater employee involvement to customize their own people practices, and are, in fact, woven into the very fabric of everyday business operations, the HR group at Men's Wearhouse (termed *human development*) can be quite small (less than a dozen employees) compared with other businesses of comparable size.

Bresler explains, "Employees do most of the HR work—so we don't need many HR folks!" For example, HR doesn't have to constantly update or spell out a myriad of competency descriptions, training courses for each role, or career paths. And since learning is primarily done through experience, informal feedback, and coaching of one another, the company doesn't support a large, centralized training function. Instead, the company's HR group focuses on setting broad policies, facilitating the sharing of great practices across businesses, and building the right culture to ensure that employees appropriately and fairly interpret the broad and simple rules.

A broad and simple rules approach works at Men's Wearhouse as well because of the nature of its employees. Its promote-from-within culture, where employees stay at the company for long periods (and many never leave until retirement), is key to building the type of trust that supports the company in giving more employee freedom and discretion. Men's Wearhouse also screens and hires people who can work effectively without being told exactly what to do and who are *servant leaders*—people who naturally lead by serving and developing others.

Interestingly, the company's HR group has never had to go through the process of rationalizing, standardizing, and harmonizing its people practices, as so many other companies have had to do in recent years. This is in part because, since it has always used broad and simple rules, its HR practices were fairly standardized from the start. Another reason is that its business is based only in the United States and Canada and has had relatively few acquisitions. With companies it has acquired, such as Moore's in 1999, it successfully replicated the same customization approach.

Since customization through broad and simple rules and employee-defined personalization is so rare in its industry, the company attracts top performers who are extremely loyal and engaged with the brand, and it has never had the trouble in attracting and retaining top talent that many other companies have had. At the level of multistore manager and above, there is almost no turnover, and below this level, turnover is significantly lower than at competitors.

Bresler explains, "People just plain like our 'contextual management' approach that gives them more freedom and discretion to customize within certain broadly defined rules and boundaries. If you go to the human development literature, you'll see this is a higher stage of development. We feel good about supporting it." The company founders believe its people philosophy of customization directly results in more motivated, productive, high-performing employees, and is the key to its success in the marketplace. To be sure, Men's Wearhouse has earned a widespread reputation as an employer of choice (it made *Fortune* magazine's 100 Best Companies to Work For list in 2007 and 2009, for example), and has consistently turned out superior results that beat the market.[17] From 2002 to 2008, for example, net sales increased 52 percent to nearly $2 billion, and net earnings increased nearly 39 percent, from $42 million to nearly $59 million (down from a whopping $147 million in 2007 before the economic downturn). (Financial results were not available for 2009 at the time of this writing.) The company has consistently far outperformed the S&P 500 and its industry peers in total return to shareholders. If you had taken $100 in 2003 and invested it in Men's Wearhouse stock, for example, by 2009, you would have had $127.77 (and $288.05 if you'd sold it a year earlier, before the economic downturn), compared with $96.00 if you'd invested it in the S&P 500 (and $163.07 if you'd sold it a year earlier).[18] Likewise, for the past six years, Men's Wearhouse has consistently outperformed the Dow Jones U.S. Apparel Retailers Group—its industry peer set.[19]

The Four Approach Model: P&G

The companies we've profiled so far in this chapter have all chosen to focus on one or a few customization approaches that work best for them. But some organizations may have specific business conditions that make a strategy of strongly pursuing all four customization approaches more or less equally the preferred route to customization. This is the case at Procter & Gamble (see figure 6-7), where the company strives to balance the need for consistency and structure (high degrees of which are easier to accomplish with the segmentation and modular choice approaches) with the need for customization and employee discretion (high degrees of which are easier to accomplish with the broad and simple rules and employee-defined personalization approaches). Drawing on all four customization approaches, P&G is able to offer customized training, customized career paths, customized places of work, customized tools to aid in on boarding to new roles, creative ways of recognition that tap into the unique motivators of each individual, and a focus on playing to everyone's personal strengths, to name just a few of its many customized talent management practices.

FIGURE 6-7

P&G's approach to customization

Customization approach	Extent approach used
Segmentation	●
Modular choices	●
Broad and simple rules	◑
Employee-defined personalization	◑

The focus on customizing HR products and services increased back in 2000. At the time, the company's performance was lagging and employee morale was struggling. A. G. Lafley, P&G's newly appointed CEO at the time, rallied the organization around the notion that "the consumer is boss" and that P&G needed to win at the two moments of truth—when consumers choose P&G products over others in the store, and when they use the product. Accomplishing this meant nothing less than learning about P&G's customers inside and out and providing them with highly relevant, tailored products and experiences.

This concept was so powerful that P&G's Beauty business began experimenting with the concept of "Winning at the Employee Moments of Truth" by developing customized HR offerings to meet the needs of its highly diverse workforce. This new approach, says Keith Lawrence, director-human resources, P&G Beauty, has provided P&G new insights into what employees really need and how the company can better meet them. He explains, "We are reapplying what we do to learn about our consumers to be more in touch and responsive to our employees as well as the business."[20]

P&G's unique culture, diversity of businesses, and types of employees have led the company to develop extensive customization using all four approaches. Segmentation and modular choice were a natural outgrowth of striving to meet the needs of its highly diverse workforce and business segments. Not only does the company employ 138,000 employees working in more than eighty different countries, but P&G markets more than 140 different brands, ranging from dog food and cosmetics to pharmaceuticals and electric razors. By using segmentation and modular choice, the company ensures that flexibility exists to make sure that local laws, consumer needs, and employee preferences are met. (However, this is done without sacrificing the core of P&G—its purpose, values, and principles—which is common around the world.)

In addition, the company has gradually added more customization practices using broad and simple rules and employee-defined personalization approaches. These have helped P&G more effectively deal with its fast changing, unpredictable business environment. Lawrence explains, "Allowing flexibility for employees and their managers to define their specific roles, work arrangements, and career paths through defining broad and simple rules or fostering employee-defined personalization helps the company respond more quickly to change."

Broad and simple rules and employee-defined personalization work for P&G because the company has worked hard to provide employees with hands-on, proactive support to handle the increased discretion they're given. But also the company's unique culture and types of employees more easily enables the trust and responsibility necessary for customization approaches like broad and simple rules and employee-defined personalization to be successful. How? Trust grows naturally because of P&G's promote-from-within philosophy, which builds trust among colleagues who work alongside one another for many years. There is also a significant investment made in building productive working relationships and fostering the skills to effectively work with one another, as well as in supporting employees in learning how to effectively handle the increased discretion that broad and simple rules and employee-defined personalization approaches allow.

P&G's ongoing work to build a high-performing organization, enabled in part through its customization initiatives, has earned the company a strong reputation as an employer of choice. The company has garnered yearly accolades from *Working Mother*, *DiversityInc.*, and *Fortune* magazines, to name a few.[21] P&G's attrition rate of 7–8 percent per year is among the best in its industry. Not only does the company report that the vast majority of its employees say that P&G is their employer of choice, but it reports that employees have high levels of engagement in their work. Ultimately, the combined customer and employee centric approach has helped the company achieve a phenomenal turnaround: since A. G. Lafley took over as chairman and CEO in 2000, P&G has seen its sales more than double, its profits triple (to more than $12 billion), and its total return to shareholders increase 300 percent compared with the 12 percent decrease most companies experienced, as represented by the S&P 500 (numbers are as of close of fiscal year 2008; fiscal year 2009 had not yet closed as of the writing of this book).[22] Although these results obviously reflect many factors, the improved productivity of its employees has contributed significantly to the stunning financial success of the company—and customization has been one important enabler of this success.

Sums up Keith Lawrence, "We have been working hard to break the mindset that there is a single path or solution; we are truly not a one-size-fits-all company. Customization in a structured and highly facilitated fashion allows us to find a unique solution at the intersection of what is important to an individual, and what is important to the business—and scaling this so it works across the company."

We've devoted this chapter to exploring why some customization approaches may work better than others, depending on an organization's unique set of business conditions and employees. Yet even if two companies choose to favor the same customization approaches, their workforce of one designs will likely look very different from one another. Just as no two individual employees will ever look precisely alike, neither will two organizations customize their people practices in precisely the same way if they hope to achieve the best results.

Two organizations that favor segmentation, for example, could choose to segment in very different ways—a company with mostly younger people, for example, won't need to segment on generation as much as a company with a wider age mix might. Or two organizations may both decide to segment based on most-critical employees, but one may identify their R&D professionals based on their strategy, and another, their sales and marketing staff.

To take another example, the exact choices an organization offers in a modular choice approach will be determined by what its employees need and value. So Tesco may need to provide options to appeal to an employee segment it calls "pleasure seekers," but another organization may not have these types of employees and therefore will offer an altogether different set of options. Or a business may have certain characteristics that limit its ability to offer some choices or practices in a particular domain; one company in our study, for example, offers many choices regarding time, but its fast-paced, highly dynamic business environment prevents it from offering extended career breaks.

Likewise, two organizations could both pursue broad and simple rules approaches in a domain like job definition, but one might do best to define the job based on outcomes, while another may prefer defining a job based on time—for example, limiting the time spent on required core job activities to allow time for customized job activities. Two companies could also support the same employee-defined personalization practice in very different ways; tech-savvy employees at a high-tech company may prefer to learn through computer-generated simulated experiences, while less tech-savvy employees at another company may learn best the old-fashioned way, through experience.

By paying careful attention to your company's unique needs and set of employees, you will be able to decide which approaches to favor as part of a general customization strategy—and to determine precisely how to implement each customization practice in the best way possible. True workforce of one organizations that will lead the labor markets won't implement just one or two one-off initiatives based on fads or the desire to copy someone else's "best practice." Rather, they will take a strategic, holistic, branded, and individualized approach to customization by extensively drawing on the approaches best suited for them.

We've seen in this chapter how four very different workforce of one pioneers have used customization to improve employee performance. And we've laid out many of the criteria to consider when deciding how to introduce more customization into your own organization to achieve similar results. (To help determine which customization approach or approaches to favor most, see our quiz, "Which Customization Approaches May Best Fit My Organization?")

Next, we'll look at many of the challenges organizations like Royal Bank of Scotland, Best Buy, Men's Wearhouse, P&G, and others may face as they seek to manage their workforce as a workforce of one. We'll present solutions to common challenges such as fairness, privacy, and control that may crop up as companies seek to navigate the new and complex terrain of customized talent management.

Which Customization Approaches May Best Fit My Organization?

Take this quiz to find out. Just check the "Yes" box if that's your answer to any of the questions posed below. Then add up only the numbers for those questions marked "Yes" in the "Total" box below. The customization approaches with the highest numbers are the ones you may wish to consider emphasizing most.

Question	Yes? If so, check here	Segmentation	Modular choices	Broad and simple rules	Employee-defined personalization
1. Does my company's business strategy or culture favor greater degrees of control over greater degrees of customization?	☐	4	3	1	0
2. Or does my company's business strategy or culture favor greater degrees of customization over greater degrees of control?	☐	0	1	3	4
3. Does my company face constant and fast change—requiring jobs, competencies, career paths, learning, and more to be constantly updated based on changing business conditions?	☐	0	1	2	2
4. Does my organization have a strong preference for a more egalitarian culture—and does it seek to achieve fairness by offering the same opportunities to everyone?	☐	0	2	1	1
5. Does my organization favor a data-driven approach and have a well-developed human capital analytic capability? Can it afford to support such a capability?	☐	2	2	1	1

(continued)

Question	Yes? If so, check here	Segmentation	Modular choices	Broad and simple rules	Employee-defined personalization
6. Has my organization gone through the process of standardizing on a common HR infrastructure and set of processes, and does it have standardized employee data?	☐	2	2	1	1
7. Do our employees tend to favor more autonomy in defining their own people practices, and do they thrive when granted it?	☐	0	0	1	2
8. Do most of my company's employees stay for a long time?	☐	0	0	2	2
9. Does my organization need to specify people practices in detail centrally due to being part of a heavily regulated industry or union environment?	☐	2	1	0	0
10. Is my company prepared to provide hands-on, proactive support to employees to handle approaches that give employees increased discretion in defining their own people practices?	☐	0	1	2	2
11. Is my company prepared to administratively support multiple variations of centrally defined people practices?	☐	2	2	0	0
Total		—	—	—	—

Workforce of One
Challenges and Solutions

Contemporary workplace trends—an increasingly diverse workforce, tougher competition for talent, employees who are accustomed to more tailored offerings as consumers—and the recognition that business results are largely attributable to employee performance will drive companies to offer more tailored, customized talent management practices in the future. We may standardize on the back end, but we will increasingly customize on the front end to provide relevant, tailored experiences for our end employees.[1]

—Beverly Tarulli, vice president of organization
and management development at PepsiCo

SCULPTING WORK TO FIT every employee—instead of requiring employees to conform to a standard mold of work—is a lofty goal. Yet we've seen that it can be achieved: in the last chapter, we've examined four companies that are actually reaching this goal. They are pioneering a groundbreaking concept of work—managing their workforces not as a single homogeneous entity, but rather with finely tuned, sophisticated attention to the often subtle differences among the people who invest their minds, hearts, and energy in their organizations day after day, year after year. These companies—and the nine other companies we cited in chapter 1 as workforce of one pioneers—offer highly personalized employment experiences and are now yielding the fruits of their labor: boosts in employees' motivation, attraction, retention, and overall contribution to the organization.

These are big payoffs, to be sure. But as we've stressed throughout this book, the road to achieving them is not easy. It is complex and demanding work; managing a workforce of one requires organizations to navigate some tricky territory. For example, when difference is recognized, appreciated, and attended to through tailored people practices, fairness may be challenged. And as organizations collect more and increasingly personal employee data toward offering more relevant people practices, privacy may be challenged too. Likewise, as an organization offers increasing discretion to employees to define their own people practices, HR managers may wonder how to maintain control and transparency around how people practices are being customized throughout the organization.

In this chapter we'll look at potential solutions to challenges in a range of areas, namely:

- **Fairness.** When people's work and employment experiences vary tremendously from person to person, how do we manage this fairly and legally?

- **Privacy.** How do we respect people's privacy when collecting information to provide more customized practices?

- **Control.** How do we ensure that people practices are appropriately customized when giving employees more choice, responsibility, and discretion?

- **Alignment of individual needs with business strategy.** How do we ensure that people practices customized for each employee also align with the business strategy?

- **Administration of variation.** How do we practically administer and manage so many practices and programs?

- **Outsourcing.** If the business case for outsourcing relies on standardization, how do we use outsourcing to help us achieve customization?

- **Building a business case.** How do we build a business case for workforce of one and balance the needs for effectiveness, efficiency, and cost?

- **Change.** How do we support the kind of cultural change needed when transforming to a workforce of one organization?

- **Unity.** How do we prevent fracturing the organizational whole when focusing on individual employees?

Let's begin with one of the most talked about and controversial challenges when it comes to managing a workforce of one: fairness.

How Do We Promote Fairness and Differentiation, Not Discrimination?

CultureRx is an organization that has some experience in customizing people practices while keeping things fair. This wholly owned subsidiary of Best Buy helps other companies implement "Results-Only Work Environments" (ROWE) using a broad and simple rules approach. The biggest snafu they encounter? The way that employees often judge other workers in terms of whether they are getting a better deal, such as when an employee leaves work at 3 p.m. to pick up his child—while his coworker silently steams, "I wish I had a kid!"[2]

CultureRx has a word for this kind of competitive comparison in the workplace: *sludge*.[3] Sludge is engrained in institutions across the world and can be dangerous indeed. When employees feel unfairly treated, this can sap their commitment and reduce their performance, satisfaction, and discretional energy to go beyond what is formally required of them, not to mention expose a company to potential lawsuits over discrimination.[4] When differences are recognized and appreciated through differentiated workforce of one practices, sludge and a feeling of inequality is sure to rear its ugly head. Only the modular choice approach is rarely affected by this phenomenon since the same set of detailed choices are offered to all.

How do you slough off sludge? In the words of Victor Hugo, "The highest equality is equity."[5] In other words, don't confuse fairness with sameness. Equality is best achieved by treating all people fairly and justly (or equitably)—which may not mean treating them all the same. (Of course, companies must comply with labor laws.) To put it simply, when people are treated the same, differences may be ignored. When they are treated equitably, differences are recognized, celebrated, and capitalized upon to help every individual realize their full potential. Because no two people are exactly the same, using equity as a starting point may be a more realistic way of achieving equal outcomes. Ensuring a positive work experience for everyone means offering *different* experiences to suit the unique needs of different people. For the open-minded employee, the transition to a more diverse workforce of one environment, infused with shared meanings of difference, can be an exciting and enriching experience.

But the question remains about how, exactly, do organizations achieve a sense of justice and fairness. According to myriad academic research on this topic, employees are most likely to feel their workplace is fair if they feel that the procedures for determining different treatment are fair; if they understand how and why decisions are made; and if the explanation is given in a sensitive, respectful manner.[6] Our own survey of employees indicates the same (see figure 7-1). Nearly all the workforce of one pioneers profiled

FIGURE 7-1

Employees support customization if reasons are logical and clear

I would support differential treatment and employee practices that vary
based on the individual if there were clear, logical, and well-communicated
reasons regarding why such differential treatment exists:

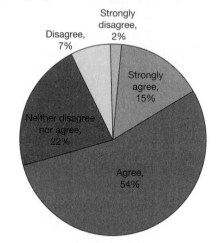

Source: Accenture workforce of one study, 2008.

in this book do a superior job at this, enabling them to differentiate their
people practices while maintaining a strong sense of fairness and justice in
their organizations.

The following are some practical steps companies can consider to help
promote a feeling of fair treatment among employees, even when they no
longer share exactly the same employment practices:

- Have a clear, documented rationale for the workforce of one
  approaches that organizational leaders adopt.

- Apply consistently any procedures used to make workforce of one
  decisions, based on accurate information.

- Make accurate, clear, and precise explanations for decisions
  available to employees, and deliver these in a sensitive manner
  (especially when outcomes appear to be unfavorable for particular
  groups or individuals).

- Grant employees a voice in decision making and in determining
  the right segments, choices, broad and simple rules, and employee-
  defined personalization practices to pursue.

Beyond those points just listed, we'd like to share several hard-won lessons from employers in our study. Before we go on, however, we'd like to explain that while countries vary around specific workplace laws, in general these lessons are universal. Moreover, because segmentation is the approach that triggers the most oft-cited problems around fairness, many of the lessons here relate to that approach. In addition, we want to be clear that we are speaking of promoting general perceptions of fairness with employees and are not addressing legal obligations or providing any legal advice. Accordingly, we are not advising on the legal position regarding any approaches outlined in this book. Companies should always consult with their legal advisers before taking any action. With this in mind, when considering issues of fairness, consider the following:

For legally protected segments, explore giving the same overall advantage to all, but in tailored ways. Accenture, for example, provides differentiated leadership training to different ethnicities but provides the same general advantage (leadership training) to all, just in slightly differentiated ways.

Ask employees to self-segment for some schemes, or make tailored programs to them optional. For segmentation schemes that segment based on personal rather than job-related characteristics (e.g., personality or health profile versus value to the organization), it is often helpful to have employees self-segment or opt in to specialized programs and practices for these segments. Likewise, an organization may offer everyone a practice or program tailored to one segment—as many companies do when inviting men to attend women's leadership events—or make segmentation practices supplemental only. Thrive Networks, a high-tech consulting firm that administers personality-based surveys, for example, only uses test results to supplement information obtained from interviews; the tests serve only as guidelines to help managers identify potential strengths in making hiring decisions.[7] The risks in this area can be seen by the law suit filed in 2004 by a former Rent-A-Center manager against Rent-A-Center, in which he claimed that the decision not to promote him was solely based on a company-administered personality test.[8]

Use documented facts to support differentiation. Differentiation should always be supported by facts as much as possible—for example, by relying on facts rather than subjective judgment to identify high performers; by relying on market pay rates and contribution to the organization to make appropriate pay decisions within a broadband pay scheme; or by deliberately specifying, documenting, and reliably testing for broader abilities or cultural fit when hiring based on broader abilities rather than narrow skills.

Provide the same opportunities for all employees whenever possible. Many people are willing to accept wide inequalities if they are coupled with equality of opportunity; thus companies should strive to provide equal opportunity whenever possible. Consider the practices used by workforce of one pioneers to provide equal opportunity—for example, Google uses coding competitions open to the general public to identify the best job candidates, and Royal Bank of Scotland still makes all benefits available to everyone, but emphasizes only certain benefits to certain segments.[9]

Continually check for nondiscrimination and fairness. No matter what customization approach your organization favors, check for fairness and potential unintended discrimination by analyzing data to ensure that no single group receives unintended preferential treatment. Companies may also survey employees regarding how fair they perceive the company's processes, and they should develop dispute processes to handle any issues that arise.

One final word on the topic of legality: organizations must tread very carefully around aspects of people management that are government regulated to ensure conformance to the law. Government regulations that affect talent management practices in the United States, for example, include laws on equal employment opportunity, affirmative action, fair labor standards, occupational safety and health, family and medical leave, and pension plans. Often, broad and simple rules can be set so that the rules' boundaries keep employees within legal limits. And in some cases, to reduce vulnerability to litigation, organizations may choose to supplement employee-defined personalization practices rather than replace them outright; for example, you may be able to avoid some issues by supplementing HR-defined performance appraisals (even if they are tailored by segment or through providing employees with modular choices) with the employee-defined personalization practice of frequent, informal feedback.

How Do We Manage Employee Needs for Privacy?

Just as companies create more relevant, customized products by collecting and analyzing a vast amount of rich consumer information, so too can companies craft more relevant and customized people practices by gathering and analyzing a range of employee information. For example, customized people practices have been created by some organizations based on scanning employee e-mail and communications (to determine bottom-up job definitions or to create expert profiling systems); collecting information on employees' health; monitoring where employees do their work (to determine their mobility profile); and looking into employees' family structure or personal value systems. All of these actions, of course, are subject to privacy laws and might give rise to privacy concerns on the part of employees or fear that they work for an Orwellian Big Brother organization. But whereas organizations in Orwell's book *1984* collected information about individuals for surveillance purposes—in order to control them in a highly totalitarian way—the collection of information for workforce of one purposes is done for nearly the opposite purpose: to liberate individuals from the constraints of ill-fitting, one-size-fits-all people practices and thereby help them flourish with highly tailored ones instead.[10]

However, questions of ethics and the limits of what companies should know about their employees are bound to crop up as companies increasingly use employee data to create more customized work experiences. Most people, of course, still expect their privacy to be respected—and feel that there are things that they absolutely consider private and would never want their organization to know. Even so, once employees understand how the collection of personal information will benefit them, and once they understand exactly what information is collected and how the information will be used and protected, employees may feel more comfortable sharing information to help their organizations help them.

Employees may also feel more comfortable sharing information if they know doing so may help their company. A solid business case can be used to help employees understand the reasons behind a company's data collection efforts. Harrah's Entertainment, for instance, justifies observing and measuring the extent to which its employees demonstrate a positive, upbeat attitude, because this behavior has been clearly linked to important revenue-driving results like customer perception of wait time.[11]

The following are some practical steps which can be considered when contemplating the collection of personal data (but they are not a guarantee of legal compliance). Any collection of data, of course, will need to be in compliance with any applicable data privacy laws. When considering these practical steps and other examples of data gathering that are referred to in this book, employers will need to ensure that their data gathering practices are in compliance with the law.

- Ensure that employee data is kept confidential—such as limiting the number of HR and other personnel who have access to such data; encrypting information; creating processes to screen for and report any security breaches; integrating IT, HR, and risk/crisis management programs; and creating a formal, written data protection policy covering HR data that is given to all staff handling employee information.

- Aggregate data collected or take advantage of technology that makes individual data anonymous.

- Analyze employee e-mail and other communications if employees grant permission to do so first.

- Educate managers and employees on the importance of employee data privacy.

- Provide a place for employees to air questions or complaints—since some data on an employee might be inaccurately interpreted by the employer.

- Give employees rights to access and correct data concerning themselves.

- Limit the amount of time you keep employee data.

- Make sure your employee data is verified and accurate.

In today's information age, information sharing can go both ways. Although companies may be increasingly collecting and analyzing employee data, the same is now true on the other side of the coin. Employees increasingly know everything about their company and their workplace practices—even things once sacrosanct (for example, members of Generation Y now think nothing of knowing one another's specific salaries).

And although there are obvious risks and dangers associated with employee data collection and analysis, it is important to remember that there is a tremendous upside as well. We can see the analogy in the consumer sphere, where analysis of consumer purchasing history has enabled the benefit of enabling companies to make suggestions as to products which viewers may wish to order. In much the same way, data collection and analysis can benefit employees. Companies, for example, provided that they comply with all applicable data privacy and other laws, can now offer employees relevant modular choices based on choices they've made and others have made who are like them. This is the positive side of employee data collection and analysis; and one that shouldn't be underestimated in terms of the value it can provide employees.

How Do We Maintain Control?

Since the time of sociologist Max Weber, control has been a central concept in organizational theory, and it is perhaps the key issue permeating our experiences of organizational life.[12] The advantage of a workforce of one approach to people management is that it does not require an organization to give up complete control in exchange for highly relevant, customized people practices. Yet it also doesn't require workers to subjugate their individual needs and desires to the collective will of the organization.

Segmentation and modular choice naturally afford high degrees of control, since the exact details of a people practice are still centrally defined. But both the broad and simple rules approach and employee-defined personalization offer organizations considerably less control. With those two approaches, individual managers or employees determine exactly how a people practice is customized, sometimes leaving HR executives and company leaders with little idea of whether talent management practices are being customized appropriately.

Workforce of one pioneers that extensively use broad and simple rules and employee-defined personalization approaches, therefore, have mastered a wide variety of control mechanisms and safeguards, as follows:

Instill guiding values, and hire people who already have them. Men's Wearhouse and Best Buy both cite the importance of instilling guiding values and hiring people who have them as key in helping employees make appropriate customization decisions. Explains Best Buy's Joe Kalkman, "When you deemphasize control and hierarchy, and command and control as we do—and when you believe that value can be created anywhere in the organization—that is a massively destabilizing approach to a hierarchy. So you have to have some sort of core and gravitational center that holds things in orbit when you peel away the traditional forms of control."[13] Best Buy relies on four core values (respect/humility/integrity; having fun while being the best; learning from challenge and change; and unleashing the power of people) to create that gravitational pull—and reduce the risks around employee flexibility in defining their own people practices. Not only does Best Buy constantly communicate these values (employees wear them on their badges, for example); employees also know that behaving consistently with these values is worth 20 percent of a score used to calculate merit increases, and 50 percent of a score used to calculate long-term incentives.

Provide supportive information, guidelines, examples, and incentives. Many of our workforce of one pioneers have found that if provided with enough information, people will naturally make the most appropriate customization decisions. This may include clearly communicating the boundaries of a broad and simple rule and providing guidelines, suggestions, and examples for how to appropriately interpret it. The same can be done for employee-defined personalization practices; IBM helps employees appropriately use new media like blogs or Second

Life by creating guidelines and policies (in both a bottom-up and a top-down fashion) regarding how to use such media.[14] When Best Buy created a competition for best video to promote retirement savings, it simultaneously provided guidelines, examples, and rewards to reinforce how to appropriately use peer-to-peer learning experiences. Explains Best Buy's Kalkman, "We reinforce appropriate behavior and reward it at every opportunity, constantly talking about it and holding people up who are good examples. It pays to be repetitive." And if a practice is frequently customized in intentionally inappropriate ways, companies like W. L. Gore adopt the same disciplinary and dismissal procedures as any other company.[15]

Educate and coach. Not only can organizations provide education regarding how to appropriately customize people practices, but they can also coach people when they encounter real customization situations. We talked to one manager, for example, who was trying to figure out how to pay someone within a broad-based pay scheme. After consulting an HR professional, he decided to pay an MBA candidate 30 percent more than was typical, because he'd received more education than others in his position. Men's Wearhouse spends a great deal of time coaching on such issues so that eventually employees feel comfortable making judgments on their own. To institutionalize such coaching, a company may redefine the role of its HR business partners as focused more on coaching and assisting line managers and employees, not just division heads, as is typical in most organizations today. Coaches may also be designated for specific practices; a company may appoint culture ambassadors and collaboration coaches to ensure that employees are sharing business-relevant knowledge and to help facilitate learning when using employee-defined learning vehicles like blogs or knowledge management systems. And coaches need not be HR professionals—Corning, for example, deliberately and strategically places superior people managers in specific places in the organization to model and teach effective people-management practices.[16]

Use peer monitoring. Many of our workforce of one pioneers rely on peers to monitor one another to ensure appropriate customization. Says Men's Wearhouse's Charlie Bresler, "We encourage observation at every level; the area managers look at the regional and district managers, and these managers look at employees and their peers. We coach the managers, and they coach each other about how to appropriately handle so much discretion."[17] The result? HR does very little monitoring. "Our people are much more effective at this than we ever would be trying to do it alone," Bresler says. Likewise, at Google and 3M, for example, peers and managers know what others are working on during their customization time, and peers or experts on blogs can monitor one another to ensure that the content is accurate and business relevant.[18]

Use HR-led analytics. HR can also use analytics to monitor practices to ensure control and quality assurance. For some practices, data may be captured, rolled up, and checked for outlying exceptions regarding exactly how a practice is customized. For example, when using a broad and simple rules approach, HR can capture individualized performance goals or which rewards managers are granting. What's more, new tracking technologies can monitor certain experience-based or peer-to-peer learning events for content and frequency. Other practices, like defining work by results instead of time using broad and simple rules, may be more difficult to monitor; Best Buy doesn't know exactly how many hours each corporate exempt employee works and where, for example (but neither does the company feel the need to know this information). For practices that allow less visibility into exactly how employees are customizing them across the organization, executives may want to rely on alternative ways to gain transparency: periodic spot checks or audits, employee surveys, exit interview data, management feedback, and using HR or senior leaders to take the pulse of the organization.

Institute approval or checking processes. Yahoo! doesn't allow people to create customized job titles without management approval, and at many companies, reviewers see postings for blogs before they go online.[19] Although perhaps it is far-fetched, we can even imagine a day when companies will support employees with increased discretion by using technology like the one Partners HealthCare has developed. The software allows doctors to make decisions by first checking to see whether they are consistent with medical best practice.[20] Such decision-support technology could conceivably be developed to provide a check on customized people practice decisions, alerting people to when a choice may be inappropriate, while also providing decision-logic guidelines and supporting information to help people make more informed choices.

Rely on filters and disclaimers. For companies worried about employees using inappropriate or derogatory material on peer-to-peer learning vehicles like blogs, there's a simple solution: use a filter to screen it out. And if you are worried about using employees as recruiters—and what they might say about the company on blogs viewed by potential job candidates—you can use disclaimers clearly stating that the views expressed are the bloggers' alone and do not necessarily represent the views of the company.

Limit certain activities to certain people. Although undermining some of the democratic potential of certain customization initiatives, an organization could also restrict some activities to only some people. Allowing only the organization's experts, for example, to post learning content on blogs could ensure that peer-provided content is accurate and trustworthy. Restricting coaching to those certified as coaches can help ensure that coaching is performed well and appropriately. Creating private, company versions of social networking sites that perform Facebook-like functions or private islands on Second Life can guard against security risks. Google uses an invitation-only social network restricted to only the elite from top schools and organizations for hiring purposes, and it provides job customization opportunities only to its engineers and managers.[21] Likewise, some companies we've studied are considering restricting employee-defined referrals to top performers—based on evidence of a strong correlation between the quality of the referring employee and that of the referral.[22]

How Do We Ensure That Employee Needs Align with Strategy?

Although workforce of one is about aligning workplace practices with the needs of individuals, clearly companies must also align these with their business's needs and strategy if they hope to achieve superior business performance. For a few companies, like Best Buy, the choice of which customization approaches to favor is deeply informed by the company's overall strategic philosophy. But our experience is that for most companies, reasons other than strategy (such as culture) inform these choices, since any of the four customization approaches can generally support and be aligned with any given strategy—and likewise can produce superior business results.

Take rewards, for example. All four workforce of one customization approaches allow variation in *how* people get rewarded (e.g., a bonus versus extra vacation days), albeit in different ways depending on the particular customization approach used. *What* employees are rewarded for, however, should always be aligned with strategy—and can be accomplished no matter what approach an organization uses. Or take learning. *How* employees learn (e.g., through listening or reading, a podcast or a lecture) has nothing to do with strategy and can be easily varied by using any of the four approaches to suit the individual's needs. *What* employees learn, however, should align with the strategy—and employees' needs and preferences as well, whenever possible.[23] By always aligning the *what* of any people practice with strategy, then, companies can rest assured when it comes to meeting the business's critical needs.

How Many Variations Can Our Organization Reasonably Handle?

Both segmentation and modular choice dramatically increase the variety of people practices that are centrally spelled out at the detailed level. So just how many variations can an organization reasonably expect to administer without devolving into so much complexity that it becomes an administrative nightmare?

This is a tricky balance to achieve, but a very important one. As Amartya Sen, the Nobel Prize winner in economics, pointed out, we want to avoid the danger of "singularization," or the "odd presumption that the people of this world can be uniquely categorized according to some singular and overarching system of partitioning of the world population . . . [this] yields a 'solarist' approach to human identity, which sees human beings as members of exactly one group."[24] The reality is that we all belong to multiple groups, both in the workplace and in our personal lives. Take Helen, for example, whom we introduced in chapter 1. We could categorize her as an American, a woman, a mother, an information systems professional, a member of the baby boomer generation, someone who learns best from reading and solitude—the list could go on. But the point is that no one category can truly capture who she is. Likewise, we need many segments or options to reflect our own evolving needs and preferences.

But since offering multiple variations can often (but not always, depending on the practice) be costly or confusing, it is important to offer the most germane, relevant, and important ones, selectively and thoughtfully choosing the right segments and choices to offer. Just as when P&G reduced the number of versions of their Head & Shoulders shampoo from twenty-six to fifteen—and then experienced an increase in sales of 10 percent (not to mention a reduction in the costs associated with the complexity of manufacturing and marketing such a variety!)—it pays to think about how granular you should go.[25] What is the value of increasing levels of granularity, relative to the cost and administrative implications for managing it? Too many segmentation schemes, or too many choices in a given area, may result in a point of diminishing returns—or at least employee confusion.

That said, we've seen how many organizations can manageably segment in a dozen or more different ways, typically using a handful of divisions per segmentation scheme (e.g., three performance-based segmentation categories or five generational categories). Technological advances have even made it possible to handle a greater number of divisional categories, even creating "segments of one"—for example, uniquely tailoring communications to potential job candidates using candidate relationship databases. And, if it is done carefully, by using sophisticated modeling technologies to support myriad modular choice options, for example, too many variations need not overwhelm individuals at all.

Offering multiple variations only becomes a problem when doing so sacrifices benefits achieved from economies of scale, or if it touches the core HR infrastructure and computer systems. It may be quite easy to offer more variations regarding place of work or recruiting programs, for example, but harder when offering variations in compensation, benefits, or performance management systems that touch core HR systems. Most enterprise systems are now flexible enough to allow configuration based on certain rules. For example, they can be configured to reflect segments or sets of choices, especially for common choices like geography or workforce; alternatively, organizations sometimes choose to use separate systems for separate segments to allow greater flexibility. Of course, integrating data from separate systems can be a challenge too.

Fortunately, every day technology is improving how well companies handle variations, fundamentally changing the equation that determines the cost and ease of supporting variation. First, as more companies start to offer more variations, software providers will build this into their software (much as they already have built in segmentation by common schemes like geography and workforce). Second, the talent management software industry is moving toward supporting more variability and complexity off of a common platform. In fact, we expect it to become increasingly easy to configure systems in any number of ways by easily adding or subtracting segments or choices, or expanding or contracting the parameters of a broad and simple rule. Third, the advent of service-oriented architecture will enable organizations to easily and seamlessly knit together data from separate computer systems that can be individually tailored for certain segments or domains of modular choice—thereby making variations easier to offer or change and much less costly to support.

Can We Outsource HR and Still Manage a Workforce of One?

Traditionally, standardized people practices are what made outsourcing HR a valuable option. The idea was that by handing over HR systems and processes to an outside provider, service improved and costs went down because of the economies of scale created by leveraging standard, commonly agreed-upon "best-practice processes" across multiple companies. But workforce of one is all about customization; how, then, do we reconcile the two?

Interestingly, outsourcing can actually greatly assist an organization in managing its workforce as a workforce of one. Many of our "pioneer" companies, like Best Buy and P&G, have successfully customized people practices for employees while outsourcing a significant portion of their HR functions. How? First, while the outsourcer still establishes a common standard platform (e.g., using a common learning management system or a talent skills database), most outsourcers can vary it significantly on the front end (e.g., populating the learning management system with specific learning choices, or configuring the talent skills database to collect data on different employee dimensions). Second, many commonly outsourced practices are back-office transactional processes like payroll or retirement plan administration. Outsourcing these processes can not only free HR up to customize front-end processes that employees really care about, but these processes rarely need customization in the first place to provide value.

Most important, for many workforce of one practices—such as offering a variety of modular choices of benefits or rewards—outsourcing may be the only viable way of reliably and cost-efficiently managing such complexity. The key is that the same processes and set of options are offered across the board to many companies, thereby allowing the outsourcer to manage such variations efficiently by taking advantage of the cost benefits that are achieved through economies of scale. Often, outsourcers and companies will cocreate a new workforce of one practice; once the infrastructure is built, the outsourcer can then take the practice to other clients. As more companies adopt more nuanced and customized people practices, not only may they get baked into talent management software, but they may get baked into outsourcing provider offerings as well, making customization an increasingly affordable and manageable proposition. All of this means that we expect outsourcing providers to take on an increasingly important role in helping organizations customize people practices. After all, many outsourcers are already moving beyond standardized back-office processes toward providing highly strategic talent management offerings that enable customization.

How Do We Build a Business Case for Customization?

Any workforce of one initiative should comprise a compelling business case. Company leaders will want to know, "Why should I care?" As we've seen in examples throughout this book, executives care because businesses thrive when they provide customized people practices that attract and retain talented, committed people who work at their full potential. Workforce of one pioneers like P&G, Best Buy, Microsoft, Google, and others are at the top of their game, often leading their industries in terms of business results.

But you may ask, Isn't it prohibitively expensive to provide customized people practices? Depending on the customization approaches used, yes, there are often some costs involved—related to things such as developing analytic capabilities, education and change management, administration, or systems costs. But for the companies we've profiled, the costs haven't been prohibitive by any means. First, some workforce of one initiatives need not be expensive at all; encouraging consistent and frequent informal feedback or personalized coaching among peers needn't cost anything, for example. And some can be even less expensive than narrowly defined one-size-fits-all practices, such as providing peer-to-peer learning options alongside or in place of classroom learning options.

Second, any costs will often pay for themselves as customization enables companies to cut ineffective workforce spending. Although companies may sometimes sacrifice some of the efficiencies that can be achieved when offering one standard solution, companies have found that even varied solutions (such as Best Buy's long-term incentives plan) can be as cost-effective as, or even more than, a universal program with lower participation.[26] Why waste resources on giving people something they do not want and that won't help them perform at their best? Providing work space to people who don't need it isn't cost effective, nor is spending a great deal of money on mass recruiting when you could produce only a few tailored messages. Likewise, although offering a variety of benefit choices may cost more to administer, it may ultimately result in a much lower total cost to serve employees: you aren't paying for unappreciated benefits that won't be used by the entire workforce.

Third, customized offerings often cost far less than the value people place on them. You get "more bang for the buck" when offering tailored rewards, for instance, since employees perceive the value of some rewards as higher than their cash value. Companies like Royal Bank of Scotland have found that even though they offer a variety of benefits, they can still purchase these less expensively than employees could because of the company's size and the economies of scale they achieve. Some studies even suggest that having highly relevant people practices that employees value can enable organizations to slash one of their biggest costs—payroll—by as much as 10 percent based on the perceived value of the practices alone.[27] Universities, for example, are notorious for paying low salaries, yet they can still hire bright young professionals because they can offer more customized jobs and work hours—which cost far less than paying higher salaries.

Last and most important, the rewards of customization for both employee and employer usually far outweigh the costs. A simple 1 percent increase in productivity, for example, typically produces more than ten times the impact of a 1 percent decrease in training costs.[28]

To create a business case, then, HR leaders should show with clear, hard facts, and in business language, the value that a workforce of one will create. For example, you can use pilot or early customization initiatives to track both workforce and business results (see table 7-1 for types of metrics to track), and you can offer "before" and "after" scenarios and analysis revealing correlations between the initiative and results. Best Buy and Royal Bank of Scotland, for example, help justify their customization efforts by showing how they reduce turnover and therefore significantly reduce costs; replacing an employee can cost one to two times an original employee's salary, not to mention associated additional training and development costs and lost productivity. Companies may also track employee commitment or the ability to hire better talent, for example; some studies suggest that by effectively managing the "employment value proposition," a company can increase its pool of potential workers by 20 percent and the commitment of its employees fourfold.[29] Based on these results, HR can tout success stories to build commitment and buy-in to roll the customization initiatives out more broadly. Best Buy, for example, works to convince skeptical managers by showing them the negative assessments of their departments, and how using broad and simple rules, like its Results-Only Work Environment, can change them. The best evidence? How other

TABLE 7-1

Building a business case for customization

Workforce metrics	Business results metrics
• Attracting talented and skilled employees	• Customer satisfaction
• Employee retention/reduced costs associated with employee turnover	• Customer retention
• Employee productivity (revenue per employee)	• Innovation (e.g., number of new products, speed to market of new products)
• Employee motivation	• Margin/profitability
• Employee absenteeism	• Performance of critical business processes
• Employee engagement/satisfaction	• Revenue/sales pipeline
• Employee proficiency	• Quality
• Time to proficiency (how quickly an employee learns job-related skills)	• Total return to shareholders
• Workforce performance (as measured by job-specific performance indicators)	• Market share

company skeptics are now their biggest supporters after achieving significantly better results from the change.

To lay the groundwork for a business case, HR leaders can also answer how the six key trends laid out in this book are specifically changing their company's business; for example: How scarce is critical talent for my organization? How have the demographics of my workforce changed? How important is the performance of our people to the success of my organization? Ultimately, the cost of inaction may be far greater than the cost of action: losing highly valued employees or getting weak performances from them is a far scarier proposition than making the kinds of changes needed to offer people relevant, tailored employment experiences that will help them and the organization perform to their potential.

How Do We Support the Cultural Change Needed?

Enjoying customized work experiences is a substantial change for most employees, often requiring that they learn new behaviors and take on new responsibilities. This is especially true when customizing using the broad and simple rules and employee-defined personalization customization approaches. Likewise, administering variety and flexible people practices that bend to suit individual needs—rather than simply administering cookie-cutter practices for efficiency's sake—will likewise require HR professionals and even functional leaders to change their behaviors and skills. For most organizations, this has required some form of change management to help people shift to a new way of relating to their organizations.

Most successful change programs supporting workforce of one aren't the traditional change management strategies that force change from the center. Rather, change is supported from the center but embedded locally and tailored to the specific needs of individuals. Any communication strategies, reporting structures, or rewards that encourage new behaviors must take into account the often different presumptions and norms of the company's various organizational groups, nationalities, seniority levels, and other factors. Ultimately, the most important job of whoever is charged with transitioning an organization to a customized talent management approach is to help others understand its value; only then will people have the motivation and desire to adopt new skills and behaviors.

How Do We Maintain Company Unity While Focusing on Individuals?

If nothing else, traditional one-size-fits-all people practices have at least helped to band people together and brand them as fellow citizens of one organization. So what happens when people practices vary from person to person? That's when other kinds of organizational "glue" are needed to create a unified culture and ensure that the company doesn't become fragmented. Here are some tips from organizations in our study on how to achieve this:

Build strong, common organizational values, mission, and goals. Although work experiences will vary, broader organizational objectives and values can help unite employees in a common purpose and culture.

Build community. By building a strong sense of community, companies can make their cultures more salient than any differing work experience an employee may have. For example, the HR department at Men's Wearhouse spends a large part of its budget on activities to enhance community and create a sense of belonging in the organization—from potlucks at managers' homes to corporate meetings that are viewed more as culture-building than as skill-building events. Organizations may also build virtual communities through forums like Second Life.

Use diversity itself and the unique ways your organization accommodates diversity as a common unifier. By touting the fact that your company offers customized work experiences in unique and differentiated ways, a workforce of one can become a unifying experience of inclusion. Microsoft did this, for example, by branding its ability to offer customized experiences as myMicrosoft.

Align customized practices with the organization's brand and values whenever possible. For many workforce of one practices, an organization can link the practice with its brand identity, thereby reinforcing the company's brand, core values, and culture. Royal Bank of Scotland's flexible benefits scheme, RBSelect, for example, reinforces its brand name while communicating the value of the company in offering employees choice. The content of some practices can even reflect the company's business and values—P&G's Beauty business offers reward choices including its own products or related experiences (like a trip to the beauty salon), for example, and outdoor gear–provider REI offers environmental-service opportunities as a way for employees to customize their work activities.[30]

Emphasize the universals that are common across the variations. Organizations can also bring workers together by emphasizing commonalities, such as the desire for fulfilling work experiences. Accenture, for example, has done a significant amount of work communicating

FIGURE 7-2

Accenture's career experience: A unified variety of employee value propositions

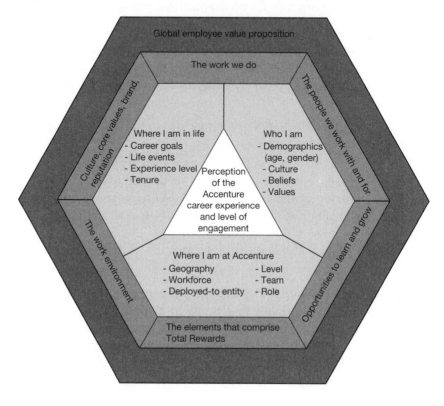

the common career experience that spans people's experiences across six people practice domains: type of work, type of people, types of learning and development opportunities, types of rewards, type of work environment, and types of values and culture. It calls its model the Accenture Career Experience (see figure 7-2). An employee's experience in each of these domains will vary based on, for example, her life stage or experience level, how old she is, her location, and what role she plays at Accenture. But across each domain, the company has clearly communicated the universal experience for all in a single set of global employee value propositions. For example, it identifies the universal value proposition related to work environment as, "Leverage a global network of exceptional resources—people, knowledge and tools—across

Managing the Workforce of One: Challenges and Solutions

Challenge	Solution
Fairness	Emphasize justice rather than sameness.
Privacy	Collect only information you plan to use, build a business case for collecting it, and consider collecting data only when you receive employee permission to do so.
Control	Use guiding values, supportive information and coaching, and monitoring and approval processes to ensure appropriate customization.
Alignment of practices with business strategy	Always align the *what* (or *content*) of the people practice with strategy (and if possible, also with the individual); how the people practice is performed can usually be aligned with the individual without reference to strategy.
Administration of variation	Strike a balance between variety and complexity by offering only the most germane options or segmentation schemes, and building the infrastructure to support variety.
Outsourcing	Use outsourcing to build a common HR platform to support customization initiatives, free up time to pursue customization, and administrate variety.
Building a business case	Track and communicate the workforce and business benefits of customization initiatives, which usually far outweigh the costs.
Change	Support change initiatives centrally, but tailor them locally. Inspire employees to change by clearly articulating the benefits of customization for them and their organizations.
Unity	Unite employees with shared organizational purpose and community. Also, create shared meanings of difference, emphasize the universals across the variations, and align customization practices with the organization's brand and values.

Accenture's diverse businesses. Work in an inclusive, dynamic, and professional environment that values each person's perspective." For employees in the consulting segment of its workforce, this will mean working in a variety of locations, but for employees in its outsourcing business, this will mean working in one primary location. Regardless of the workforce segment or location, Accenture fosters a team-focused environment. Defining such common experiences will unite people and create a single brand proposition for all.

We've seen in this chapter that administering customized people practices needn't be a difficult, overwhelming, or costly proposition. It merely requires organizations to rise to a higher and more sophisticated level of functioning, which may mean some growing pains at first. (See "Managing the Workforce of One: Challenges and Solutions.") But the effort will be well worth it, not only for employees who will have more positive work experiences, but also for companies—which will likely see the benefits of improved workforce performance directly affect the bottom line.

Let's turn now to how you as an HR professional can get started managing your workforce as a workforce of one. We'll look at the specific skills and capabilities you'll need to develop, and we'll lay out an action plan to get you started on your journey.

8

A Call to Action for HR

Building Your Workforce of One Capability

> *We need to break the mind-set in the field of HR that there is a single path or solution. By finding the intersection of what is important to an individual and what a company needs through a customized approach to talent management, companies will begin to reap greater levels of business success and employee engagement than ever before.*[1]

—Keith Lawrence, director, P&G Beauty Human Resources

W E THINK OF MANAGING a workforce as a workforce of one as no less than revolutionary—an approach to talent management that is fundamentally different from business as usual. When people practices are no longer generic, one-size-fits-all practices merely reflecting the lowest common denominator, but rather become highly relevant, nuanced, and granular to reflect the diverse needs of every individual, an altogether new relationship emerges between an organization and its people. The notion of managing "human resources" fundamentally transforms.

No longer is human resources something that a company "does" for its employees through delegation to a centralized HR group. Rather, no matter which approach you use, it becomes an individualized, close-to-the-action responsibility of every person in the organization. For an organization managing its workforce as a workforce of one, people management becomes everybody's job. No longer a specialized, stand-alone function, people management becomes a broad corporate competency in which HR and the line work together to customize practices to benefit not only the organization as a whole but also every individual. We view this as the next stage in managing an organization's people for optimal performance, and one that follows the developmental stages of other important breakthroughs in management.

With quality improvement, for example, organizations progressed from centralized inspection to zero defect to Six Sigma, which makes quality improvement part of everyone's job. Likewise, with information management, organizations progressed from centralized data collection to data warehousing to business analytics; today information management is part of many managers' jobs. Just as information management, quality improvement, and other fields such as financial management and customer relationship management have become integrated throughout the organization, so is it time now for such integration of human resource management through a workforce of one approach.

Explains Debra Hunter Johnson, former vice president of human resources at American Airlines from July 2003 to January 2007 and currently director of law and human resources, Reciprocity Restaurant Group, "Over time, as human capital management became a centralized specialization under the domain of HR, we started taking away some of managers' people management responsibilities so that they could 'focus on the business' . . . It is time we give people management back to managers, where the biggest performance improvements can be made through a more customized and personalized approach."[2]

Fortunately, there's real evidence that such a shift is indeed occurring. Organizations are increasingly taking talent management activities traditionally performed by HR and turning them over to line management.[3] As the need for a more flexible and tailored approach to talent management grows, we predict this trend will continue.

Ironically, in order to support a more integrated talent management model, HR will need to step up to take a more active and prominent role than ever. When employees take on more responsibility for talent management, it might seem like a foregone conclusion that HR could then take on less responsibility for talent management—by adopting a more laissez-faire, hands-off approach that relegates to employees the responsibility for developing and maximizing their own performance. Yet nothing could be further from the truth: organizations will, in fact, need to take a hands-on, highly supportive stance to ensure that people practices are customized in the most optimal fashion for both the employee and the business. HR, as the group responsible for people, is best positioned to do this. But to take on this role, HR will require a new mandate—as well as a whole host of new skills and capabilities and perhaps even an entirely new structure—than has been traditionally assigned it.

A New Mandate for HR

For nearly seventy years, HR has acted almost exactly opposite from a workforce of one approach. As the primary setter and enforcer of narrow, one-size-fits-all rules, it had a mandate to maintain strict control over the workforce; deliver low-cost, easy-to-manage administrative HR services; and ensure fairness (and avoid lawsuits) through equal treatment.[4] One human resources executive told us, "Formalization and standardization of people policies and practices is really done more for HR than for employees. I'd guess 40 percent of HR's inflexibility is necessary because of legal constraints, risk mitigation, and the need for senior executives to have a consistent view of their talent. But the other 60 percent is probably due to the simple fact that it makes HR's job easier." Standardization, uniformity, and rote solutions may be easier to manage, but they do not make sense when workforces are increasingly diverse and complex, and when organizations must compete on attracting and retaining superior talent that performs at its best.

HR professionals, therefore, need to adopt a whole new approach. Instead of focusing on efficiently delivering administrative HR services, HR must shift to focus on capitalizing on people's differences to provide the best talent management solutions for each employee—thereby contributing to stellar results for the bottom line. HR will thus become a truly *strategic* function integral to the way the company competes. At Best Buy, for example, HR is no longer just an administrative support function—rather, it is fully focused on strategic differentiation and transformational company change to its customer-centricity model. Two of HR's major mandates at Best Buy? One, to recognize the unique talents of each employee, and to deploy those talents in a manner that maximizes the employee's energy to drive business outcomes. And two, to reengineer the talent system, and develop other HR capabilities, for personalization rather than for sameness. As we've seen from Best Buy and other case examples, control and fairness can still be achieved—albeit in more sophisticated ways than the "blunt hammer" approach of sameness.

Aspects of HR's new mandate might sound familiar. Many HR organizations have successfully transformed from being primarily a transactional, administrative function to becoming what is now commonly known as a *strategic business partner*. (HR has accomplished this largely by moving administrative functions to outsourcing providers.) Yet what we are talking about moves well beyond the common conception of what it means to be a strategic business partner. A workforce of one approach requires that HR adopt the role of employee performance improver—something that few HR organizations, even ones that define themselves as strategic business partners, have yet to adopt, according to research studies.[5] For most HR professionals, the process of *transformation*, as the process of becoming a strategic business partner is commonly called, has meant redefining the definition of the HR "customer" from the traditional focus on the employee to an almost exclusive focus on the management ranks, with the goal of furthering strategic business initiatives. Although focusing on such strategic initiatives is an important and laudable achievement for HR, to really achieve the kind of business benefits that can ensue from customized people practices, HR needs to broaden its definition of its customer—namely, to once again include the *employee*. But this will be in a much deeper way than past mandates to merely address employee grievances or protect their rights. Being there for employees and improving their performance may be the ultimate way of serving the needs of the CEO and senior managers: as employee performance improves, so will business results. As Julian Atkins, head of HR at Coventry Building Society, explains, "HR shouldn't just be about facing the CEO; it should be about facing the employees."[6]

All of this may well result in human resources functions looking more and more like marketing functions. Just as marketing exists to serve customers with highly relevant offerings that ultimately create value for the business, workforce of one HR organizations will exist to fundamentally understand and serve employees with highly relevant offerings that will improve their engagement, motivation, retention, and performance. Already, we're seeing this move in many of our workforce of one pioneers. We believe it is no coincidence, for instance, that Microsoft's head of HR, Lisa Brummel, was once one of Microsoft's highly valued product managers; that Charlie Bresler, Men's Wearhouse's head of HR (called "human relations" at the company), is also head of marketing; or that Royal Bank of Scotland's HR leader Neil Roden once worked in sales and marketing. Sometimes, whole HR functions are moved to or blended with marketing—such as how The Container Store moved employee recruiting to its marketing department.[7] Other times, marketing staff are borrowed or permanently moved to the human resources function: Royal Bank of Scotland, Best Buy, and P&G's Beauty business have all recruited marketing experts to help them develop the kind of insights into employees that marketers have traditionally developed for customers.

Given HR's increasing similarity to marketing, it should come as no surprise that HR professionals will need to develop a raft of new skills and capabilities.

New Skills and Capabilities to Manage the Workforce of One

Although the particular skills HR will need may vary somewhat, depending on which customization approaches an organization favors, we will explore here some universal skills and capabilities on which HR managers can rely regardless of the approach emphasized.

Specifically, HR professionals will need to develop the kind of insights marketers use to create business results, market and brand the organization's customization initiatives, and actively support individuals in their customization efforts. They will also need to adopt the process of "cocreation" that many marketing and product development departments now pursue with their customers. And they will have to become just as adept at using technology to support customization as marketing professionals have become. Finally, they will need to work toward finding new ways to unite employees when they have more varied employment experiences than ever before.

Developer of Insights into Employees—and Translator of Insights into Results

The most important new skill HR can develop is the art and science of insight into its people: understanding how the needs, preferences, and activities that drive performance potential vary among types of individuals in the organization. Traditionally, HR's approach has been more "product-out" than "consumer-in." That is, conclusions about how to deliver offerings are made without the benefit of insight from consumers—the employees. In marketing departments, consumer insight is critical. So too should it be with human resource departments, with every employee interaction being used as an opportunity to listen and understand.

At P&G, for example, HR strives to understand employees inside and out by relying on a variety of marketing concepts such as focus groups, surveys, blogs, data analysis and analytics, and other approaches to determine what is meaningful and relevant for its employees. As a result, the company has an extensive talent database, with information related to employee's interests, experiences in the company, training, languages, geographic preferences, and strengths—all on top of more common demographic and employee data such as tenure, compensation history, gender, ethnicity, and level.

Keith Lawrence, director, P&G Beauty human resources, explains, "We make it a top priority to know our employees. Not only do we have extensive data for each individual (just like for the consumers we serve) but we also expect our HR team to understand and experience the daily lives of our employees—just as we expect our marketing experts to deeply appreciate the daily lives of consumers. We expect HR staff to immerse themselves in the business. They take temporary assignments working in an operating plant, go on sales calls, visit the stores, and use shopping trips to the store to understand our products and how well they meet the needs of our consumers."

How to Really Know Your Employees

If knowing your employees is the very foundation for providing a customized experience for them, how do you do it? First, HR professionals should strive to collect information beyond the typical demographic or skill set variables—to include a deep understanding of personality traits, behaviors, cultural differences, values, and aspirations. Just as marketers care more about customer *behavior* and *values* than demographic variables such as whether the customer is a man or a woman, for example, so too should human resources professionals. Second, just as marketers care about the "whole customer" and how the company's product might be used in a person's everyday life, so too should HR strive to know the "whole employee" by looking at him outside of his company role. HR can then better tailor people practices—including work-life practices, benefits, or jobs that may harness hidden strengths and interests. (Of course, any gathering of data will need to be carried out in accordance with local applicable data privacy and employment laws.)

To this end, HR can apply a variety of consumer research techniques. Many companies find it helpful to use some methods concurrently, using "soft" data, like one-on-one interviews, to create a rich, deep understanding to support more "hard" data, such as surveys. Techniques include:

- Surveys and polls
- Employee focus groups

One of the most important ways P&G gets to know employees is to test hypotheses regarding employees to determine what works best. For example, after testing the use of iPods to improve information sharing within part of the Beauty business, it was discovered that members of Generation Y tended to use them more frequently than others. They leveraged this insight in designing future communication programs.

There are many ways of really getting to know employees (see "How to Really Know Your Employees"), from Microsoft's "listening tour" to blogs to more traditional survey techniques. When possible, information about employees should be documented, using information systems to create a rich and central repository of employee information to be mined to create optimal employee experiences. Of course, companies should always do so

- One-on-one interviews
- Entrance and exit interviews
- Use of technology or systems to track things like job mobility, life events (e.g., having a baby), or where employees are working
- Having employees and managers document information (e.g., their interests, aspirations, compensation and work histories, skills, strengths, and reward preferences)
- Ethnography and observations
- Blogs, wikis, discussion groups, and online panels (these can be read on your own or analyzed through using technology that extracts content summaries)
- Mock markets (see the section on cocreation in this chapter)
- Town halls
- External market research (e.g., to understand generational differences)
- Advisory boards
- Assessments (e.g., for strengths, existing knowledge, personality, or broader abilities)
- Input from HR business partners dedicated to serving business units

Since a workforce continuously evolves and changes, you will always need ongoing input from these sources to ensure that the organization fine-tunes its customization practices for relevance.

in a manner respectful to employees, and make sure to obey any privacy laws. But by relying on facts rather than faith, assumptions, or imitations of others, an organization is much more likely to achieve highly relevant people practices that most closely fit the needs and preferences of its own set of employees.

Once HR knows its employees inside and out, this knowledge can then be mined, analyzed, interpreted, and translated into action—for example, to create the most germane way to segment the workforce, to uncover workers' needs and preferences for use in creating a menu of choices, or to define the parameters of a broad and simple rule. Often, this means looking at the data from multiple angles—looking at how or whether different segments react differently to different rewards, for example. Statistical techniques often used in consumer research, like conjoint analysis, can also help an organization make sense of the data by allowing insights into the trade-offs people make when choosing among offerings.

The results of offering customized work experiences should then be tracked as well, by relying on before-and-after scenarios or on employee self-reports of improved performance or motivation, or by using statistical analysis to create correlations or causality between practices, workforce performance metrics, and business results. According to the results, HR can continually refine and adjust customized practices, creating a continual cycle of hypothesis, experimentation, measurement, and refinement to create optimal results. When significant data is collected, one could even begin to predict how a particular change may affect employee behavior *before* implementing the change—predicting, say, how a new incentive plan may affect a particular segment's productivity or engagement, or forecasting how offering one additional modular choice in benefits may impact turnover.

Although segmentation and modular choice approaches lend themselves most to an analytic, data-driven approach, even companies that rely more on employee-defined personalization and broad and simple rules for customization will need metrics and data analysis. These will not only reveal how the practices create business value, but will also enable an organization to effectively monitor the practices to ensure that employees are customizing appropriately. But most HR organizations will need to develop and learn an entirely new analytic capability to support a workforce of one approach. In our initial study of more than sixty organizations, for example, we learned that only 11 percent of organizations interviewed felt they did a good job of measuring their people practices to make informed decisions about their workforce.[8]

One common barrier to developing an analytic capability is the fact that many HR professionals today haven't needed analytic skills to do their jobs. To remedy this, in many workforce of one pioneers—such as Royal Bank of Scotland, Procter & Gamble, Intel, Tesco, and Capital One—whole groups are now solely responsible for analyzing employee data in increasingly sophisticated ways to gain insight toward creating customized, relevant people practices.[9] Lack of systems integration and consolidated data, data quality issues, and lack of easy data access are other common barriers. Technology such as data warehouses that integrate employee and business data from various sources can help support this capability, as can a user-friendly portal through which HR staff, leaders, and managers can access data and do their own analyses. Royal Bank of Scotland, for example, has a data warehouse that integrates data from thirty computer systems, and recently collaborated with the marketing and IT departments to develop a Human Capital Toolkit—an online system of measurements and resources that allow staff outside of the analytics group to easily collect data or make comparisons within the masses of accumulated data. The investment in resources for the tool and in its analytic capabilities has paid itself back many times over in improved business performance.

Marketer and Brander of Customized Work Offerings

Just as marketing professionals work to inform employees of customized experiences and products, so must HR professionals. Toot your own horn—especially if you offer highly unique or unusual customization opportunities for your employees relative to your competitors. Often, organizations are offering their people many customized work experiences, but fail to communicate them and their value both for employees and for the business as a whole. Microsoft brands its HR experience myMicrosoft; Deloitte & Touche LLP brands its customized career experience Mass Career Customization™. [10] Don't underestimate the power of branding and marketing customized people offerings; not only will it attract and retain talented employees, but it will likely improve employee performance as well. If people aren't aware that they can customize their jobs, they aren't likely to do so—and the business benefits that can ensue from capitalizing on someone's unique strengths won't follow.

We recommend calling on marketing experts, for example, to present your organization's unique approach to customization to both prospective and current employees, and to help translate it into what it means for them. One useful tool to market people practices, for example, is what's known as a *total rewards portfolio*, which presents all the broad benefits an employee can expect to achieve from working at a company—from learning and development opportunities, to health and retirement benefits, to rewards and compensation—in a single integrated package. This can be tremendously helpful when it comes to communicating and promoting a specific person's customization "package" and unique "employment deal."

Of course, the more innovative and valuable your customized employment offerings, the better off you are from a marketing standpoint. As Keith Lawrence explains, to remain an employer of choice, P&G must continually craft new and innovative customized offerings "that better meet the ever changing needs of our business and employees than other companies."

Supporter of Employee Customization Experiences

A workforce of one approach to talent management requires employees to take a more active role in fully, proactively, and responsibly participating in making customization decisions. As the people who know themselves—and their subordinates—best, frontline employees and managers are the only ones who can ensure that people practices truly fit them (or their employees). Just as frontline employees and managers have become more responsive to customers to improve customer satisfaction, frontline employees and managers must now take on more responsibility for ensuring that people practices are responsive to employees to improve both job satisfaction and performance. Indeed, the fact that managers are in the position to respond to the unique needs of their local environment is perhaps the most critical reason why so many studies—our own included—have found managers to be among the most important elements in improving employee productivity, performance, loyalty, and engagement.[11]

Managers may be instrumental, for example, in determining which employees or positions should be categorized into various workforce segments, or they may coach an employee about which modular learning-style option might work best for her. Likewise, they may be heavily involved in employee-defined personalization practices like providing coaching, informal feedback, and experience-based learning opportunities for their subordinates; testing potential new employees in real or simulated work environments; or discussing employees' personal strengths, weaknesses, and interests with other managers to identify new opportunities for their subordinates.

Likewise, employees may independently define their learning content when using an employee-defined personalization approach, or customize their jobs through interpreting a broad and simple rule. Or they might customize when and where they work by selecting the right modular choices for themselves, or else self-segment—as they might do by telling their company what life stage they're in so that HR can group them appropriately. Even if an employee is not able to customize a people practice directly, she can still often offer important input that will help the person making customization decisions, like telling her manager or HR representative about the kinds of rewards to which she responds best.

Of course, all of this depends on HR providing guidance, tools, and coaching to support employees and their managers in taking increased responsibility for customizing talent management practices. This is true whether they are self-segmenting, choosing from a menu of modular choices, interpreting a broad and simple rule, or completely defining their own people practices. Specifically, HR can provide support in two useful ways. First, it can help employees best participate in customization decisions by helping them thoroughly understand themselves and what will work best for them or for a particular subordinate. If someone doesn't know his strengths, interests, and passions, how can he truly customize his job? If he doesn't know how he learns best, how can he pick the best learning style option for himself? This is the very foundation of providing great customization—yet few people are consciously aware of their individual strengths or clear on their goals and purpose in life.

Fortunately, HR can provide tools to help people develop self-awareness. It can test for broad abilities or strengths, for example, or allow people to collect feedback from others to improve their self-awareness. At Accenture, a Personal Engagement List tool kit helps employees reflect on their personal professional priorities and the values that drive their engagement (e.g., determining what's most important to them—their actual work and development opportunities or the rewards and recognition they receive). Managers and career counselors then discuss the list with their subordinates and help them better tailor their people practices accordingly. Once people have a better idea of who they are, they can cultivate and communicate their own "brand" throughout the company, thereby helping others better tailor work experiences for them.

Second, clear communication and education about the organization's customization practices, how they support employees, and why employees will now have varying work experiences is a must. This will ensure both that people practices are customized appropriately and that the organization instills a strong sense of fairness. Some form of change management also may be needed, as well as plenty of examples of appropriate and inappropriate customization, what-if scenarios, and role models to follow. And if customization efforts ever go awry—say, if a manager makes an inappropriate salary decision, or if an individual uses peer-to-peer learning vehicles like blogs for nonbusiness purposes—then the HR group should defend employees against inappropriate measures or take action to ensure that inappropriate decisions are reversed.

HR must also help employees understand that they fully own each decision, and that they must take full responsibility for the outcomes and implications of their decisions. This is easier said than done. If one person decided to zigzag her way through an organization on a highly customized, horizontal career path, for example, and the consequence of this choice was that she did not develop highly specialized skills that are valued by the organization, she would need to accept this and not be jealous of someone who chose a different route. Although in a workforce of one, HR will administer people practices fairly, employees must now come to accept and even appreciate the fact that employment deals will vary.

Managers and HR professionals have an especially important role to play here in making sure employees understand the consequences of their actions, and in articulating why specific individuals have different employment experiences compared with others.

HR can also offer support in the form of extensive coaching around how to customize appropriately. Likewise, organizations can support employees by providing self-assessments and tools to help them get clearer on their goals and needs, decision support tools to help them make the most effective choices, and plenty of information so they can make more informed decisions. For organizations using segmentation practices, personalized portals for each segment could be created, and managers could be given user-friendly online "dashboards." If a manager has five employees, each with different performance management practices, for example, an overview screen could describe each segment, the tailored practices designed to support each, and a list detailing which employees belong to which segments.

Call center support may also need to be transformed, so that staff may answer each employee's questions or so that an employee is routed to a specific staff member based on the segment to which they belong. Call center staff may also need to advise employees on the specific modular choices offered or clarify the boundaries of a broad and simple rule. At Accenture, for example, employees input their employee number, and the HR call center employee then knows the caller's job level and workforce (e.g., consulting, outsourcing, IT solutions, or corporate support roles) and can provide customized treatment accordingly. It's easy to imagine providing differentiated support based on a number of other segments as well.

Finally, HR must support customization by holding managers accountable for people development. After all, managers are the people who often customize people practices for their employees and contribute significantly to employee development. After decades of Frederick Taylor–inspired efforts to break down complex activities into simple, standardized tasks and to consolidate them into areas of HR expertise, it will require effort to reorient managers to accept people management as integral to their jobs. Managers are no different from anyone else; they need new incentives to take on new responsibilities. That's why, for example, at Procter & Gamble, managers' compensation, stock options, performance ratings, and assignments are tied to their success in recruiting, developing, and retaining high-performing employees.[12]

Cocreator of People Practices with Employees

Just as leading organizations now cocreate new products and services with their customers, leading workforce of one organizations will often cocreate people practices with their employees. You may ask employees what is most important to them, as employees are asked at Best Buy, to help you make decisions about what and how to customize, and you may ask employees to contribute information about themselves to help you make the right set of modular choices available, determine the most germane segments or the appropriate boundaries of a broad and simple rule, or even determine which employee-defined practices to foster and how.

One company in our study, for example, involved sales managers in defining compensation practices for the sales workforce employee segment. Companies may also gather input through surveys or focus groups, blogs, or wikis to help their organizations determine what and how to customize. At Best Buy, the online employee community Blue Shirt Nation is used for this purpose; executives monitor it to ensure they are providing relevant and highly valued people practices. When Best Buy restricted one of its modular benefits choices of a highly valued employee discount, for example, employees flooded the Watercooler (an internal message board) and Blue Shirt Nation (an internal social network) with protests. HR swiftly responded—and the benefit was reinstated in a matter of days, not weeks. One can even imagine using other innovative technologies to get input in cocreating people practices; just as Google and Best Buy have mock prediction markets for employees to assess ideas like customer demand for new products and services, one could have markets to determine the most valued modular choice options, for example.[13]

Of course, companies can do it the old-fashioned way as well, by collecting and disseminating practices that have worked for people and supporting these organization-wide. At Men's Wearhouse, says Charlie Bresler, "We rely on individuals to invent, reinvent, and coinvent people strategies. It's an interactive, iterative process. HR ideas about maximizing people performance come directly from the field. They're further developed by [HR] operators who come from the field themselves and who are sensitive to the field. It's like ping-pong. It goes back and forth, but nothing becomes a suggested practice unless it makes sense for the field. It's organic; it's organized chaos."[14] To facilitate this process, annual meetings of line managers responsible for multiple stores are held so managers can share experiences that have worked in individual stores, such as effective ways to coach and model sales behavior, or how to effectively hire someone.

Creator of Unity Within Diversity

As your people begin to have a far more variable relationship with your company throughout their careers, you will need to unite them through a common understanding of the organization's values, culture, and goals. Every customization decision an employee, manager, or HR staff member makes should be rooted in the bedrock of the organization's values, mission, strategy, and goals; it will be your responsibility to work with your organization's senior leaders to ensure that these are clearly understood and embraced by all.

Advanced User of Technology

The customization strategies we've discussed throughout this book wouldn't be possible without the technological advances of recent years. Technology has been the sea change that's enabled the workforce of one to emerge. Clearly, HR leaders must become adept at using it to develop insight into employee needs, track the impact of customization on performance, support employees in their customization efforts through modeling and decision support technologies, and administer multiple variations of people practices, to name just a few applications. And of course, technology is also key for actually creating customized talent management offerings themselves—everything from role-based portals and peer-to-peer learning vehicles like blogs and wikis, to time-trading applications, self-coaching applications, and modularly configured learning.

Toward a New HR Organization

What, then, might a workforce of one HR organization look like—given its new mandate and set of skills required to manage a workforce as a workforce of one? As we've discussed, it may have a dedicated analytics group, as well as dedicated people and resources to support and coach people in their customization experiences. To design and administer a greater variety of practices when using segmentation or modular choice approaches, HR may sometimes also require additional people to stay abreast of multiple variations in each domain. Dedicated HR staff may even represent the needs of each segment—certainly if using a segmentation approach to customization, but also perhaps when using other approaches as well. One can imagine how an organization offering modular choices like Tesco might appoint someone to ensure that the choices offered appeal to the pleasure seeker segment. (Recall from chapter 3 that Tesco offers choices with respect to benefits, compensation, training, and development to meet the needs of five distinct segments: pleasure seekers, want-it-alls, work-life balancers, live-to-work employees, and work-to-live employees.)[15] In this scenario, employees may be supported less by functional heads of various pieces—learning, recruiting, and so on—and instead by people who represent the unique needs of each segment. Ideally, these people would even be members or previous members of the segment.

Designating HR staff in this way effectively knocks down internal HR functional silos, which is critical for transforming from a producer-focused HR organization to a customer-focused—or an employee-focused—organization. Just as marketing organizations must often break down organizational silos to bring together representatives of multiple offerings, products, and channels to meet a customer need, so must HR silos break down to meet employee needs. The focus will then be on how organizations serve various employee segments in improving their performance, rather than on how cost-effectively each internal functional program is administered. Workforce of one HR organizations will thus need to adopt an integrated approach to talent management, where HR processes and data across the entire employee experience (from defining talent needs to talent discovery to developing and deploying talent) are integrated to enable an organization to strategically look at the employee as a *whole*, rather than as a series of fragmented parts—and to then customize practices accordingly.

To thoroughly understand employees and improve performance, HR will increasingly need to knock down not only internal HR silos but also the entire functional silo of HR itself. HR must thoroughly understand employees and the business in which they work. To achieve this integration, HR managers at The Container Store are given responsibility for other areas of the company, such as store operations; they are also encouraged to take positions at the store level.[16] At other workforce of one pioneers, people rotate from the business into HR and from HR into the business. At Men's Wearhouse, HR comprises people with business rather than HR backgrounds. The group works so closely with store operations to improve overall workforce and store performance that, in the words of Charlie Bresler, "the two functions are nearly inseparable."

All of this is to say that to truly improve employee performance through customized offerings, HR must become comfortable working in areas outside traditional HR domains. It may be just as involved in creating general work environments and fostering specific cultures as it would be involved in creating traditional human resources programs. For example, HR may help set up an open physical work space that encourages learning through observation and shadowing, as Forrester Research does; or help in creating personal networking opportunities, as Nike does by sponsoring employee sports activities and other networking events (e.g., an African American employee network).[17] Or HR may need to collaborate closely with IT to create many employee-defined personalization practices, like self-coaching applications, or with the facilities management department to craft modular choices regarding workplace and setting.

The need for HR to collaborate closely with other functions in improving workforce performance may even some day lead to the fusion of IT,

HR, and real estate functions. Indeed, at Capital One, the chief human resources officer oversees both the corporate real estate and human resources organizations. And at many organizations, like British Telecommunications (BT) and Sun Microsystems, separate workplace effectiveness groups composed of cross-functional representatives (e.g., from HR, IT, finance, facilities, and line managers) already exist.[18] We expect that this may be the wave of the future for organizations that adopt a more employee-centric approach to HR.

Embarking on Your Journey to a Workforce of One

So how can you begin introducing more customization in your own organization? Improving employee attraction, retention, and performance begins with five simple steps (see figure 8-1).

1. **Assess the unique needs of your organization and employees.** Anyone setting out to manage their workforce as a workforce of one must first take the time to assess the unique conditions of both their company and their employees. This means thoroughly getting to know employees in a detailed manner and asking questions like these: Where do our employees value customization most—in their career paths, their schedules, or their job duties? Are they mostly of the same generation, or do we have multiple generations to contend with? Knowing your employees inside and out by getting the answers to these questions and others is the very foundation of creating a customized work experience.

2. **Determine your primary customization approaches.** To proactively create a well-thought-out, coordinated customization design uniquely optimized for your own organization, you should next use chapter 6 as a guide to help you when determining which customization approach or set of approaches you may wish to emphasize most.

FIGURE 8-1

Five simple steps to jump-start your workforce of one

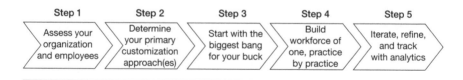

Step 1	Step 2	Step 3	Step 4	Step 5
Assess your organization and employees	Determine your primary customization approach(es)	Start with the biggest bang for your buck	Build workforce of one, practice by practice	Iterate, refine, and track with analytics

3. **Start with the biggest bang for your buck.** Although we believe that extensive customization can produce significant benefits for both an organization and its employees, a few well-chosen initiatives can sometimes be far more fruitful than a handful of those that don't matter quite as much. Well-chosen customization initiatives are especially important at the beginning of an organization's customization journey; their success will build momentum and support for more. A simple cost-benefit analysis can help determine how (or whether) to customize in each practice area and to set priorities. Best Buy and Microsoft, for example, both rely on extensive research (step 1) to determine the few key areas where employees most need customization and flexibility, and where the most rewards in engagement, motivation, and performance will hence ensue. Microsoft's vice president of HR, Lisa Brummel, for example, used her inaugural employee listening tour, survey data, focus groups, town halls, and exchanges with employees in her blog to determine Microsoft's main priorities for customization, including a flexible work environment, benefits and compensation, and performance management and rewards. Consider, too, costs and ease of implementation; it may be easy and inexpensive to add wikis or blogs to encourage informal peer-to-peer learning, for example, but more expensive to create specific, tailored learning programs based on segment when tailoring management training to the needs of different ethnicities, for example.

4. **Build a workforce of one, practice by practice.** The organizations we've studied have built a more customized people management approach initiative by initiative, one at a time, no matter what their starting point. As discussed earlier in the book, you'll need to look carefully at each particular people practice domain to determine whether the customization approaches your organization favors are suitable for that particular area.

   For more innovative or unusual initiatives, most executives start out with pilots in one corner of the organization to build the business case and test the concept before scaling it more broadly. Deloitte's Mass Career Customization initiative, Intel's segmentation of workers by mobility profile, and Capital One's Flexible Work Solutions initiative all started out that way.[19] Some, like Best Buy's results-only workplace initiative and peer-to-peer learning blog Blue Shirt Nation, may even begin as "guerrilla" operations initially unknown to, and unsanctioned by, management.

As companies become more comfortable with workforce of one practices—and as these practices become more necessary and doable because of changes in the workforce, technological and HR infrastructure advances, and resolution of control issues—organizations may continue to add more customization practices, one by one. It gets easier over time, as organizations learn to deal with greater complexity, and employees start to feel comfortable with difference, choice, and discretion.

5. **Iterate, refine, and track with analytics.** Both P&G and Microsoft iterate their people practices as they do their products; and as your organization builds a workforce of one, you'll likewise want to continually refine it. You may have different employees over time—a new generation in the workforce after Generation Y, or different employees due to different businesses you enter or geographies you penetrate—and you may need to refine your specific customization practices accordingly and sometimes even switch customization approaches altogether. You will need to continually monitor both your business and employee needs to make sure you are using the most germane segmentation schemes or offering the most relevant modular choices, adding and subtracting some as time goes by, for example. And you'll need to ensure that the parameters and "guardrails" are set where they should be if you are using the broad and simple rules approach. Employee-defined personalization may need less top-down monitoring to ensure relevance, as it fluidly and organically responds to business and employee needs. But you'll still need to experiment with and refine employee-defined personalization practices to be certain they're working as intended and are consistently and appropriately used. You should also track business results to check that customization is producing the desired benefits.

By getting started on your customization journey today, and by taking action now to transform your HR organization to drive a fundamentally new way of managing people (see "Do You Have the Capability to Manage a Workforce of One?"), your company can go a long way toward resolving many of the pressing challenges companies face today: too many disengaged, dissatisfied, or poorly performing employees; increasing competition from all fronts; and most important, the need to continually improve business results. Maximizing the potential of your organization's most important asset—its people—in this way only makes good business sense. When companies manage their workforces as a workforce of one, no longer are people viewed merely as numbers, but rather as individuals with unique needs and preferences who are capable of making optimal frontline decisions for themselves and their subordinates within a structured and controlled framework. Ultimately, organizations that open the window of opportunity for employees to enjoy work experiences that are completely tailored to them open the window of opportunity for their organizations to perform at their best—running on the engine of committed, engaged, and high-performing talent.

Do You Have the Capability to Manage a Workforce of One?

Take this quiz to find out. Just circle the number to the right of the question that best applies to you. Each response is on a sliding scale of 1–5, with the points 1, 3, and 5 defined for you. (For example, you may circle the number 4 if your organization falls somewhere between the defined points of 3 and 5.) Add up the numbers circled and place in the "Total" box. Then use the "How Do You Measure Up?" scoring guide for a high-level view of how close your HR organization may be to effectively managing its workforce as a workforce of one.

Question	1	2	3	4	5
1. What is your HR mandate, and how are you measured?	HR as an efficient deliverer of administrative HR services		HR as a "strategic business partner" to further strategic business initiatives only		HR as a primary driver of business results through the role of "people performance improver"
2. Do you have the skills and resources to effectively drive strategic HR-enabled value?	We do not have a mandate to drive strategic value through HR, or we do but don't have the skills, time, or resources to deliver on it.		We have a mandate to drive strategic value through HR and we have the skills to do so, but we don't have the time or resources to deliver on it.		We have a mandate to drive strategic value through HR and have the skills, time, and resources to deliver on it.
3. Who is your primary HR customer?	Primarily focused on the HR department, not the employee. Our mind-set is more "product-out" than "consumer-in"		Management ranks only		Management ranks and employees, with the latter as a way of meeting management's goals of business improvement through improved employee performance
4. How do you currently achieve control?	Through creating the same detailed people practices for everyone and ensuring compliance with them		Through some customized practices and some standardized ones, and more through encouraging than policing		Through using one or more of the four workforce of one approaches, and supporting them with alternative safeguards such as values, supportive information, and education
5. Have you adopted marketing mind-sets and knowledge and applied them to your people practices?	No, we have no one with a marketing background, and we rarely partner or interface with marketing.		Some; we sometimes partner with marketing or borrow marketing staff for certain projects, and have a small number of people with marketing mind-sets.		Yes, we have HR leaders and employees with marketing backgrounds or mind-sets, and we often partner with marketing to learn their skills.

Question	1	2	3	4	5
6. Do you have an employee insight capability?	No, we make decisions about HR offerings based on our own ideas in a "product-out" way.		We make some decisions based on employee insights (i.e., insights related to employee level or performance).		Yes, we make decisions about HR offerings based on extensive insights and research into employees.
7. Can you translate employee insights into action and results?	No, we don't have the capability to translate employee insights into action, or use analytics to track the impact of initiatives on results.		We sometimes translate employee insights into action, and only sometimes use analytics to analyze the results of our people initiatives.		Yes, we use analytics to translate insights into action and continuously improve our people programs.
8. Do you market and brand your talent offerings?	No, we rarely, if ever, market and brand our HR offerings as we might our products.		We are working on getting better in this area, and are starting to choose a few HR offerings to market and brand.		Yes, we extensively market and brand our offerings, and we have a well-developed capability in this area to help us communicate the employee value proposition.
9. Do you have strong communication, education, and change management capabilities?	No, we need to work on these areas.		We are about average in this area, and still need to improve.		Yes, we have clear and well-developed channels for communicating and educating our employees as well as proven change management methods.
10. Can your HR staff act as coaches to employees in their customization efforts?	Our HR staff are skilled in administration, not coaching.		We have the skills to be effective coaches, but we don't have enough HR staff to coach employees—only senior managers.		Yes, we have enough skilled HR staff to actively coach not just senior leaders in the business, but employees as well.

	1	2	3	4	5
11. Do you have tools and capabilities to help employees develop self-insight?	No, we don't offer any help for employees to understand themselves and their motivations better.		We offer a limited number of tools, workshops, tests, and other ways to help employees understand what is important to them and what they need to be successful at work.		Yes, we have a lot of tools, workshops, tests, and other ways to help employees understand what is important to them and what they need to be successful at work.
12. Can you effectively support employees in their customization efforts?	We don't have the ability to offer employees decision support, information, and modeling tools to help them make informed choices, nor can our call center handle additional complexity.		We have some ability to offer decision support, information, and modeling tools to help employees make informed choices, and we may be able to somewhat modify our call centers to handle additional complexity.		Yes, we have the ability to offer decision support, information, and modeling tools to help employees make informed choices; we can also modify our call centers to handle additional complexity.
13. Do your leaders, managers, and employees spend time and effort on people development?	Our people are focused on getting their everyday jobs done to the exclusion of developing others.		Our people spend some time and effort on people development.		We've developed robust processes that support our employees in effectively and consistently developing one another.
14. Do you have the capabilities to "cocreate" talent management offerings with employees?	No, we only know how to create talent management offerings by ourselves.		We sometimes cocreate talent management offerings—mostly by conducting traditional research as to what employees want.		Yes, we know how to engage employees to cocreate talent management offerings with us in leading and sophisticated ways, and we do so often.
15. How adept are you at using advanced and leading-edge technology?	We don't have a well-developed IT capability to support talent management.		We are good at using technology to support efficient HR administration, and we are working to use IT to strategically support more of our talent practices.		We are on the cutting edge of using new technology to support talent management, and have superior IT skills to support furthering customization with technology.

16. How integrated are your HR processes and functional areas?

1 — We have so many functional silos within HR that rarely do we communicate or coordinate with one another. HR processes are stand-alone with little integration.

2

3 — We are organized by functional area (e.g., in a center of excellence), but we do a fair job of integrating talent management across functional boundaries.

4

5 — We have broken down HR silos and have an integrated talent management approach so that we can most effectively bring together different offerings to meet different employee needs; we may even have dedicated people to serve the needs of each employee segment (even if we don't favor segmentation).

17. How integrated is HR with other functions (e.g., IT, facilities) that seek to improve employee performance?

1 — HR and other departments seeking to improve employee performance rarely work together on performance improvement initiatives.

2

3 — HR sometimes works with departments like IT or real estate on joint performance improvement initiatives.

4

5 — We are extensively integrated with other functions, like IT or facilities, that seek to improve performance; these functions may be merged together, or we may have extensive cross-functional teams.

18. How much does HR understand and integrate with the business?

1 — Our HR staff has little business exposure.

2

3 — We are working hard to get better at understanding the business we serve, and we have succeeded in giving our HR staff some exposure to the business.

4

5 — HR thoroughly understands the business; we may have a significant number of HR staff who came from the business, we may rotate HR staff into the business, or we may jointly assign HR and business tasks to our people.

19. Does HR work outside traditional HR domains to improve performance?

1 — We tend to create and administer traditional HR programs only.

2

3 — We sometimes get involved in people performance initiatives that aren't typical HR programs.

4

5 — Yes, we are good not just at creating specific HR programs, but at fostering general work environments and cultures, or in creatively coming up with new ways to improve performance that aren't typically considered "HR."

Total

How Do You Measure Up?

- **If you scored between 19 and 43:** Your HR organization may require significant change to support customization, but you can still get started on your customization journey now.

  Like most HR organizations, yours may need to develop many new skills and capabilities to support a workforce of one approach, and it may need a new mandate and structure as well. But you can start immediately on your customization journey by adopting the mind-set of treating employees as you do your customers and by pursuing some "quick win" customization initiatives that build on the infrastructure or capabilities you do have. This will help you build a business case for beginning the long-term work of transforming the HR organization to support a more nuanced, sophisticated approach to managing talent.

- **If you scored between 44 and 69:** You have many of the capabilities needed to effectively support customization, and can begin to introduce a number of customization initiatives today.

  Although your HR organization still has some work to do if it hopes to fully support a customized talent management model, you have already developed many of the skills and capabilities necessary. You can consider pursuing multiple customization initiatives at once, if you desire, while still working to fully transform your HR function so that it can most effectively support customization.

- **If you scored between 70 and 95:** You have strong capabilities to manage your workforce as a workforce of one, and can immediately start extensive customization.

  Your HR organization is already well suited to managing a workforce of one and thus will require much less transformation than most HR organizations. Customization of talent management practices will be much easier for you, since you already have many of the key skills and capabilities. You therefore may want to pursue customization more aggressively and extensively to get a leg up on the competition—and more quickly enjoy the potential rewards and benefits of a customized talent management approach.

Conclusion

The Future of Workforce of One

WE BEGAN THIS BOOK WITH a vision: organizations designed to fit you, rather than demanding that you fit them. Instead of treating a workforce as a single homogeneous entity, organizations would treat each employee as a "workforce of one" with unique needs, aspirations, and preferences to optimize the performance of every individual contributing to their organizations—and thereby contribute to the kinds of business results that propel companies far ahead of the competition.

It only makes sense when people, a key driver of value and business results in today's knowledge-based economy, are given rewards they really care about, they are more motivated. When they can learn how they learn best, they are better skilled; and when they are offered workplaces that suit their unique needs for concentration or collaboration, they are more productive. When they can customize their jobs and careers, they harness their unique strengths and make better, fuller contributions to their organizations. Our employee survey confirms this: people are more attracted to companies that would provide customized people practices, and they're more likely to remain there and perform at their best.

Throughout this book, we've shown this vision isn't just a pipe dream—we have documented more than a dozen organizations that are already turning this vision into a living, breathing reality. We've provided many examples of how companies are achieving a customized work experience today—not by secretive, one-off side deals between manager and employee, but rather in a consistent, scalable, and manageable fashion: through segmenting the workforce, offering employees a range of modular choices, defining broad and simple rules, and/or fostering employee-defined personalization. And in many of these organizations, we've seen the hard evidence that such strategies pay off—customization has helped them become an employer of choice and better attract, retain, and maximize the performance of their people. By creating a unique approach to customization that is optimized for their specific organizations and employees, these companies have earned an important competitive advantage that may be difficult to replicate by others.

As we look to the future, we predict that many of the trends driving organizations to create customized work experiences today will only grow stronger tomorrow, pushing more organizations toward creating an ever-better fit between people practices and individuals. Workforces will only grow more diverse on every conceivable dimension, including diversity in life pursuits, values, and expectations of work—thereby making it less and less likely that an organization will be able to satisfy its workforce's needs in one single way. And as intangible assets like an organization's people represent increasingly more of an organization's value—and as jobs grow increasingly complex and therefore more difficult to standardize in an industrial-age fashion—we expect one-size-fits-all people practices to become obsolete and, increasingly, even harmful to the bottom line. Advances in customization in the consumer sphere will also push organizations toward such advances in the work sphere; as people receive more and more relevant, tailored experiences in their role as consumers, so will they demand these same sorts of refined and granular experiences as employees.

We also predict that customization will become increasingly easier to manage and implement as time goes by. Technology advances will make it easier to administrate variety, support employees in organically defining their own people practices in a bottom-up rather than top-down fashion, and help employees make the most relevant decisions through sophisticated modeling tools and decision-support systems. Customization options will soon be baked into both software and outsourcing offerings, allowing a company to more cost-effectively offer customized work experiences. Control issues also will continue to develop in ways other than the "blunt hammer" approach of sameness and conformity to a single standard.

In addition, we expect that some of the more innovative advances in customized work experiences today will become mere "hygiene factors" offered by everyone tomorrow—propelling organizations to increasingly create altogether new and competitively differentiated ways of offering people customized work experiences. The specific people practices we've profiled in this book are therefore likely to change. But the four general customization approaches will not, as they represent broader "metaconcepts" that can encompass both current customization practices and ones developed in the future.

Our goal in this book was to create a general framework for customization that will give you the tools and guidelines to innovate and creatively come up with your own customized work experiences. We challenge you to take one of the four metaconcepts of segmentation, modular choice, broad and simple rules, and employee-defined personalization and create brand-new ways of offering your employees highly relevant employment experiences. In this way, at its heart, this book was meant to be a durable, long-lasting framework for continual innovation.

We can only speculate what the future might hold for new customized people practices that may develop as organizations creatively apply the four customization approaches profiled in this book. For one, as scientists continue to understand the drivers of human behavior and performance—even down to the DNA level—we expect organizations to keep refining how they segment employees or provide them with modular choices. One recent article, for example, revealed a startling scientific discovery further supporting the fact that we must take an individualized approach to improving human performance: a full 30 percent of us do not carry the *specific DNA* needed to be able to learn from our mistakes—a quality that was long thought to be universal among all of us![1] Scientists are now talking about not only an era of *personalized medicine* (matching drugs to people's DNA) but a brand-new era of genomics that may lead people to tailor *experiences*—from parenting practices to learning practices in schools and organizations—just as we tailor drugs based on an individual's specific genetic makeup.

Another area where we expect to see significant advances is in using intelligent systems to monitor and understand employees' work, learning, or behavior—thereby enabling highly personalized coaching, learning opportunities, rewards, and more, based on a bottom-up understanding of every individual's ever-evolving specific needs and situation. Systems, for example, could monitor the preferred work patterns of each individual, enabling highly sophisticated scheduling based on the ebbs and flows of an individual's personal energy level and how it matches the workday's rhythms.

The possibilities are truly endless, and we look forward to seeing what the future holds to help organizations become even better at capitalizing on individual differences, driving ever-greater levels of individual and business performance. Even the workforce of one pioneers profiled in this book recognize that their journey toward offering more relevant and tailored work experiences has really just begun. Indeed, we are just embarking on a new era in how we manage talent—an era where individuals get the opportunity to develop to their fullest through work experiences that uniquely fit them, and an era where organizations will reap vast rewards through a more sophisticated people management approach. We challenge you to apply the principles you've learned in this book to your own organization: to do no less than lead your industry into the future and propel your organization to new heights in workforce and business performance.

How Many Employees Have Customized Work Experiences?

FIGURE A-1

How many employees have customized work experiences?

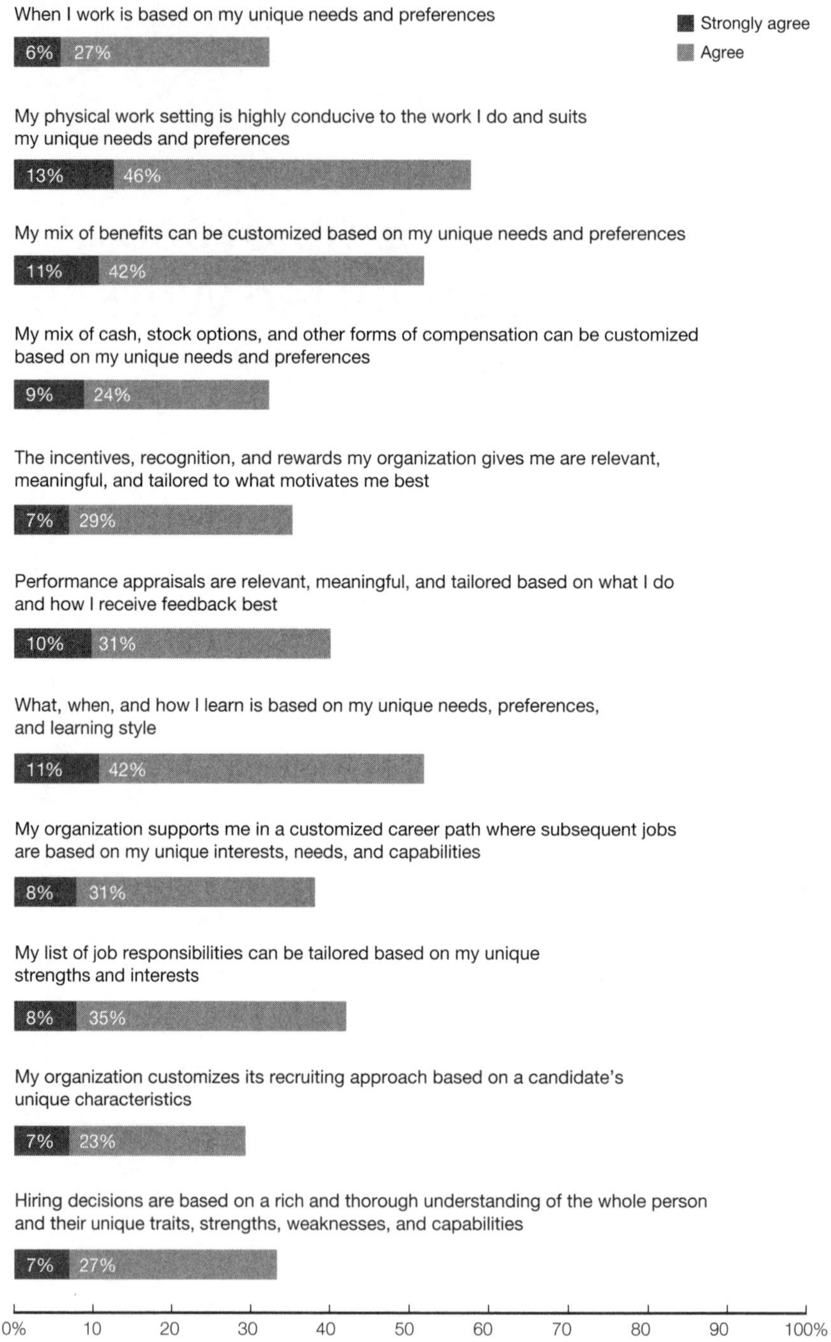

■ Strongly agree
▨ Agree

When I work is based on my unique needs and preferences
6% 27%

My physical work setting is highly conducive to the work I do and suits my unique needs and preferences
13% 46%

My mix of benefits can be customized based on my unique needs and preferences
11% 42%

My mix of cash, stock options, and other forms of compensation can be customized based on my unique needs and preferences
9% 24%

The incentives, recognition, and rewards my organization gives me are relevant, meaningful, and tailored to what motivates me best
7% 29%

Performance appraisals are relevant, meaningful, and tailored based on what I do and how I receive feedback best
10% 31%

What, when, and how I learn is based on my unique needs, preferences, and learning style
11% 42%

My organization supports me in a customized career path where subsequent jobs are based on my unique interests, needs, and capabilities
8% 31%

My list of job responsibilities can be tailored based on my unique strengths and interests
8% 35%

My organization customizes its recruiting approach based on a candidate's unique characteristics
7% 23%

Hiring decisions are based on a rich and thorough understanding of the whole person and their unique traits, strengths, weaknesses, and capabilities
7% 27%

0%   10   20   30   40   50   60   70   80   90   100%

Source: Accenture workforce of one study, 2008.

Notes

Introduction

1. See, for example, work by Baruch Lev, such as "Sharpening the Intangibles Edge," *Harvard Business Review*, June 2004, 109–116; as well as the work of economist Laurie Bassi, such as "How's Your Return on People?" (with Daniel McMurrer), *Harvard Business Review*, March 2004, 18.

2. See the following articles and white papers: Susan Cantrell et al., "Measuring the Value of Human Capital Investments: The SAP Case," *Strategy & Leadership* 34, no. 2 (2006): 43–52; Susan Cantrell, Harold Scott, and Peter Cheese, "Focusing HR on Growth at Harley-Davidson," *Strategic HR Review* 5, no. 2 (2006); James M. Benton, Susan Cantrell, and Meredith A. Vey, "Making the Right Investments in People," *Accenture Outlook* 16, no. 3 (2004): 64–73; and Susan Cantrell et al., *The Accenture Human Capital Development Framework: Assessing, Measuring and Guiding Investments in Human Capital to Achieve High Performance* (New York: Accenture, 2005), http://www.accenture.com/Global/Research_and_Insights/Institute_For_High_Performance_Business/By_Subject/Talent_and_Leadership/ThePerformance_old.htm.

3. Peter Cheese, Robert J. Thomas, and Elizabeth Craig, *The Talent Powered Organization: Strategies for Globalization, Talent Management, and High Performance* (London: Kogan Page, 2008). The survey was conducted in March 2008.

4. Lucy Kellaway, "The Next Little Thing," *The World in 2006* (a publication by the *Economist*), 2006.

Chapter 1

1. Cheryl Kozak, interview by Susan Cantrell, January 22, 2008.

2. Best Buy was ranked as one of the top fifty places to work by Glass Door, an online community that offers career advice to employees and that compiles its list based on company reviews and ratings from employees, http://www.glassdoor.com/blog/2009/01/fortune-announces-best-places-to-work-how-does-it-compare. Best Buy was also named a *Forbes* Company of the Year in 2004, and it has repeatedly made *Fortune*'s Most Admired Companies list in recent years (Mark Tatge, "Fun and Games," *Forbes*, January 12, 2004; and http://money.cnn.com/magazines/fortune/mostadmired/2009/index.html).

3. The improvement in revenues and earnings per share are based on data from 2003 to 2009, and were obtained from Best Buy's annual reports or 10-K. We also compared Best Buy's stock prices to major indexes and industry peers from the start of the economic downturn in September 2008 to July 2009.

4. Joe Kalkman and Tina Decker, interview by Susan Cantrell on May 10 and June 16, 2008.

5. Stan Davis, *Future Perfect* (Reading, MA: Addison-Wesley, 1987).

6. Best Buy's "unique store approach" focuses on serving the specific needs and interests of customer segments each store tends to attract. Customized colors and personalized messages can be chosen for Nike athletic shoes at nike.com (see http://nikeid.com). Customers can create and order their own custom LEGO brick design (see http://factory.lego.com). Capital One offers customized credit cards (see http://www.capitalone.com/cardlab). The term *market of one* was coined by James H. Gilmore and B. Joseph Pine, *Markets of One* (Boston: Harvard Business School Press, 2000).

7. C. K. Prahalad and M. S. Krishnan, *The New Age of Innovation: Driving Cocreated Value Through Global Networks* (New York: McGraw-Hill, 2008). The notion of "personalized cocreation" is also discussed by C. K. Prahalad and Venkat Ramaswamy, *The Future of Competition: Co-Creating Unique Value with Customers* (Boston: Harvard Business School Press, 2004).

8. Clayton M. Christensen, Michael B. Horn, and Curtis W. Johnson, *Disrupting Class: How Disruptive Innovation Will Change the Way the World Learns* (New York: McGraw-Hill, 2008).

9. For more on the concept of a talent-powered organization, see Peter Cheese, Robert J. Thomas, and Elizabeth Craig, *The Talent Powered Organization: Strategies for Globalization, Talent Management, and High Performance* (London: Kogan Page, 2008).

10. Hewitt Associates, *Preparing for the Workforce of Tomorrow* (Lincolnshire, IL: Hewitt Associates, February 2004), http://www.hewittassociates.com/_MetaBasicCMAssetCache_/Assets/Articles/workforce_tomorrow.pdf.

11. See, for example, Keith H. Hammonds, "Why We Hate HR," *Fast Company*, August 2005; Jack and Suzy Welch, "So Many CEOs Get This Wrong," *BusinessWeek*, July 7, 2006; and "Is Your Leadership Department Friend or Foe? Depends on Who's Asking the Question," Knowledge@Wharton, August 10, 2005, http://knowledge.wharton.upenn.edu/article.cfm?articleid=253.

12. *Human Resource Institute study:* Reported by the Institute for Corporate Productivity (formerly the Human Resource Institute) and HR.com, as cited in "No Silver Bullet for Performance Management," *T+D*, February 2007. Also, the Society for Human Resource Management has concluded that more than 90 percent of performance appraisal systems are a failure, as reported by Bob Nelson, "Are Performance Appraisals Obsolete?" *Compensation and Benefits Review* 32, no. 3 (2000): 39–42; and by Jeff Weekley and Jeff Labrador, "Making Performance Management Relevant," *Kenexa Connection*, http://events.kenexa.com/newsletter/oldver/2007043.asp?uid=&tbl=test. *Study on employee satisfaction with training:* Ellen Balaguer, Peter Cheese, and Christian Marchetti, *The High-Performance Workforce Study 2006* (New York: Accenture, 2007), http://www.accenture.com/Global/Consulting/Talent_and_Organization/Workforce_Performance/R_and_I/HighPerformaceStudy2006.htm.

13. For example, a meta-analysis of twenty-four longitudinal studies showed that the improvement in 360-degree feedback ratings over time is generally small; the authors conclude this is because some feedback recipients are more likely to respond positively to this practice than others. See James Smither, Manuel London, and Richard Reilly, "Does Performance Improve Following Multisource Feedback? A Theoretical Model, Meta-Analysis, and Review of Empirical Findings," *Personnel Psychology* 58(2005): 33–36. Another study suggests that leadership development efforts that rely on generic, commercial best-practice products often fail because they do not take into account the unique business problems that different individuals face; see Douglas A. Ready and Jay A. Conger, "Why Leadership Development Efforts Fail," *MIT Sloan Management Review* 17, no. 5 (2003): 22–24. Yet another study shows that personalized, noncash rewards are viewed as more effective than impersonal cash rewards in achieving eight out of ten corporate goals (study by the Forum for People Performance Management and Measurement at Northwestern University in Evanston, IL; as reported

by Charlotte Huff, "Recognition That Resonates," *Workforce Management*, September 2006, 25).

14. Thomas H. Davenport and Jeanne Harris, *Competing on Analytics* (Boston: Harvard Business School Press, 2007).

15. Christa Degnan Manning, Marianne D'Aquila, and Karen Carter, *Human Capital Management Market Sizing Report, 2007–2012* (Boston, MA: AMR Research, June 23, 2008).

16. Don Tapscott, "Meet the Net Generation" (PowerPoint presentation, New Paradigm Research Summary, November 2007).

17. Julie Connelly, "Youthful Attitudes, Sobering Realities," *New York Times*, October 28, 2003.

18. John W. Budd, *Employment with a Human Face: Balancing Efficiency, Equity, and Voice* (Ithaca, NY: ILR Press, 2004).

19. See Denise Rousseau, "The Idiosyncratic Deal: Flexibility Versus Fairness," *Organizational Dynamics* 29, no. 4 (200): 260–273; and John Kimberly and Hamid Bouchikhi, "The Customized Workplace," in *Management 2C: New Visions for the New Millennium*, ed. Subir Chowdhury (Upper Saddle River, NJ: Financial Times/Prentice Hall, 1999).

20. For example, psychologist Howard Gardner shows how individuals can vary in the types of intelligences they have in his groundbreaking book *Frames of Mind: The Theory of Multiple Intelligences* (New York: Basic Books, 1983). Also, an Accenture study of 1,029 full-time employees found that although respondents had about the same amount of increased work, some suffered significantly more than others and reacted to stress differently. "Are Your Harried Employees Enjoying Life or Headed to the Doctor's Office?" Accenture Management Report, 2006, http://www.accenture.com/Global/Consulting/Talent_and_Organization/Workforce_Performance/R_and_I/AreOffice.htm. Another study found that only some people learn from stressful experiences and others do not, based on variations in genetic makeup; see Sharon Begley, "But I Did Everything Right!" *Newsweek*, August 9, 2008. Also, psychologist David McClelland found that different people have different learned needs, causing them to have different motivations, like those for achievement, affiliation, or power; see David C. McClelland, *The Achieving Society* (New York: Van Nostrand Reinhold, 1961).

21. High person-environment fit was shown to improve organizational commitment and job satisfaction by Amy L. Kristof-Brown, Ryan D. Zimmerman, and Erin C. Johnson, "The Consequences of Individuals' Fit at Work: A Meta-Analysis of Person-Job, Person-Organization, Person-Group, and Person-Supervisor Fit," *Personnel Psychology* 58, no. 2 (2005): 28–342. High person-environment fit was shown to improve organizational citizenship behaviors by Daniel J. Comeau and Richard L. Griffith, "Structural Interdependence, Personality, and Organizational Citizenship Behavior: An Examination of Person-Environment Interaction," *Personnel Review* 34, no. 3 (2005): 30.

22. C. G. Jung, *Psychological Types*. Collected Works, vol. 6 (Princeton, NJ: Princeton University Press, 1976).

23. Thomas H. Davenport, *Thinking for a Living: How to Get Better Performances and Results from Knowledge Workers* (Boston: Harvard Business School Press, 2005).

24. William Bridges, *Jobshift: How to Prosper in a Workplace Without Jobs* (Reading, MA: Addison-Wesley, 1994).

25. See, for example, work by Baruch Lev, such as "Sharpening the Intangibles Edge," *Harvard Business Review*, June 2004, 109–116; as well as the work of economist Laurie Bassi, such as "How's Your Return on People?" (with Daniel McMurrer), *Harvard Business Review*, March 2004, 18.

26. As of spring 2008.

27. Balaguer, Cheese, and Marchetti, *The High-Performance Workforce Study 2006*; and Economist Intelligence Unit (in cooperation with Development Dimensions International), *The CEO's Role in Talent Management* (Larkspur, CA: Economist Intelligence

Unit, May 2006), http://www.eiu.com/site_info.asp?info_name=eiu_CEO_role_in_talent_management&rf=0.

28. For data on our own study, see Susan Cantrell et al., *The Accenture Human Capital Development Framework: Assessing, Measuring and Guiding Investments in Human Capital to Achieve High Performance* (New York: Accenture, 2005), http://www.accenture.com/Global/Research_and_Insights/Institute_For_High_Performance_Business/By_Subject/Talent_and_Leadership/ThePerformance_old.htm; and James M. Benton, Susan Cantrell, and Meredith A. Vey, "Making the Right Investments in People," *Accenture Outlook* 16, no. 3 (2004): 64–73. For other empirical evidence linking people processes and programs to business results, see Brian E. Becker and Mark A. Huselid, "High Performance Work Systems and Firm Performance: A Synthesis of Research and Managerial Implications," *Research in Personnel and Human Resources Management* (1998); Nick Bontis and Jac Fitzenz, "Intellectual Capital ROI: A Causal Map of Human Capital Antecedents and Consequents," *Journal of Intellectual Capital* 3, no. 3 (2002): 223–247; David Ulrich and Wayne Brockbank, *The New HR Agenda: 2002 Human Resource Competency Study* (Ann Arbor: University of Michigan Business School, 2003); and Bruce N. Pfau and Ira T. Kay, *The Human Capital Edge* (New York: McGraw-Hill, 2002).

29. For a description of this research, see the description of the measurement tool we developed to assess organizations' people practices in the introduction of this book.

30. "The Search for Talent," *Economist*, October 7, 2006; Cornelia M. Ashby, *Higher Education: Science, Technology, Engineering, and Mathematics Trends and the Role of Federal Programs* (Washington, DC: United States Government Accountability Office, May 3, 2006), http://www.gao.gov/new.items/d06702t.pdf; Jill Schildhouse, "Working Hard to Avoid the Labor Shortage," *Inside Supply Management* 7, no. 3 (2006): 22; and data from the following sources: Employment Policy Foundation, projections of census from the Bureau of Labor Statistics, and the Bureau of Economics.

31. David Terkanian, "Lifetime 'Career' Change," *Occupational Outlook Quarterly* 50, no. 2 (2006): 27; and David Smith and Deepak Malkani, *What Employers Need to Know About the Class of 2008: Shaping Recruitment and Retention Strategies to Achieve High Performance* (New York: Accenture, 2008).

32. Pete Engardio, "A Guide for Multinationals; One of the Great Challenges for a Multinational Is Learning How to Build a Productive Global Team," *BusinessWeek*, August 20, 2007.

33. William Whyte, *The Organization Man* (New York: Simon & Schuster, 1956).

34. Steve Hamm, with Joshua Schneyer, "International Isn't Just IBM's First Name," *BusinessWeek*, Davos Special Report, January 28, 2008, 36; and "The New Organization," *Economist*, January 19, 2006.

35. As cited by Elissa Tucker, Tina Kao, and Nidhi Verma, "Next-Generation Talent Management: Insights on How Workforce Trends Are Changing the Face of Talent Management," *Business Credit* 107, no. 7 (2005): 20.

36. Michelle Conlin, with Jessi Hempel, "UnMarried America," *BusinessWeek*, October 20, 2003, 06.

37. See, for example, Ken Dychtwald, Tamara J. Erickson, and Robert Morison, *Workforce Crisis: How to Beat the Coming Shortage of Skills and Talent* (Boston: Harvard Business School Press, 2006); and Warren G. Bennis and Robert J. Thomas, *Geeks and Geezers* (Boston: Harvard Business School Press, 2002).

38. Merrill Lynch, *New Retirement Survey: A Perspective on the Baby Boomer Generation* (New York: Merrill Lynch, 2005).

39. Families and Work Institute, *Generation and Gender in the Workplace* (New York: American Business Collaboration, 2004), http://familiesandwork.org/eproducts/genandgender.pdf.

40. International Data Corporation, *Worldwide Mobile Worker 2007–2011 Forecast and Analysis*, IDC Report 20983 (Framingham, MA: International Data Corporation, January 2008).

41. Ira May and Joyce P. Pedrasa, "Use of Contingency Work Force to Give Firms Flexibility, Efficiency in Face of Competition," *BusinessWorld*, October 6, 2006.

42. Greig Aitken, interview by Susan Cantrell, March 10, 2008.

43. Denise Rousseau, "Let's Make an I-Deal," American Management Association e-newsletter, Performance and Profits, August 2006, http://www.amanet.org/performance-profits/editorial.cfm?Ed=324.

44. Happy Meal is a registered trademark of McDonald's.

45. For a list of Accenture's employer of choice awards, see: http://www.accenture.com/Global/About_Accenture/Company_Overview/Awards_and_Recognition/GreatPlaceto Work.htm. Performance is measured by stock price from 2003–2008, per Accenture annual report 2008.

46. Jim Romeo, "Answering the Call," *HR Magazine*, October, 2003.

47. Ashlea Ebeling, "Corporate Moneyball," *Forbes*, April 23, 2007, 102.

48. Information regarding Capital One's work environment was obtained through an interview of Capital One's Matt Schuyler by Thomas H. Davenport. Used with permission.

49. Dan Sussman, "Now Hear This," *T + D*, September 1, 2005, 57.

50. *Developing leaders:* Fay Hansen, "Building Better Leaders . . . Faster," *Workforce Management*, June 9, 2008, 25. *Best place to work:* Capital One appeared on *Fortune* magazine's "Best Companies to Work For" list in 2007, http://money.cnn.com/magazines/fortune/bestcompanies/2007/full_list/.

51. *Personal Pursuits program:* Sherry E. Sullivan and Lisa A. Mainiero, "Kaleidoscope Careers: Benchmarking Ideas for Fostering Family-Friendly Workplaces," *Organizational Dynamics*, February 2007, 45.

52. *Modular choices:* Danielle Sacks, "Scenes from the Culture Clash," *Fast Company*, January–February 2006, pg. 72; *Segmentation:* Segmentation by generation is referred to in chapter 2. Segmentation by geography is referred to in Mary Brandel's article, "Fishing in the Global Talent Pool," *Computerworld*, November 20, 2006, 33. *Job rotation:* "Best Practices," *Training Magazine*, March 1, 2005, 68. *Coaching:* "A Living, Breathing People Strategy," *T+D*, October 2007, Vol. 61, No. 10, pg. 42. *Employee referrals:* Mary Brandel, "Fishing in the Global Talent Pool," *Computerworld*, November 20, 2006, 33. *Recruiting content:* Lindsey Gerdes, "The Best Places to Launch a Career," *BusinessWeek*, September 24, 2007, 48. *Talent-interest databases:* Nick Van Dam, "Strategic Capability Building Through Talent Management," presentation to the International Consortium for Executive Development Research, Seattle, WA, May 23, 2006.

53. For a list of specific awards, see http://www.deloitte.com/dtt/leadership/0,1045,sid%253D2251,00.html accessed July 20, 2009.

54. Lynda Gratton, *The Democratic Enterprise* (Upper Saddle River, NJ: Financial Times/Prentice Hall, 2004); 119–124.

55. *Modular choices:* Gratton, *The Democratic Enterprise*, and Nic Patton, "Supermarket Sweep," *Personnel Today*, July 5, 2005, 19. *Diversity training courses:* Hayley Pinkerfield, "It's Good to Talk," *Human Resources*, January 2007, 19.

56. *Shift-swapping scheme:* Pinkerfield, "It's Good to Talk." *Job try-outs and employee-identified job recruits:* Patton, "Supermarket Sweep." *Apprenticeship program:* Tom Lloyd, "Shopping for Apprentices," *Human Resources*, March 1, 2005, 26.

57. *HR guidelines:* Jennifer Koch Laabs, "Thinking Outside the Box at the Container Store," *Workforce*, March, 2001. *Basis of compensation:* "Kip Tindell," interview, *Chain Store Age*, August 1, 2004, 28; and Patrick Mirza, "Challenging HR Assumptions," *Human Resources*, July–August 2003, 8.

58. *Employee-defined recruiting:* Container Store's recruiting practices are described by: Jennifer Taylor Arnold, "Customers as Employees: Your Best Job Candidates Might Be Right in Front of You," *HR Magazine*, April 2007, 76; Mike Duff, "Top-Shelf Employees Keep Container Store on Track," *DSN Retailing Today*, March 8, 2004, 7; Jennifer Koch Laabs, "Optimas 2001—General Excellence: Thinking Outside the Box at the Container Store," *Workforce*, March 2001, 34–38; and "Kip Tindell." *Customized career paths and job fit:* Laabs, "Thinking Outside the Box at the Container Store."

59. As reported on the company Web site, http://www.containerstore.com/careers/index.jhtml;jsessionid=0PEAAEVKTEDRNQFIAILSM5GAVABBQJVC?message=/repository/secondaryMessages/fortune.jhtml.

60. *Employee projects:* Bala Iyer and Thomas H. Davenport, "Reverse Engineering Google's Innovation Machine," *Harvard Business Review*, April 2008, 58. *Recruiting and hiring:* Todd Raphael, "At Google, the Proof Is in the People," *Workforce*, March 2003, 50–51; and Josey Puliyenthuruthel, "How Google Searches—for Talent," *BusinessWeek Online*, April 11, 2005, http://www.businessweek.com/magazine/content/05_15/b3928076.htm. *Experience-based learning:* John Sullivan, "Search Google for HR," *Workforce Management*, November 19, 2007, 42.

61. Ashlea Ebeling, "Corporate Moneyball," *Forbes*, April 23, 2007, Vol. 179, No. 9, pg. 102.

62. Sullivan, "Search Google for HR."

63. *Turnover:* Sullivan, "Search Google for HR." *Employee-generated revenue:* Dominic Rushe, "Can Google Break Windows?" *The Sunday Times* (London), July 12, 2009.

64. http://money.cnn.com/magazines/fortune/bestcompanies.

65. *Diversity:* For a list of awards in this area won by Pepsi, see http://www.pepsico.com/PEP_Company/Honors/index.cfm. *Leadership development:* The Hay Group and *Chief Executive* magazine rank PepsiCo as number 3 in the 2006 Top 20 Best Companies for Leaders, as referenced on the Pepsi Web site at http://www.pepsico.com/PEP_Company/Honors/index.cfm#. *Employer of choice:* For a list of awards in this area won by Pepsi, see http://www.pepsico.com/PEP_Company/Honors/index.cfm. *Profitability:* http://money.cnn.com/magazines/fortune/fortune500/2009/full_list/. "The *BusinessWeek* 50—The Best Performers," *BusinessWeek*, April 6, 2009.

66. GORE-TEX is the registered trademark of W. L. Gore & Associates.

67. Andy Moore, "Simply the Best," *Personnel Today*, June 8, 2004, 22; Patrick J. Kiger, "Power of the Individual: Small Groups Big Ideas," *Workforce Management*, February 27, 2006, 23–27; and Tamara J. Erickson and Lynda Gratton, "What It Means to Work Here," *Harvard Business Review*, March 2007, 104.

68. *Best Place to Work:* http://www.gore.com/en_xx/aboutus/fastfacts/index.html accessed July 20, 2009.

69. http://money.cnn.com/magazines/fortune/bestcompanies.

70. Hewitt, *Preparing for the Workforce of Tomorrow*.

71. For example, 1,118 senior HR practitioners saw the HR function as having moved from off-the-shelf schemes to strategic, tailored solutions. See Penny Tamkin, Wendy Hirsh, and Claire Tyers, *Chore to Champions: The Making of Better People Managers*, IES Research Networks Report 389 (Brighton, England: Institute for Employment Studies, May 2003). Also, only 3 percent of U.S. senior-level HR executives in one study say that they never tailor retention efforts to an individual's needs; 9 percent say they always do, 33 percent say they frequently do, and 45 percent say they sometimes do. Survey conducted by career management services firm Lee Hecht Harrison, as described in Sheree R. Curry, "Retention Getters," *Incentive* 79, no. 4 (2005).

Chapter 2

1. Nancy Reardon, interview by Susan Cantrell, July 25, 2005.

2. See, for example, Ken Dychtwald, Tamara J. Erickson, and Robert Morison, *Work force Crisis: How to Beat the Coming Shortage of Skills and Talent* (Boston: Harvard Business School Press, 2006).

3. Pete Engardio, "A Guide for Multinationals; One of the Great Challenges for a Multinational Is Learning How to Build a Productive Global Team," *BusinessWeek*, August 20, 2007, 48.

4. Jennifer Reingold and Diana Brady, "Brain Drain," *BusinessWeek*, September 20, 1999, 112–126; and Ken Dychtwald, Tamara Erickson, and Robert Morison, "It's Time to Retire Retirement," *Harvard Business Review*, March 2004, 48.

5. Lindsey Gerdes, "The Best Places to Launch a Career," *BusinessWeek*, September 24, 2007, 48.

6. Keith Lawrence, from interviews (six total) by Susan Cantrell (and sometimes David Smith) in February, March, and April 2008.

7. Trevor Blackman, interview by Susan Cantrell, February 18, 2008.

8. Andrés Tapia, "Ask Our Expert: Communicating the Value of Benefits to a Diverse Workforce," Hewitt Associates, Knowledge Center, http://www.hewittassociates.com/Intl/ NA/en-US/KnowledgeCenter/ArticlesReports/ArticleDetail.aspx?cid=4318&tid=3660. For gender-based differences, see Alison M. Konrad et al., "Sex Differences and Similarities in Job Attribute Preferences: A Meta-Analysis," *Psychological Bulletin* (July 2000). Also see the quote from Andrés Tapia on this topic in Hewitt Associate's introduction to Preparing for the Workforce of Tomorrow (Hewitt Associates: February 2004) at http://www. hewittassociates.com/Intl/NA/en-US/KnowledgeCenter/ArticlesReports/Article Detail.aspx?cid=1734.

9. Sylvia Ann Hewlett, *Off-Ramps and On-Ramps: Keeping Talented Women on the Road to Success* (Boston: Harvard Business School Press, 2007).

10. Dalila Asha Stitz, interview by Susan Cantrell, February 9, 2009.

11. Lori Lucas and Barb Hogg, *Breaking Down the Barriers: Insights on Boosting 401(k) Plan Participation and Interaction* (Lincolnshire, IL: Hewitt Associates, 2004), http://www.hewittassociates.com/_MetaBasicCMAssetCache_/Assets/Articles/ breaking_down_barriers.pdf.

12. Andrés Tapia, *Multicultural Marketing of Employee Benefits* (Lincolnshire, IL: Hewitt Associates, 2008), http://www.hewittassociates.com/_MetaBasicCMAssetCache_/ Assets/Articles/2008/Multicultural_Marketing_for_Employee_Benefits.pdf.

13. Amy Joyce, "They Open More Doors for Women; These 4 Companies Are Noted for Inclusion," *Washington Post*, February 4, 2007.

14. Thomas L. Friedman, *The World Is Flat* (New York: Farrar, Straus and Giroux, 2005).

15. "Recruiting from a Global Talent Pool," Corporate Executive Board Report, May 2001.

16. Mary Brandel, "Fishing in the Global Talent Pool," *Computerworld*, November 20, 2006, 33.

17. Society for Human Resource Management, *Multinational Corporations in China: Finding and Keeping Talent* (Alexandria, VA: Society for Human Resource Management Research Department, October 2007), http://www.shrm.org/research/staffresearch_published/Mult inational%20Corporations%20in%20China%20Finding%20and%20Keeping%20Talent.pdf.

18. Mary Brandel, "Fishing in the Global Talent Pool," *Computerworld*, November 20, 2006, 33.

19. Towers Perrin, *Winning Strategies for a Global Workforce*, Towers Perrin Workforce Study Executive Report (Stamford, CT: Towers Perrin, 2006), http://www.towersperrin.com/tp/getwebcachedoc?webc=HRS/USA/2006/200602/GWS.pdf.

20. Greig Aitken, interview by Susan Cantrell, March 10, 2008.

21. Ellen Balaguer, Peter Cheese, and Christian Marchetti, *The High-Performance Workforce Study 2006* (New York: Accenture, 2007), http://www.accenture.com/Global/Consulting/Talent_and_Organization/Workforce_Performance/R_and_I/HighPerformaceStudy2006.htm.

22. Ibid.

23. This study was cited by Edward E. Lawler III and David Finegold, "Individualizing the Organization: Past, Present, and Future," *Organizational Dynamics* 29, no. 1 (2000): 1–15.

24. As quoted in "Future Success Powered by Employees," *DSN Retailing Today*, January 2006, 22.

25. Jill Smart, Accenture's human resources officer, interview conducted by Susan Cantrell during a presentation on Accenture' employee value propositions, February 4, 2008.

26. For more on how these segments share distinct attributes, see Thomas H. Davenport, *Thinking for a Living* (Boston: Harvard Business School Press, 2005); and Richard Florida, *The Rise of the Creative Class* (New York: Basic Books, 2002).

27. Lee Clow, chairman and worldwide creative director of TBWA\Chiat\Day, interview by Susan Cantrell, June 27, 2001.

28. Erik Berggren and Jason Corsello, "Talent Management 2017," SuccessFactors Research Report, http://www.successfactors.com/research/talent-2017.

29. "The Rise of the High-Performance Learning Organization," Accenture Management Report, 2007, http://www.accenture.com/NR/rdonlyres/8D6D739C-D7C5-4308-86CC-E1F24F2865E6/0/RiseofHighPerfLearningOrg_FullResearchReport.pdf.

30. Ricardo Semler, *Maverick: The Success Story Behind the World's Most Unusual Workplace* (New York: Grand Central Publishing, 1995).

31. Respectively, Dychtwald, Erickson, and Morison, "It's Time to Retire Retirement," 48–57; and Erin White, "The New Recruits: Older Workers," *Wall Street Journal*, January 14, 2008.

32. Larry Huston and Nabil Sakkab, "Connect and Develop: Inside Procter & Gamble's New Model for Innovation," *Harvard Business Review*, March 2006.

33. Robert D. Hof, "The End of Work as You Know It," *BusinessWeek*, August 20, 2007, 80.

34. Ibid.

35. GE's practice is described by Anne Freedman in "Master of HR," *Human Resource Executive*, October 2004.

36. Helen Handfield-Jones, "Cutting Through the Fog: Navigating the Messy Wars for Talent," in *Workforce Wake-Up Call*, eds. Robert P. Gandossy, Elissa Tucker, and Nidhi Verma (Hoboken, NJ: Wiley, 2006).

37. Ibid.; John W. Boudreau and Peter M. Ramstad, *Beyond HR* (Boston: Harvard Business School Press, 2007); and Mark A. Huselid, Richard W. Beatty, and Brian E. Becker, " 'A Players' or 'A Positions?' " *Harvard Business Review*, December 2005.

38. Ellen Balaguer et al., "Driving High-Performance Through Mission-Critical Job Families," Accenture Management Report, 2006, http://www.accenture.com/NR/rdonlyres/308CC09D-87C0-4DFA-8D39-9496DDEBDA5B/0/1527054_Mission_Critv02.pdf.

39. Boudreau and Ramstad, *Beyond HR*.

40. Leaders are considered to be those companies in which the three functions their executives deem to be most important perform at the highest levels. Balaguer, Cheese, and Marchetti, *The High-Performance Workforce Study 2006*, http://www.accenture.com/Global/Consulting/Talent_and_Organization/Workforce_Performance/R_and_I/HighPerformaceStudy2006.htm.

41. Edward Lawler writes about how he sees skills-based pay as the trend of the future in his book *Talent: Making People Your Competitive Advantage* (San Francisco: Jossey-Bass, 2008).

42. Peter Cappelli has written about such an approach in "A Market-Driven Approach to Retaining Talent," *Harvard Business Review*, January–February 2000.

43. Howard Gardner, *Frames of Mind: The Theory of Multiple Intelligences* (New York: Basic Books, 1983); and David Kolb, *Kolb Learning Style Inventory v 3.1* (Philadelphia: Hay Group Transforming Learning, 2007), http://www.haygroup.com/tl/Questionnaires_Workbooks/Kolb_Learning_Style_Inventory.aspx.

44. Heather Atkinson, "Creating a 'Three-Dimensional' HR Strategy at Hallmark Cards," *Strategic HR Review* 4 (2005): 8.

45. Starbucks' and Apple's personality testing was referenced by Kira Vermond, "Résumé? Forget It. Take This Test Instead," *Globe and Mail Update*, November 30, 2007, http://www.reportonbusiness.com/servlet/story/RTGAM.20071130.wkiravermond1201/BNStory/robAtWork/home. The number of companies using personality tests was reported by Annie Murphy Paul, *The Cult of Personality* (New York: Free Press, 2004).

46. For more on the Myers-Briggs Type Indicator, see Isabel Briggs Myers, *Gifts Differing: Understanding Personality Type* (Palo Alto, CA: Davies-Black Publishing, 1995).

47. Tom Hennigan, interview by Susan Cantrell and Jane Linder, February 9, 2005.

48. Marcus Buckingham and Donald O. Clifton, *Now, Discover Your Strengths* (New York: Free Press, 2001); and Marcus Buckingham, *Go Put Your Strengths to Work* (New York: Free Press, 2007).

49. Susan Cantrell and Thomas H. Davenport, *It Fits Like a Glove: Aligning Work Settings with Worker Needs to Drive Performance*, Accenture Institute for Strategic Change (now called Accenture Institute for High Performance Business) Research Note (Cambridge, MA: Accenture, August 23, 2001).

50. Susan Cantrell, *Choices in Workplace Design for High-End Knowledge Work*, Accenture Institute for Strategic Change Research Note (Cambridge, MA: Accenture, April 3, 2001).

51. Rick Wartzman, "Conditioning the Corporate Athlete," *BusinessWeek*, May 22, 2008, http://www.businessweek.com/print/managing/content/may2008/ca20080522_077037.htm.

52. Betty Sosin, "Getting Personal," *HR Magazine*, June 2005.

53. Jeremy Smerd, "Diagnosing the Workforce," *Workforce Management*, September 10, 2007, 35.

54. Sharon Klun, interview by Susan Cantrell, February 26, 2008.

55. Phred Dvorak and Jaclyne Badal, "This Is Your Brain on the Job," *Wall Street Journal*, September 20, 2007.

56. Louise Lee, "Boosting Our Gray Matter," *BusinessWeek*, August 20, 2007, 86.

57. Ibid.

58. Tamara Erickson and Ken Dychtwald, "The New Employee/Employer Equation," report by The Concours Group, Age Wave, and Harris Interactive, 2004.

59. The initial scheme was profiled by David W. De Long, "Intel's Workplace Environment Program: Confronting the Conflict Between Cost and Effectiveness," Accenture Institute for Strategic Change Research Note (Cambridge, MA: Accenture, October 26, 2001). The updated description of the scheme was described in an article by Thomas H. Davenport and Paula Klein, "Rethinking the Mobile Workforce," *Optimize*, August 1, 2005, 26.

60. Ashlea Ebeling, "Corporate Moneyball," *Forbes*, April 23, 2007.

61. All information about Harrah's, including the John Bruns quote, came from Robert J. Thomas, *Harrah's Entertainment: Instilling a Customer-Focused Mindset*, Case Study (Wellesley, MA: Accenture Institute for High Performance Business, October 2005).

62. Martha J. Frase, "Stocking Your Talent Pool," *HR Magazine*, April 2007, 66.

63. "The 10 Most Forward-Thinking Leaders in Workforce Management," *Workforce Management*, March 13, 2006, 1.

64. U.S. Office of Personnel Management, *Career Patterns* (Washington, DC: U.S. Office of Personnel Management, June 2006), http://www.opm.gov/hcaaf_resource_center/careerpatterns/CPGuideV1.pdf.

65. Erin White, "Personality Tests Aim to Stop 'Fakers,' " *Wall Street Journal*, November 6, 2006.

66. Susan Cantrell and Nicole Di Paolo Foster, *Techniques for Managing a Workforce of One: Segmentation*, Accenture Institute for High Performance Business Research Note (Boston: Accenture, January 2007).

Chapter 3

1. Greig Aitken, interview by Susan Cantrell, March 10, 2008.

2. See http://www.capitalone.com/cardlab/.

3. Susan Cantrell and Nicole Di Paolo Foster, *Techniques for Managing a Workforce of One: Modular Choice*, Accenture Institute for High Performance Business Research Note (Boston: Accenture, January 2007).

4. Gary Kirchner, "The Navy's New War," *Training* 42, no. 7 (2005): 30.

5. Lynda Gratton, *The Democratic Enterprise* (Upper Saddle River, NJ: FT Prentice Hall, 2004), 147–152.

6. Susan Cantrell and Thomas H. Davenport, *It Fits Like a Glove: Aligning Work Settings with Worker Needs to Drive Performance*, Accenture Institute for Strategic Change (now Institute for High Performance Business) Research Note (Boston: Accenture, August 23, 2001).

7. Kay Baldwin-Evans and Charles Jennings, "Taking a Bold Approach to Organizational Learning," *Strategic HR Review* 6, no. 5 (2007): 28.

8. Tom Hennigan, interview by Susan Cantrell and Jane Linder, February 9, 2005.

9. Sherry E. Sullivan and Lisa A. Mainiero, "Kaleidoscope Careers: Benchmarking Ideas for Fostering Family-Friendly Workplaces," *Organizational Dynamics* 36, no. 1 (2007): 45.

10. For example, AT&T ran a program like this called AT&T Resource Link a decade ago; see Jeffrey L. Bradach and Nicole Sackley, "AT&T Resource Link: Revisioning the Managerial Workforce," Case 497004 (Boston: Harvard Business School, 1996).

11. Robert Morison, Tamara Erickson, and Ken Dychtwald, "Managing Middlescence," *Harvard Business Review*, March 2006, 78–86.

12. Sarah E. Needleman, "The Latest Office Perk: Getting Paid to Volunteer," *Wall Street Journal*, April 28, 2008.

13. See, for example, the study of 235 managers by the Forum for People Performance Management and Measurement at Northwestern University in Evanston, IL, as reported by Charlotte Huff, "Recognition That Resonates," *Workforce Management*, September 11, 2006, 25.

14. Carlson Companies' rewards are described by Diane Cadrain, "Cash vs. Non-Cash Rewards: In the Land of Employee Rewards, Cash Isn't Necessarily King," *HR Magazine*, April 2003; and Brooker Barrier, "Carlson Restaurants Aims to Please Workers with Rewards Program," *Nation's Restaurant News*, October 9, 2006, 42. Unreal Marketing was profiled by Melinda Ligos, "Some Bosses Let Workers Choose Their Own Bonuses," *New York Times*, December 19, 2004.

15. Disney was profiled by Leon Rubis, "Show and Tell," *HR Magazine*, April 1998, 100; Baptist Health of Florida was profiled by John Sullivan, "Personalizing Motivation," *Workforce Management*, March 27, 2006, 50.

16. See http://www.thanks.com.

17. Barrier, "Carlson Restaurants Aims to Please."

18. Huff, "Recognition That Resonates," Watson Wyatt study cited in Sheree R. Curry, "Retention Getters," *Incentive* 179, no. 4 (2005): 18.

19. "Microsoft's Meet-My-Mood Offices," as part of "How to Make a Microserf Smile," *BusinessWeek*, September 10, 2007.

20. Ibid.

21. Information regarding Capital One was initially obtained through an interview of Capital One's Matt Schuyler by Thomas H. Davenport (date unknown), used with permission. Updated information was obtained from the company itself in February 2009.

22. Ibid.

23. Chuck Slater, "Solving the Real Productivity Crisis," *Fast Company*, January 2004.

24. Sullivan and Mainiero, "Kaleidoscope Careers."

25. According to a 2006 benefits survey from the Society for Human Resource Management, as cited by Maureen Jenkins, "Say Goodbye—If Only for a While," *Black Enterprise*, April 2007, 62.

26. Sonja Sherwood, "Next-Generation Benefits (Part II)," *DiversityInc.*, February 14, 2006, http://www.diversityinc.com/public/95.cfm.

27. Jacob Goldstein, "As Doctors Get a Life, Strains Show," *Wall Street Journal*, April 29, 2008.

28. GMAT stands for Graduate Management Admission Test.

29. Accenture 2006 survey of middle managers in Europe, the United States, and Australia; *Ignore at Your Peril the Plight of Your Company's Middle Managers*, http://www.accenture.com/Global/Research_and_Insights/By_Subject/Talent_and_Organization/Human_Resources_Mgmt/IgnoreManagers.htm.

30. Katherine McIntire Peters, "Looking for Leaders," *Government Executive*, August 1, 2007, 17.

31. Barb Cole-Gomolski, "Dual Career Paths Reduce Turnover," *Computerworld*, February 22, 1999, 24.

32. Fran Smith, interview by Susan Cantrell, July 21, 2005.

33. Erik Berggren and Jason Corsello, "Talent Management 2017," SuccessFactors Research Report, http://www.successfactors.com/research/talent-2017.

34. Cari Tuna, "Pay, Your Own Way: Firm Lets Workers Pick Salary," *Wall Street Journal*, July 9, 2008.

35. Liz Hill, global benefits, Dell, "Build Your Own Health Plan Options for Employees at Dell" (presentation at The Gathering Conference, Hewitt Associates, 2004), as cited by Elissa Tucker, *Human Capital Relationship Management*, Hewitt Associates Management Report (Lincolnshire, IL: Hewitt Associates, 2007).

36. Trevor Blackman, interview by Susan Cantrell, February 18, 2008.

37. Gratton, *The Democratic Enterprise*, 158–161.

38. Information on greeters from Linda Jane Coleman, Marie Hladikova, and Maria Savelyeva, "The Baby Boomer Market," *Journal of Targeting, Measurement & Analysis for Marketing* 14, no.3 (April 2006): 191.

39. http://walmartstores.com/Careers/7750.aspx

40. Mass Career Customization is a trademark of Deloitte & Touche LLP. All information in this chapter regarding Deloitte's Mass Career Customization framework came from Cathleen Benko and Anne Weisberg, *Mass Career Customization* (Boston: Harvard Business School Press, 2007).

41. All information presented on Tesco in this section comes from Gratton, *The Democratic Enterprise*, 119–124; and Gabrielle Monaghan, "Businesses Have to Prioritise Workplace Flexibility," *Irish Times*, October 13, 2006.

Chapter 4

1. This quote and all subsequent quotes from Charlie Bresler in this chapter were obtained in a series of interviews with him conducted by Susan Cantrell in January and February 2008.

2. Gretchen M. Spreitzer, "Social Structural Characteristics of Psychological Empowerment," *Academy of Management Journal* 39, no. 2 (1996): 483–504.

3. Richard Normann, *Reframing Business: When the Map Changes the Landscape* (San Francisco: Jossey-Bass, 2001).

4. Alexandra DeFelice and Marshall Lager, "A Century of Customer Love," *Customer Relationship Management*, June 1, 2005.

5. Debra Hunter Johnson, interview by Susan Cantrell, August 4, 2005, and quoted by Susan Cantrell and Nicole Di Paola Foster in *Techniques for Managing a Workforce of One: Flexible Policies*, Accenture Institute for High Performance Business Research Note (Boston: Accenture, February 2007).

6. Jennifer Koch Laabs, "Thinking Outside the Box at the Container Store," *Workforce*, March 2001.

7. Patrick J. Kiger, "Flexibility to the Fullest," *Workforce Management*, September 25, 2006, 1.

8. Frank Jossi, "Clocking Out," *HR Magazine*, June 2007, 46.

9. Divisions were chosen because they were otherwise unaffected by company reorganizations or other initiatives.

10. This quote and all subsequent quotes from Joe Kalkman, interviews by Susan Cantrell, May 10 and June 16, 2008.

11. Amy L. Kristof-Brown, Ryan D. Zimmerman, and Erin C. Johnson, "The Consequences of Individuals' Fit at Work: A Meta-Analysis of Person-Job, Person-Organization, Person-Group, and Person-Supervisor Fit," *Personnel Psychology* 58, no. 2 (2005): 281–342.

12. 3M and Google were profiled by Virginia Matthews, "Thinking Space," *Personnel Today*, January 16, 2007, 22; and Google was profiled by Bala Iyer and Thomas H. Davenport, "Reverse Engineering Google's Innovation Machine," *Harvard Business Review*, April 2008, 58.

13. George Cahlink, "Fewer Hands on Deck," *Government Executive*, June 1, 2004, 68. Reprinted with permission from *Government Executive*, June 1, 2004. Copyright 2009 by National Journal Group, Inc. All rights reserved.

14. Patrick J. Kiger, "Acxiom Rebuilds from Scratch," *Workforce Management*, December 1, 2002.

15. GORE-TEX is a registered trademark of W. L. Gore & Associates.

16. W. L. Gore's practices described in this paragraph were described by Andy Moore, "Simply the Best," *Personnel Today*, June 8, 2004, 22; Patrick J. Kiger, "Power of the Individual: Small Groups Big Ideas," *Workforce Management*, February 27, 2006, 23–27; and Tamara J. Erickson and Lynda Gratton, "What It Means to Work Here," *Harvard Business Review*, March 2007, 104.

17. Jessie McCain, interview by Susan Cantrell, July 27, 2005, and quoted by Susan Cantrell and Nicole Di Paolo Foster, *Techniques for Managing a Workforce of One: Individualized Management Practices*, Accenture Institute for High Performance Business Research Note (Boston: Accenture, February 2007).

18. Richard Karlgaard, "Talent Wars," *Forbes*, October 31, 2005, 45.

19. Report by Polly Labarre, CNN, March 3, 2008.

20. Debra Shipman, "Can We Learn a Few Things from Google?" *Nursing Management* 37, no. 8 (2006): 10–12.

21. "Google Keeps Thumbing Its Nose at the Street," *MarketWatch*, October 18, 2007, http://www.marketwatch.com/news/story/googles-hiring-binge-slap-wall/story.aspx?guid=%7B7227A536%2DD8D3%2D49F4%2DA12E%2DD626A2406F3E%7D&dist=msr_3.

22. Robert J. Thomas, *Marriott: Building a Winning Mindset, Brand and Organization*, Accenture Institute for High Performance Business Case Study (Wellesley, MA: Accenture, January 2006).

23. Interview with Container Store CEO Kip Tindell, "Kip Tindell," *Chain Store Age*, August 1, 2004, 28; and Patrick Mirza, "Challenging HR Assumptions," *Human Resources*, July–August 2003, 8.

24. Moore, "Simply the Best"; Erickson and Gratton, "What It Means to Work Here."

25. Kiger, "Power of the Individual."

26. Sylvia Ann Hewlett, *Off-Ramps and On-Ramps: Keeping Talented Women on the Road to Success* (Boston: Harvard Business School Press, 2007).

27. Hoshin planning was developed in Japan and is hierarchical in nature, with the corporate objectives determining the corporate strategies, which, in turn, are supported by lower-level strategies that cascade down the organization. In effect, the goals of every individual are customized to support the goals of the next person up in the hierarchy. Every strategy further consists of tactics or actions that need to be undertaken to accomplish the strategy.

28. Beverly Tarulli, interview by Susan Cantrell, April 12, 2008.

29. "The Performance Review Mistake Everyone's Making—Will Your Organizations Avoid the 'One Size Fits All' Pitfall?" (*Talent Management* webinar sponsored by Saba, January 22, 2008), http://www.talentmgt.com/events/Webinars/2007/December/159/index.php.

30. Susan Cantrell and James M. Benton, *The Five Essential Practices of a Talent Multiplier* (Wellesley, MA: Accenture, August 2005), http://www.accenture.com/Global/Research_and_Insights/Institute_For_High_Performance_Business/By_Subject/Talent_and_Leadership/talentmultiplier.htm.

31. Ellen Balaguer, Peter Cheese, and Christian Marchetti, *The High-Performance Workforce Study 2006* (New York: Accenture, 2007), http://www.accenture.com/Global/Consulting/Talent_and_Organization/Workforce_Performance/R_and_I/HighPerformaceStudy2006.htm.

32. David Packard, *The HP Way: How Bill Hewlett and I Built Our Company* (New York: HarperCollins, 1996).

33. Cantrell and Foster, *Techniques for Managing a Workforce of One: Flexible Policies.*

34. Lina Echeverría, interview by Susan Cantrell, February 4, 2005.

35. This quote and all subsequent quotes from Julian Atkins and information about Coventry Building Society in this chapter came from an interview conducted by Susan Cantrell on August 1, 2005, and as written by Cantrell and Foster, *Techniques for Managing a Workforce of One: Flexible Policies.*

36. Ann Pomeroy, "Everyone Has a Contribution to Make," *HR Magazine*, June 2007, 14.

37. Mark Tatge, "Fun and Games," *Forbes*, January 12, 2004.

38. Moore, "Simply the Best."

39. Tom Hennigan, interview by Susan Cantrell and Jane Linder, February 9, 2005.

40. Ilana Polyak, "Money Talks, But Is Anyone Listening?" *Workforce Management*, August 2003, 26.

Chapter 5

1. Joe Kalkman, interview by Susan Cantrell, May 10 and June 16, 2008.

2. Tesco's market is profiled by Hayley Pinkerfield, "It's Good to Talk," *Human Resources*, January 2007, 19; JetBlue's market is profiled by Tamara J. Erickson and Lynda Gratton, "What It Means to Work Here," *Harvard Business Review*, March 2007, 104–112.

3. Erickson and Gratton, "What It Means to Work Here."

4. Thomas H. Davenport, "IDEO—A Work Setting That Maximizes Innovation," Accenture Institute for Strategic Change Research Note (Cambridge, MA: Accenture, June 8, 2001).

5. All information on Wieden+Kennedy comes from interviews conducted with Dan Wieden and his staff and as written about by Susan Cantrell, *Wieden+Kennedy's "Factory"*

Approach to Creativity, Accenture Institute for Strategic Change (now Accenture Institute for High Performance Business) Research Note (Boston: Accenture, August 17, 2001).

6. F. B. Czarnomski, *The Eloquence of Winston Churchill* (New York: Signet, 1957).

7. The U.S. Department of Labor based this conclusion in part on a comprehensive study conducted by the Education Development Center in Newton, Massachusetts, in 1997; see Kevin Dobbs, "Training on the Fly," *Sales and Marketing Management*, November 2000. See also Morgan W. McCall Jr., Michael M. Lombardo, and Ann M. Morrison, *The Lessons of Experience: How Successful Executives Develop on the Job* (Lanham, MD: Lexington Books, 1988).

8. After-action reviews are structured reviews for analyzing *what* happened, *why* it happened, and *how* it can be done better, by the participants and those responsible for the project or event—as defined by Wikipedia, http://en.wikipedia.org/wiki/After_Action_Review.

9. Susan Cantrell and Nicole DiPaolo Foster, *Techniques for Managing a Workforce of One: Individualized Management Practices*, Accenture Institute for High Performance Business Research Note (Boston: Accenture, 2007).

10. Steven Spear, "Learning to Lead at Toyota," *Harvard Business Review*, May 2004.

11. Cantrell and Di Paolo Foster, *Techniques for Managing a Workforce of One*.

12. Anne Laurent, "Virtually There," *Government Executive*, October 1, 2007, 13.

13. Robert J. Thomas, *Crucibles of Leadership: How to Learn from Experience to Become a Great Leader* (Boston: Harvard Business Press, 2008).

14. The Container Store's practices are described by Jennifer Taylor Arnold, "Customers as Employees: Your Best Job Candidates Might Be Right in Front of You," *HR Magazine*, April 2007, 76; Mike Duff, "Top-Shelf Employees Keep Container Store on Track," *DSN Retailing Today*, March 8, 2004, 7; Jennifer Koch Laabs, "Optimas 2001— General Excellence: Thinking Outside the Box at the Container Store," *Workforce*, March 2001, 34–38; and "Kip Tindell," *Chain Store Age*, August 1, 2004, 28.

15. Emilio J. Castilla, "Social Networks and Employee Performance in a Call Center," *American Journal of Sociology* 110, no. 5 (2005): 1243–1283; and 2004 Chartered Institute of Personnel and Development survey results, as cited in "Employee Referral," *Bulletpoint*, April 2006, 14.

16. Todd Raphael, "At Google, the Proof Is in the People," *Workforce*, March 2003, 50–51.

17. Lina Echeverría, interview by Susan Cantrell, February 4, 2005.

18. Booz Allen Hamilton 2006 survey of seventy-three companies, as cited by Jeanette Borzo, "Taking On the Recruiting Monster," *Fortune Small Business*, May 2007, 89.

19. Lindsey Gerdes, "The Best Places to Launch a Career," *BusinessWeek*, September 24, 2007, 48.

20. Information regarding Jobster and ADP were obtained from Borzo, "Taking On the Recruiting Monster."

21. Erickson and Gratton, "What It Means to Work Here."

22. Erin White, "Walking a Mile in Another's Shoes," *Wall Street Journal*, January 16, 2006.

23. Cantrell and Foster, *Techniques for Managing a Workforce of One*.

24. White, "Walking a Mile in Another's Shoes."

25. Josey Puliyenthuruthel, "How Google Searches—For Talent," *BusinessWeek Online*, April 11, 2005, http://www.businessweek.com/magazine/content/05_15/b3928076.htm.

26. See, for example, Gerald Olivero, Denise K. Bane, and Richard E. G. Kopelman, "Executive Coaching as a Transfer of Training Tool: Effects on Productivity in a Public Agency," *Public Personnel Management* 26, no. 4 (1997): 461–469; S. Graham, J. F. Wedman, and B. Garvin-Kester, "Manager Coaching Skills: Development and Application," *Performance Improvement Quarterly* 6, no. 1 (1993): 2–13; Julia Marber, "Are There Any Tangible Benefits to Coaching and Are There Any Positive Financial Returns?" Clear

Coaching Limited, 2007, http://www.coachfederation.org/NR/rdonlyres/D639C5BD-F593-4B5B-B837-ED7EC0E0AF0C/7758/037WhatarethebenefitsofcoachingSummary Feb07.pdf; and Center for Creative Leadership study, cited in "Executive Commentary by Elaine Biech," *Academy of Management Executive* 17, no. 4 (2003).

27. Dan Tynan, "20 Tips to Get Promoted," *InfoWorld*, October 16, 2006, 32.

28. Study performed by mentoring solutions provider Menttium Corporation of Minneapolis, as cited in "Executive Commentary by Elaine Biech."

29. This quote and all subsequent references to Charlie Bresler in this chapter were obtained in a series of interviews with him conducted by Susan Cantrell in January and February 2008.

30. "AC Milan Lab/Jean-Pierre Meersseman," *Journal of Applied Kinesiology*, no. 18 (2004).

31. Thomas H. Davenport and John Glaser, "Just in Time Comes to Knowledge Management," *Harvard Business Review*, July 2002.

32. These examples are described in Lynda Gratton and Sumantra Ghoshal, "Managing Personal Human Capital: New Ethos for the 'Volunteer' Employee," *European Management Journal* 21, no. 1 (2003).

33. For more information on these emerging technologies, see Jane C. Linder, *How Do Things Really Work Around Here?* Accenture Institute for High Performance Business Research Note (Boston: Accenture, 2005).

34. Chris Taylor, "What's in a Name?" *Sales & Marketing Management* 158, no. 1 (2006): 31–35.

35. Thomas W. Malone, *The Future of Work* (Boston: Harvard Business School Press, 2004).

36. Nick Van Dam, "Strategic Capability Building Through Talent Management" (presentation to the International Consortium for Executive Development Research, Seattle, WA, May 23, 2006).

37. Steve Hamm, with Joshua Schneyer, "International Isn't Just IBM's First Name," *BusinessWeek*, January 28, 2008, 36.

38. Richard Nelson Bolles, *What Color Is Your Parachute?* (Berkeley, CA: Ten Speed Press, 1972); and Marc Gunther, "Mr. MTV Grows Up," *Fortune*, April 17, 2006, 110.

39. Patricia Sellers, "The Most Wanted Man on the Planet," *Fortune*, February 16, 2009, 80–84.

40. Glenn Rifkin, "The In-Depth Interview: Mitchell Kapor," *Computerworld*, December 9, 1991, 73–74.

41. Eric Schmuckler, "From Nick to Mick," *Working Woman*, October 1996, 30–33.

42. Patricia Sellers, "The 50 Most Powerful Women in American Business," *Fortune*, October 12, 1998, 76–98; and Craig Johnson, "The Rise and Fall of Carly Fiorina: An Ethical Case Study," *Journal of Leadership & Organizational Studies* 15, no. 2 (2008): 188–189.

43. Noreen O'Leary, "A Remembrance of Things Past," *Adweek*, July 26, 1999, 4–5.

44. Bill Jenson, *Work 2.0: Rewriting the Contract* (New York: Perseus Books, 2002).

45. Ricardo Semler, *Maverick: The Success Story Behind the World's Most Unusual Workplace* (New York: Grand Central Publishing, 1995).

46. For a good summary of the research on the benefits of job rotations, see Michael A. Campion, Lisa Cheraskin, and Michael J. Stevens, "Career-Related Antecedents and Outcomes of Job Rotation," *Academy of Management Journal* 37, no. 6 (1994): 1518–1542.

47. Ricardo Semler, *Maverick: The Success Story Behind the World's Most Unusual Workplace* (New York: Grand Central Publishing, 1995).

48. All information on the U.S. Navy in these two paragraphs is from George Cahlink, "Fewer Hands on Deck," *Government Executive*, June 1, 2004, 68. Reprinted with permission from *Government Executive*, June 1, 2004. Copyright 2009 by National Journal Group, Inc. All rights reserved.

49. Ed Frauenheim, "Your Co-Worker, Your Teacher: Collaborative Technology Speeds Peer-Peer Learning," *Workforce Management*, January 29, 2007, 19.

50. This quote and all subsequent ones in this chapter from Sharol Tarbini come from an interview with her conducted by Susan Cantrell on February 10, 2005, and as quoted by Cantrell and Foster, *Techniques for Managing a Workforce of One.*

51. Cantrell and Foster, *Techniques for Managing a Workforce of One.*

Chapter 6

1. This quote and all subsequent quotes from Charlie Bresler in this chapter are from a series of interviews with him conducted by Susan Cantrell in January and February 2008.

2. Harrah's data-driven approach is discussed in a case study by Robert J. Thomas, *Harrah's Entertainment: Instilling a Customer-Focused Mindset* (Wellesley, MA: Accenture Institute for High Performance Business, October 2005).

3. This reference to Tina Decker and all subsequent references and quotes by her are from interviews with her and Joe Kalkman conducted by Susan Cantrell on May 10 and June 16, 2008.

4. Cheryl Kozak, interview by Susan Cantrell, January 22 and 28, February 5 and 11, 2008.

5. This quote and all subsequent quotes and references to Greig Aitken are based on an interview with him conducted by Susan Cantrell on March 10, 2008.

6. For example, Royal Bank of Scotland Retail Banking ranked number 7 on the list of 100 Best Companies to Work For 2007, *Sunday Times* (London), March 11, 2007.

7. 2007 Royal Bank of Scotland annual report.

8. Ibid.

9. Interview with Joe Kalkman and Tina Decker conducted by Susan Cantrell on May 10 and June 16, 2008.

10. Interview with Jim Asplund, conducted by Susan Cantrell, February 13, 2009.

11. Patrick J. Kiger, "Flexibility to the Fullest: Throwing Out the Rules of Work," *Workforce Management*, September 25, 2006, 1.

12. Ibid.

13. Assuming the money was invested at the close of Best Buy's fiscal year on February 28, 2003 (adjusted close). 2009 data reflects the adjusted close of fiscal year end February 28, 2009. S&P 500 data also reflects the adjusted close on the same dates.

14. Best Buy 2003 Annual Report and 2009 10-K.

15. Ibid.

16. Mark Tatge, "Fun and Games," *Forbes*, January 12, 2004; and Kate Bonamici, "The List of Industry Champs," *Fortune*, February 20, 2006, http://money.cnn.com/magazines/fortune/fortune_archive/2006/03/06/8370680/index.htm and http://money.cnn.com/magazines/fortune/mostadmired/2009/full_list/.

17. See http://money.cnn.com/magazines/fortune/bestcompanies/2009/full_list; and http://money.cnn.com/magazines/fortune/bestcompanies/2007/index.html.

18. Assuming the money was invested at the close of Men's Wearhouse's fiscal year on February 2003. Figures for 2009 are based on the close of fiscal year five years later on January 30, 2009. Close price adjusted for dividends and splits.

19. Men's Wearhouse annual reports 2007 and 2008.

20. This quote and all subsequent quotes in this chapter from Keith Lawrence from interviews (six total) by Susan Cantrell (and sometimes David Smith) in February, March, and April 2008.

21. P&G's list of honors include being voted as one of *Fortune*'s Top 100 Best Companies to Work five times since 2002; ranked fifth in the 50 Top Companies for Diversity list by *DiversityInc.* magazine in 2008; and named one of *Working Mother* magazine's Best

Companies for Working Mothers five times since 2000. Awards and recognitions list on Procter & Gamble's Web site at http://www.pg.com/content/pdf/04_news/media_tools/ Awards_n_Recognition.pdf.

22. Net sales for fiscal year 2000 were $39,951 million and for fiscal year 2008, $83.503 million. Net earnings were $3.363 million for fiscal year 2000, and $12,075 million for fiscal year 2008. Includes restructuring program changes that, on an AT basis, totaled $68 million, $1,475 million, $705 million, and $538 million for FYs 2000, 2001, 2002, and 2003, respectively. If you had invested $100 in 2000 in the S&P 500, you would have $88.00 8 years later, compared to $252.20 if you had invested that $100 in P&G stock. Assumes each $100 was invested in P&G common stock and the S&P 500 index on market close June 30, 2000 (the end of P&G's fiscal year). Returns reflect the value of that $100 on June 30, 2008.

Chapter 7

1. Beverly Tarulli, interview by Susan Cantrell, April 2, 2008.

2. CultureRx is described by Frank Jossi, "Clocking Out," *HR Magazine*, June 2007, 46.

3. Ibid.

4. Suzanne S. Masterson et al., "Integrating Justice and Social Exchange: The Differing Effects of Fair Procedures and Treatment on Work Relationships," *Academy of Management Journal* 43, no. 4 (2000): 738–748; and Jason A. Colquitt et al., "Justice at the Millennium: A Meta-Analytic Review of 25 Years of Organizational Justice Research," *Journal of Applied Psychology* 86, no. 3 (2001): 425–445.

5. Victor Hugo, *Les Miserables* (Paris: A. Lacroix, Verboeckhoven & Ce, 1862), vol. 4, bk. 1, chap. 4.

6. Gerald S. Leventhal, "What Should Be Done with Equity Theory? New Approaches to the Study of Fairness in Social Relationships," in *Social Exchange: Advances in Theory and Research*, eds. Kenneth Gergen, Martin Greenberg, and Richard Willis (New York: Plenum Press, 1980); and Robert J. Bies and John S. Moag, "Interactional Justice: Communication Criteria of Fairness," in *Research on Negotiation in Organizations*, vol. 1, ed. Roy J. Lewicki, Blair H. Sheppard, and Max Bazerman (Greenwich, CT: JAI Press, 1986).

7. Diane E. Lewis, "Companies Turn to Personality Profiles for Hiring," *Boston Globe*, January 9, 2005.

8. Ibid.

9. Josey Puliyenthuruthel, "How Google Searches—For Talent," *BusinessWeek Online*, April 11, 2005, http://www.businessweek.com/magazine/content/05_15/b3928076.htm.

10. George Orwell, *Nineteen Eighty-Four: A Novel* (London: Secker & Warburg, 1949).

11. Robert J. Thomas, *Harrah's Entertainment: Instilling a Customer-Focused Mindset*, Case Study (Wellesley, MA: Institute for High Performance Business, October 2005).

12. Max Weber's most famous work, in which he discusses control in modern organizations and his famous "iron cage" thesis (the increasing rationalization of human life, which traps individuals in an "iron cage" of rule-based, rational control), is *Economy and Society: An Outline of Interpretive Sociology* (Berkeley: University of California Press, 1978).

13. This quote and all subsequent quotes of Joe Kalkman in this chapter come from interviews with him conducted by Susan Cantrell on May 10 and June 1, 2008.

14. Eric Krell, "HR Challenges in Virtual Worlds," *HR Magazine*, November 2007, 85.

15. Andy Moore, "Simply the Best," *Personnel Today*, June 8, 2004, 22.

16. Susan Cantrell and Nicole Di Paolo Foster, *Techniques for Managing a Workforce of One: Management Practices That Recognize the Individual*, Accenture Institute for High Performance Business Research Note (Boston: Accenture, February 2007).

17. This quote and all subsequent quotes from Charlie Bresler are based on a series of interviews with him conducted by Susan Cantrell in January and February 2008.

18. Virginia Matthews, "Thinking Space," *Personnel Today*, January 16, 2007, 22.

19. Chris Taylor, "What's in a Name?" *Sales and Marketing Management*, January–February 2006, 31–35.

20. Thomas H. Davenport and John Glaser, "Just in Time Comes to Knowledge Management," *Harvard Business Review*, July 2002.

21. Aili McConnon, "Social Networking Is Graduating—and Hitting the Job Market; How Do the Online Rolodexes Stack Up?" *BusinessWeek*, September 10, 2007, 4; and Bala Iyer and Thomas H. Davenport, "Reverse Engineering Google's Innovation Machine," *Harvard Business Review*, April 2008, 58.

22. Valery Yakubovich and Daniela Lup, "Stages of the Recruitment Process and the Referrer's Performance Effect," *Organization Science* 17, no. 6 (2006): 710–723.

23. The only exception to this is when a company seeks to offer learning opportunities solely as a recruiting or retention benefit. In these cases, the content of learning does not need to be aligned with strategy and the business goals of the organization.

24. Martyn Sloman, "The World of Learning Evolves Globally," *T+D*, December 2007, 53.

25. Barry Schwartz, "Self-Determination: The Tyranny of Freedom," *American Psychologist* 55, no. 1 (2000): 79–88.

26. The cost of Best Buy's long-term incentives plan is discussed in "Future Success Powered by Employees," *DSN Retailing Today*, January 2006, 22.

27. Corporate Executive Board report cited in "Masters of the Universe," *Economist*, October 7, 2006.

28. Thomas Kraack, "The 'Other 80 Percent': Increasing Workforce Productivity in an Age of Scarcity" (white paper, Accenture, 2007).

29. Corporate Executive Board report cited in "Masters of the Universe."

30. REI is discussed in "Too Little Talent," *Chain Store Age*, August 2006, 28.

Chapter 8

1. This quote and all subsequent quotes in this chapter from Keith Lawrence are from interviews (six total) by Susan Cantrell (and sometimes David Smith) in February, March, and April 2008.

2. Debra Hunter Johnson, interview by Susan Cantrell, August 4, 2005.

3. Chartered Institute of Personnel and Development, *HR Survey: Where We Are, Where We're Heading* (London: Chartered Institute of Personnel and Development, October 2003); and Penny Tamkin, Wendy Hirsh, and Claire Tyers, *Chore to Champions: The Making of Better People Managers*, IES Research Networks Report 389 (Brighton, England: Institute for Employment Studies, 2003).

4. For a good history of the human resource department in the United States, see Stanford Jacoby, *The Embedded Corporation* (Princeton, NJ: Princeton University Press, 2004).

5. See, for example, Chartered Institute of Personnel and Development, *HR Survey*; and Mercer Human Resource Consulting, *Transforming HR for Business Results: A Study of US Organizations* (New York: Mercer Human Resource Consulting, 2003).

6. Julian Atkins, interview by Susan Cantrell, August 1, 2005.

7. Patrick Mirza, "Challenging HR Assumptions," *Human Resources*, July–August 2003, 8.

8. Susan Cantrell et al., *The Accenture Human Capital Development Framework: Assessing, Measuring and Guiding Investments in Human Capital to Achieve High Performance* (New York: Accenture, 2005), http://www.accenture.com/Global/Research_and_Insights/Institute_For_High_Performance_Business/By_Subject/Talent_and_Leadership/The Performance_old.htm.

9. Susan Cantrell and Susan Miele, *The Workforce of One: The Role of Human Resources*, Accenture Institute for High Performance Business Research Note (Boston: Accenture, April 2007); and Lynda Gratton, *The Democratic Enterprise* (Upper Saddle River, NJ: Financial Times/Prentice Hall, 2004).

10. Mass Career Customization is a trademark of Deloitte & Touche LLP. Cathleen Benko and Anne Weisberg, *Mass Career Customization* (Boston: Harvard Business School Press, 2007).

11. Our study involved using statistical analysis to analyze thirty-five hundred employee surveys at over sixty organizations (see the introduction); results revealed that a greater proportion of human capital activities that involve managers are correlated with improved workforce performance than activities that do not involve managers. Likewise, The Gallup Organization determined that the single most important variable in employees' productivity and loyalty is the quality of their relationship with their direct manager; see Marcus Buckingham and Curt Coffman, *First Break All the Rules: What the World's Greatest Managers Do Differently* (New York: Simon & Schuster, 1999). The Conference Board also determined that a positive relationship with one's manager is one of the strongest drivers of employee engagement; see John Gibbons, *Employee Engagement: A Review of Current Research and Its Implications* (New York: The Conference Board, November 2006).

12. Susan Cantrell and Susan Miele, *The Workforce of One: The Role of Human Resources*, Accenture Institute for High Performance Business Research Note (Boston: Accenture, April 2007).

13. Google's market is discussed in Bala Iyer and Thomas H. Davenport, "Reverse Engineering Google's Innovation Machine," *Harvard Business Review*, April 1, 2008.

14. This quote and all subsequent quotes from Charlie Bresler are from a series of interviews with him conducted by Susan Cantrell in January and February 2008.

15. "Softening the Sell," *Employee Benefits*, September 7, 2004.

16. Jennifer Koch Laabs, "Optimas 2001—General Excellence: Thinking Outside the Box at the Container Store," *Workforce*, March 2001, 34–38.

17. Both Forrester Research's and Nike's practices are profiled by Susan Cantrell and Nicole Di Paolo Foster, *Workforce of One: Management Practices That Recognize the Individual*, Accenture Institute for High Performance Business Research Note (Boston: Accenture, February 2007).

18. Thomas H. Davenport et al., *The Art of Work: Facilitating the Effectiveness of High-End Knowledge Workers* (Cambridge, MA: Accenture Institute for Strategic Change, 2002).

19. Benko and Weisberg, *Mass Career Customization*; and Thomas H. Davenport and Paula Klein, "Rethinking the Mobile Workforce," *Optimize*, August 1, 2005, 26.

Conclusion

1. Sharon Begley, "But I Did Everything Right!" *Newsweek*, August 9, 2008.

Index

Note: Page numbers followed by *f* denote figures; those followed by *t* denote tables.

abilities boundaries in broad and simple
    rules, 111
Accenture, 5
    broad and simple rules use, 118
    coaching and mentoring, 142
    company unity and customization,
        207–209
    customization approach, 44, 160
    employee-defined personalization, 131
    minority group research, 66
    modular choices offered, 94, 97
    segmentation of the workforce, 70, 75, 76
    support of customization
        experiences, 221
    as a workforce of one pioneer, 44
AC Milan, 141
Acterna, 75
Acxiom, 115
Aerospace Corporation, The, 71
Aitken, Greig, 36, 68, 172, 174
Allyn, Jennifer, 67
Anderson, Brad, 11, 121, 176
Asplund, Jim, 177
Atkins, Julian, 121, 214
Automatic Data Processing (ADP), 139
Avis Budget Group, 120, 135

baby boomers, 63
Baptist Health of Florida, 93
behaviors and values as a segmentation
    scheme, 77–78
benefits
    defining in broad and simple rules,
        117–118
    offering choice in, 100–101

Best Buy
    alignment of employee needs with
        strategy, 200
    broad and simple rules use, 113,
        114–116, 121, 125, 126
    business background, 11
    business impact of customization
        approach, 178–179
    customization approach, 12–13, 42, 46,
        164, 175–179, 227
    employee-defined personalization,
        134, 139
    innovative practices, 13
    mentoring and coaching, 141
    modular choices offered, 100
    practices that maintain control,
        197–198, 199
    segmentation of the workforce, 70
    strengths-based approach impact,
        114–115
    support of customization experiences,
        223
    view of HR as a strategic function, 213
    as a workforce of one pioneer, 46
Blackman, Trevor, 66, 101
blogs, 150
Blue Shirt Nation, 134
Booz Allen Hamilton, 91
Bresler, Charlie, 117, 119, 122, 141, 151,
    180, 182, 198, 214, 223
Brinton, Jackie, 118
British Telecommunications (BT), 69–71
broad and simple rules
    advantages to, 122–123, 124, 127
    at Best Buy, 175–179 (*see also*
        Best Buy)

broad and simple rules (*continued*)
business environments conducive to, 122, 177, 180, 182
business environments not conducive to, 173
challenges for employees and managers, 125
defining competencies, 120–122
defining jobs and careers, 114–116
defining pay and benefits, 117–118
defining results, 113
described, 41–42, 110
disadvantages of, 123–126
employees' reaction to, 123
hiring the whole person, 116–117
job fit's relation to employee engagement, 114–115
at Men's Wearhouse, 179–183 (*see also* Men's Wearhouse)
performance goals and, 118–120
pioneering companies, 46–47
recommendations for customizing using, 127–128
rewards allocated by management, 120
software programs for cascading performance goals, 119–120
types of constraining boundaries, 111
ways to introduce, 112
Brummel, Lisa, 117, 214, 227
Bruns, John, 78
BT (British Telecommunications), 69–71
Buckingham, Marcus, 74
building a workforce of one
analytics as a tool, 228
assessing workforce needs, 226
building a strategic program over time, 227–228
capability quiz, 229–234
choosing customization initiatives, 227
determining customization approach, 226
elements of a workforce of one HR organization, 224–226
fundamental transformation of human resources function, 211–212
HR as a strategic function, 213
HR's increasing similarity to marketing, 214
new definition of HR customer, 214
skills and capabilities needed (*see* skills and capabilities for a workforce of one)

Campbell Soup Company, 73
Capital One, 95
as a workforce of one pioneer, 44
career development and choice, 98–99
Carlson Companies, 93
challenges and solutions for a workforce of one
administration of variation, 201–202
alignment of employee needs with strategy, 200–201
business case for customization, 203–206
cultural change support, 206
fairness, 191–194
maintaining company unity, 206–209
maintaining control, 197–200
outsourcing HR, 202–203
overview, 190, 209
privacy requirements and, 194–196
rewards of customization, 205
change, how workforce of one enables, 166–167
checkout line phenomenon, 138
Christensen, Clayton, 14
Clow, Lee, 70
coaching and mentoring and customization, 140–142
collaborative filtering, 89–90
compensation
employee-defined, 147
offering choice in, 99–100
The Container Store
breaking down of HR silo, 225
customization approach, 46
pay and benefits rules, 118
referrals for recruiting emphasis, 137
as a workforce of one pioneer, 46
control, 150–151, 153, 158, 159*f*, 168*t*, 171*f*
Corning, 120, 138, 198
Coventry Building Society, 90, 121
culture and customization
at Best Buy, 177
challenge of cultural change support, 206
cultural differences as a consideration in segmentation, 68
customization design while considering culture, 160–162
at Men's Wearhouse, 180, 182, 207
at Procter & Gamble, 185
at Royal Bank of Scotland, 173, 207

CultureRx, 191

customer customization, 28–29

customization design considerations
  amount of change inherent to the organization, 166–167
  broad and simple rules only model, 179–183
  broad and simple rules plus employee-defined personalization model, 175–179
  business impact at Best Buy, 178–179
  business impact at Men's Wearhouse, 182–183
  business impact at Procter & Gamble, 185
  business impact at Royal Bank of Scotland, 174–175
  culture and values, 160–162
  customization approaches compared, 159*t*, 168*t*
  deciding how many approaches to use, 168–170
  deciding which approaches to use, 170–171, 186, 187–188*t*
  existing HR infrastructure and resources, 164–165
  four approach model, 183–185
  number of different businesses and geographies, 167
  primary variables to consider, 168*t*
  regulatory or union environment, 165–166
  segmentation plus modular choice model, 172–175
  strategic philosophy and, 158, 160
  types of employees, 162–164

customization imperative
  approaches to customization overview, 40*f*
  case example of how standardized practices can fail, 20–21
  current move toward a workforce of one approach, 49–50
  current use of customized work experience, 240*f*
  customization revolution in marketing to customers, 14
  customization's impact on employee attraction and retention, 33, 34*f*
  customized work experience at Best Buy, 11–13
  defining broad and simple rules, 41–42

diagnostic tools, conditions that make a company suitable, 53–57
diagnostic tools, deciding if your company would benefit, 51–53
diversity dimensions to address, 17–19
diversity of the workforce and, 35–36
elements that affect its suitability, 39
elements that that make it viable, 36–39
employees' desire for customized experiences, 28–29, 32*f*
employees' views of how well organizations accommodate different diversity profiles, 19
employees' views on diversity accommodations, 22*t*
evolution of talent management, 25*f*
examples of, 43
fostering employee-defined personalization, 42–43
HR's loyalty to standardized policies, 19, 23
key trends driving the workforce of one overview, 26*f*
knowledge work's impact on HR, 29–31
link between business performance and people performance, 31, 33
offering modular choices, 41
pioneering companies, 43–48
potential benefits of, 14–16, 23–25
segmenting the workforce, 40–41
technology's enabling of customization, 26–28
workers' view of relevance of HR practices, 16, 17*t*

Davis, Stan, 14
Decker, Tina, 13, 165, 177, 178
Dell, 100
Deloitte Touche Tohmatsu, 5, 63, 101, 102, 144
  as a workforce of one pioneer, 44–45
diagnostic tools
  conditions that make a company suitable, 53–57
  deciding if your company would benefit, 51–53
  deciding what customizations approaches fit best, 187–188
  deciding if your company can manage a workforce of one, 229–234
Disney, 73, 93

diversity, 17–22, 35–36, 66–67, 207
Dow Chemical, 63
downframing, 110
Dychtwald, Ken, 77

Echeverria, Lina, 120, 138
Eli Lilly, 67
employee-defined personalization
    advantages to, 147–148, 149
    at Best Buy, 175–179
    compensation and, 147
    customized career journeys examples, 145
    described, 42–43, 129–130, 151–152
    disadvantages of, 148–150
    experience-based learning, 135–136
    jobs and careers, 143–146
    mentoring and coaching, 140–142
    peer-to-peer learning, 131–135
    performance feedback and recognition, 142–143
    pioneering companies, 46–47
    privacy and fairness issues, 150–151
    recommendations for customizing using, 152–153
    relationship recruiting, 136–139
    software programs for, 150
    time trading, 131
    try-before-you-buy hiring, 139–140
    ways to introduce, 132–133
enterprise resource planning (ERP), 28
Erickson, Tamara, 77
Ernst & Young, 96, 138
experience-based learning, 135–136

Facebook. See also social networks
    employee-defined personalization and, 147
    fairness and privacy issues and, 150, 200
    influence on customization movement, 13, 43, 72, 138, 145
    peer-to-peer learning and, 131, 133
    for recruiting, 138
fairness and customization
    employee-defined personalization and, 150–151, 160–161
    employees' perception of fairness, 191–192
    equality versus equity, 191
    legal issues, 194

lessons learned, 193–194
    perception of fairness in broad and simple rules, 122–123
    perception of fairness in modular choices, 104, 160–161
    perception of fairness in segmentation, 83, 160
    steps that promote a feeling of fair treatment, 192
Fiorina, Carly, 145
flex benefits schemes, 101
Ford, 136
Forrester Research, 136, 140, 148
Freston, Tom, 145
Future Perfect, 14

Gates, Bill, 116
gender and ethnicity as a segmentation scheme, 66–68
geographical location as a segmentation scheme, 68–69
Google
    broad and simple rules use, 115, 117
    customization approach, 46
    employee-defined personalization, 138
    peer monitoring and, 199
    technology use, 223
    try-before-you-buy hiring, 140
    as a workforce of one, 46–47

Hallmark Cards, 74
Hardek, Moira, 114, 122
Harrah's Entertainment, 78, 161, 195
Hartford Financial Services Group, 83
Hayes, David, 100
health and well-being as a segmentation scheme, 75–76
Hennigan, Tom, 74, 90, 123, 136
Hewlett, Sylvia Ann, 66
Hewlett-Packard, 143, 144
human resources (HR)
    companies' adherence to generic practices, 2–3, 23–25, 213
    consideration of existing HR infrastructure and resources, 164–165
    current fundamental transformation of, 211–212
    elements of a workforce of one HR organization, 214–226
    increasing similarity to marketing, 214

knowledge work's impact on, 29–31
loyalty to standardized policies, 19, 23
new definition of HR customer, 214
viewed as a strategic function, 213
workers' view of current level of
   customization, 240*f*
workers' view of relevance of practices,
   16, 17*t*

IBM, 35, 96
IDEO, 132
India and workforce segmentation, 68
InnoCentive, 72
Intel, 76, 77, 79
International Data Corporation (IDC), 35

JetBlue Airways, 67, 131
Jobster, 138–139
Johnson, Debra Hunter, 110, 212

Kalkman, Joe, 114, 134, 177, 197, 198
Kapor, Mitchell, 145
Kelly Services, 93
Klun, Sharon, 76
Kluster, 72
knowledge work, 29–31
Kozak, Cheryl, 169

Lafley, A. G., 184
Lawrence, Keith, 64, 184, 185, 215, 219
Laybourne, Geraldine, 145
learning
   consideration in segmentation schemes,
      74–75
   offering choice in, 88–90
life stage or generation as a segmentation
   scheme, 63–66
Limited Brands, 73

Macy's, 97
market-based segmentation, 74
Marriott, 92, 117
McCain, Jessie, 116
McMurry, 79
Men's Wearhouse, 5
   broad and simple rules use, 117, 119,
      179–183

business impact of customization
   approach, 182–183
company unity and customization, 207
customization approach, 47
employee-defined personalization,
   136, 151
mentoring and coaching, 141
practices that maintain control, 197, 198
support of customization experiences,
   225
as a workforce of one pioneer, 47
mentoring and coaching, 140–142
Microsoft
   broad and simple rules use, 116, 117, 227
   company unity and customization, 207
   employee-defined personalization,
      133, 139
   employee retention and
      customization, 33
   mentoring and coaching, 141
   modular choices offered, 94–95, 96,
      99, 100
   performance feedback and
      recognition, 142
   pioneering HR strategies, 48
   segmentation of the workforce, 68, 83
   as a workforce of one pioneer, 48
Millennials, 63, 97
modular choices
   advantages of, 104–105, 106
   in benefits, 100–101
   in career development, 98–99
   in compensation, 99–100
   data analysis use with, 105
   described, 41
   disadvantages of, 105–107
   fairness issues and, 191
   for hourly workers, 97
   in learning, 88–90
   offering interrelated choices at once,
      101–103
   overview, 89–91
   peoples' desire for choice, 87–88
   perception of fairness inherent in, 104
   in performance appraisals, 93–94
   pioneering companies, 44–45
   recommendations for customizing
      using, 108
   in rewards and recognition, 92–93
   at Royal Bank of Scotland, 172–175
   segmentation versus, 104
   in work activities and projects, 90–92

modular choices (*continued*)
  in work space, 94–96
  in work time, 96–98
Myers-Briggs Type Indicator, 74

Navistar, 99
The New Age of Innovation, 14
Nike
  employee-defined personalization, 146,
    148, 150
  modular choices offered, 96
Nivi, Hossein, 136
Nordstrom, 110

Ogilvy, David, 145
OPM (U.S. Office of Personnel
    Management), 78
organizational scope boundaries in broad
    and simple rules, 111
The Organization Man, 35

Partners HealthCare, 141, 199
peer-to-peer learning, 131–135
PepsiCo
  broad and simple rules use, 119
  employee-defined personalization use, 47
  segmentation of the workforce, 75
  as a workforce of one pioneer, 47
performance appraisals
  in employee-defined personalization,
    142–143
  offering choice in, 93–94
PNC Financial Services Group, 92
Prahalad, C. K., 14
PricewaterhouseCoopers, 64, 67, 97
Principal Financial, 72
privacy issues, 194–196. *See also* fairness
    and customization
Procter & Gamble, 5
  broad and simple rules use, 123
  business impact of customization
    approach, 185
  company unity and customization, 207
  customization approach, 183–185
  efforts to understand employees, 215
  modular choices offered, 105
  pioneering HR strategies, 48
  segmentation of the workforce, 64, 75
  talent management focus, 31
  as a workforce of one pioneer, 48

recruiting and customization, 136–139
REI, 207
relationship recruiting, 136–139
Rent-A-Center, 193
reputation management companies, 139
Results-Only Work Environment (ROWE),
    Best Buy, 12–13, 46, 125, 126, 175,
    178, 191, 205, 227
results or outcome boundaries in broad
    and simple rules, 111
rewards and recognition
  allocated by management in broad and
    simple rules, 120
  offering choice in, 92–93
Roden, Neil, 214
role or type of workforce as a
    segmentation scheme, 69–71
ROWE. *See* Results-Only Work
    Environment
Royal Bank of Scotland, 5
  business impact of customization
    approach, 31, 174–175
  company unity and customization, 207
  customization approach, 45, 161,
    172–175
  modular choices offered, 96, 101
  reaction to diversity in the workforce, 36
  segmentation of the workforce,
    65, 68, 80
  as a workforce of one, 45

Schulze, Dick, 121
Second Life, 133
segmenting the workforce
  advantages to segmentation,
    80–81, 82
  based on employee's needs and
    desires, 84
  by behaviors and values, 77–78
  cultural differences as a
    consideration, 68
  customizing practices for
    nonemployees, 72
  described, 40–41, 62, 82
  differentiation versus discrimination, 62
  disadvantages to segmentation,
    81–84
  extended workforce consideration,
    71–72
  fairness issues and, 160, 193
  by gender and ethnicity, 66–68
  by geography, 68–69

by health and well-being, 75–76
by learning style and personality type,
    74–75
by life stage or generation, 63–66
modular choices versus, 104
multiple segmentation schemes use,
    78–80
pioneering companies, 44–45
possible schemes, 64–65
recommendations for customizing
    using, 85–86
by role or type of workforce, 69–71
at Royal Bank of Scotland, 172–175
segmenting employees before they are
    hired, 79
by value of the employee, 72–74
work environment best suited to, 173
Semco, 71, 146
Sen, Amartya, 201
servant leaders, 182
service-oriented architecture (SOA), 28
Shaw, Bill, 117
Singapore Armed Forces, 98
skills and capabilities for a workforce
    of one
    barriers to developing an analytic
        capability, 218–219
    cocreation of people practices with
        employees, 222–223
    creation of unity within diversity,
        223–224
    developing insights into employees,
        215–219
    marketing and branding customized
        offerings, 219
    metrics and data analysis use,
        216–218
    support of customization experiences,
        220–222
    techniques for getting to know
        employees, 216–217
    technology use, 224
Skyline Construction Inc., 100
sludge in the workplace, 191
Smart, Jill, 70
smart push, 90
Smith, Fran, 99
SOA (service-oriented architecture), 28
social networks. See also Facebook
    customization approach and, 152
    influence on customization movement,
        28, 178
    for recruiting, 138

software programs for customization. See
    technology
Sprint Nextel, 78
Steelcase, 75
Stitz, Dalila Asha, 67
strategic boundaries in broad and simple
    rules, 111
SuccessFactors, 71, 99
Sun Microsystems, 77, 141

talent databases, 144
Taleo, 143
Tapscott, Don, 28
Tarbini, Sharol, 150
Tarulli, Beverly, 119
TBWA/Chiat/Day, 70
technology
    as an enabler of customization, 23–25,
        26–28, 148
    innovative uses of, 223
    service-oriented architecture, 28
    social networks and, 138, 178
    software for broad and simple rules,
        119–120
    software for employee-defined
        personalization, 143, 150
    using to build a workforce of
        one, 224
Tesco
    customization approach, 45
    employee-defined personalization, 131
    modular choices offered, 102–103
    as a workforce of one pioneer, 45
Thanks.com, 93
3M, 115, 199
Thrive Networks, 193
time or money boundaries in broad and
    simple rules, 111
time trading, 131
Time Warner, 118
Toyota, 136
Travelers, 169–170
Trilogy Software, 146
try-before-you-buy hiring, 139–140

Unipart, 71
Unisys, 90
United States and workforce
    segmentation, 68
University Health Care System, Augusta,
    Georgia, 76

University of Pittsburgh Medical Center, 66, 67
Unreal Marketing, 93
upframing, 110
U.S. Army, 98
U.S. Department of Homeland Security, 136
U.S. Navy, 90, 115, 147
U.S. Office of Personnel Management (OPM), 78

value-based segmentation, 72–74
values-based boundaries in broad and simple rules, 111
Vikre, Lee, 79
volunteer work as a work choice, 92

Waiden, John, 70
Wal-Mart, 102
The War for Talent, 73
Whole Foods, 140
Wieden+Kennedy, 134–135
W.L. Gore, 116, 118, 122, 198
  as a workforce of one pioneer, 47
work activities and projects, offering choice in, 90–92
workforce of one
  benefits of, 15, 25, 29, 31–34, 93, 96, 203–206

building (*see* building a workforce of one)
challenges and solutions (*see* challenges and solutions for a workforce of one)
company pioneers, 44–48
described, 2
embarking on the journey, 226–228
employee reports of customization, 240*f*
four customization approaches, 39–43
four approaches, 39–43
future of, 235–238
increased presence of, 48–50
as the new management imperative (*see* customization imperative)
research methods, 4–6
skills and capabilities needed (*see* skills and capabilities for a workforce of one)
strategies used, 6, 44–49, 158–187
value in customizing HR practices, 3–4
why it works, 36–39
work space and choice, 94–96
work time and choice, 96–98

Yahoo!, 143, 199

Zimmer, George, 180
ZoomInfo, 139

About the Authors

Susan M. Cantrell is a Fellow at the Accenture Institute for High Performance and President/CEO of The Cantrell Group, a research and consulting organization. Susan is an award-winning author who has written or cowritten over thirty articles or book chapters for such publications as the *Wall Street Journal*, *MIT Sloan Management Review*, *Strategy & Leadership*, *Across the Board*, *Strategic HR Review*, and *Talent Management* magazine. Her work has been widely referred to in publications such as the *Financial Times*, *CIO* magazine, and *Les Echos*. Susan has been a regular contributor to *Outlook Journal*, an Accenture client-focused publication, and has authored over fifty Accenture white papers, management reports, and research notes. She has been a judge on award panels for publications such as *BusinessWeek* and is a frequent speaker on improving human performance at work.

David Smith is a Managing Director of the Accenture Talent & Organization Performance practice. He specializes in designing and developing talent and organization performance strategies and solutions for clients. David has more than twenty years' experience working across the broad Accenture client base serving *Fortune* 500 companies. He is a frequent speaker at industry conferences and events, has authored or coauthored several articles and papers, and is sought after to contribute his opinions and viewpoints on talent management and organization performance issues in publications such as the *Wall Street Journal*, *T+D*, *HR News*, and *Talent Management* magazine. David also is a regular contributor to the Accenture client-focused journal of high performance, *Outlook Journal*.